Concepts and Practice of Architectural Daylighting

CONCEPTS AND PRACTICE OF ARCHITECTURAL DAYLIGHTING

Fuller Moore

Illustrations by

Gregory Anderson

 Van Nostrand Reinhold Company
_____ New York

Printed in the United States of America

Designed by Mary McBride

Van Nostrand Reinhold Company Inc.
135 West 50th Street
New York, New York 10020

Van Nostrand Reinhold Company Limited
Molly Millars Lane
Wokingham, Berkshire RG11 2PY, England

Van Nostrand Reinhold
480 La Trobe Street
Melbourne, Victoria 3000, Australia

Macmillan of Canada
Division of Canada Publishing Corporation
164 Commander Boulevard
Agincourt, Ontario M1S 3C7, Canada

16 15 14 13 12 11 10 9 8 7 6 5 4 3 2 1

Library of Congress Cataloging in Publication Data

Moore, Fuller.
    Concepts and practice of architectural daylighting.

    Includes index.
    1. Daylighting.   2. Architectural design.   I. Title.
NA2794.M66   1985   729'.28   84-29929
ISBN 0-442-26439-9

CONTENTS

FOREWORD

Daylighting is the most recently rediscovered realm of architecture. Once inseparable from the practice of fine building design, lighting by natural means began to be regarded as anachronistic early in the twentieth century when electric lighting became both practical and economical. Instant, safe, predictable, and absolute, artificial lighting has tended to overwhelm building design since the industrial revolution. Electricity has also made possible constant illumination levels that do not reflect the natural rhythms and the unpredictable variations of each day's new light.

The recent escalation of energy costs and the parallel rising concern about depletable resources have rekindled ancient design skills in bioclimatic and ecotechnic approaches to the built environment. Passive solar heating—the picture window facing the sun with calculated overhang and night insulation covers—is the most widely popularized and easily understood of these rediscovered design techniques. Passive and hybrid cooling seems less potent and more abstruse. But daylighting is at once the newest and the most ancient, the most obviously simple and the most subtly complex of these rediscovered lighting strategies.

Professor Fuller Moore, who is also a practicing architect, brings the broad sweep of architectural daylighting design into a systematic format. A well-versed educator, he has provided a timely bridge from the academic sphere to the realm of practical applications. Because the concepts of natural lighting are related to passive heating and cooling, several of the analysis and design tools are almost identical as well. This integration of methods parallels the ideal of architecture as a unity—lighting is perceived not as a plug-in, turn-on, switch-off apparatus, but as a dynamic, interactive architectural element. For instance, the lighting design aesthetics of Alvar Aalto's libraries and churches reveal a gallery of daylighting typologies.

The presentation of mathematical theory in conjunction with graphic illustration is perhaps this book's greatest strength. The visual analogies, the charts and diagrams, and the graphic analyses of photographs can be "read" almost without words. Current research, new products, step-by-step exercises, recent case studies, and the latest design tools provide a comprehensive overview of one of the most vital and most overlooked areas of current architectural design.

Not all of architectural daylighting, however, is new—the physics have not changed. Standard design methods, such as physical models and the BRS method, are carefully explained, although they have been around a long time. What *is* new is a fresh enthusiasm coupled with a concern for design quality, and a diversity of compatible design approaches suitable to many kinds of projects. Intended as a practical introduction for the serious professional, this comprehensive work brings together a full range of design tools, as well as practical hints. Surely, it can no longer be claimed about daylighting that we know so much and practice so little.

Jeffrey Cook, Professor
College of Architecture and Environmental Design
Arizona State University

PREFACE

This book is based on the simple premise that most people like daylight illumination. The reasons may be subjective and difficult to quantify, but given a choice, most people would choose a daylit building over its electrically lit counterpart. Yet architects continue to depend on electric lighting for most of their commercial and institutional projects. I believe that there are three reasons for this: (1) recently, illumination has been the sole domain of engineering specialists who do not consider daylighting to be cost-effective, (2) daylight is considered by most architects as an uncontrollable amenity (and thus unacceptable for task illumination), and (3) most architects do not understand the principles of daylight illumination sufficiently to introduce them early in the schematic design phase.

The primary goal of this book is to familiarize the practicing architect with the concepts and the analytical procedures needed to design daylit buildings confidently. It is not a poetic tribute to the joys of daylit buildings, in spite of the fact that these joys are perhaps the fundamental and best reason for using daylight. (Other authors, especially Richard Peters, have presented this aspect eloquently.) It can better be described as a collection of concepts and design tools intended to justify (through performance and economic analyses) an otherwise only intuitively attractive design direction.

In this book, mathematical theory has been replaced wherever possible with analogies and graphic explanations. Graphic and computer design tools have been emphasized in lieu of tables and formulae. In North America, the Libbey-Owens-Ford sun angle calculator has been responsible for the architectural profession's familiarity with the equidistant projection of the skydome, and that format has been adopted throughout because of its inherent suitability for analysis of daylighting. Finally, English units have been used because it is doubtful that the building industry will convert to the metric system before this book becomes obsolete.

I am grateful to the Design Arts Program of the National Endowment of the Arts for their support of my earlier studies of the implications of daylighting on architectural form, particularly through the study of the works of Alvar Aalto and Louis I. Kahn. In addition, I would like to thank Doug Balcomb, Harvey Bryan, Jeff Cook, Leo Dwyer, Greg Franta, Kerri Hunter, Scott Johnston, Hayden May, Marietta Millet, Ed Mazria, Dick Peters, John Reynolds, Claude Robbins, Alvin Sain, Sergio Sanabria, and Steve Selkowitz for their encouragement and advice. My wife, Kay, with her optimism and help, made the marathon rewarding and enjoyable. But perhaps the greatest sacrifice was made by sons Justin and Michael, who yielded Pac-man to the word processor on our microcomputer. Now *that's* what I call support.

Fuller Moore, A.I.A.
February, 1984

Concepts and Practice of Architectural Daylighting

PART I: LIGHT

Chapter 1:
Historical Response

PREINDUSTRIAL ARCHITECTURE

Throughout most of architectural history, daylight has been the primary source of light, supplemented by burned fuels. In addition to illumination, daylight has been symbolic of cleanliness, purity, knowledge, and heaven. Generally speaking, in climates where daylight is plentiful and predictably bright, architects have responded by decreasing opening sizes or using a diffusing medium in the openings (grilles, and translucent or tinted glazing).

To a remarkable degree, past architecture tended to admit light only where it was wanted. Windows and roof openings were given special prominence within the structure. As a result, there were rather great changes in light levels within a building (and in many cases within a space). Usually the presence of openings and correspondingly bright areas signified that a special "event" (such as an altar in a church) occurred within that region.

ANCIENT EGYPT

In ancient Egypt, the presence of blinding sunlight and glaring, bleached exterior surfaces void of vegetation minimized the size of wall and roof openings. The opening size was further limited by the restricted structural spanning capability of the stone used for post-and-beam construction of the monumental temples of the period. The thickness of the masonry walls served to soften and diffuse sunlight by multiple side reflection as well as provide massive thermal storage to reduce the excessive daily temperature swings characteristic of desert climates. In some large temples, light was introduced to the interior through clerestory openings fitted with carved stone grilles to soften the light. In others, light reached the interior through roof slits and small window openings, as well as through entrance doors (fig. 1-1). In the Great Temple of Ammon the quantity of light was intentionally varied to reinforce the axial sequence through the great Hypostyle Hall and finally to the darkest inner sanctum.

Urban housing in ancient Egypt utilized an inner courtyard (atrium) that has since characterized Middle Eastern residences. In addition to providing light to inner rooms, it provided a primary work space, a private social area for the family, and a sleeping area during summer months.

1-1. Great Temple of Ammon, Karnak, 1530–323 B.C.: (a) plan at Hypostyle Hall; (b) section through Hypostyle Hall; (c) detail showing auxiliary light slits; (d) Hypostyle Hall clerestory; (e) inner hall roof apertures. (After Fletcher, 1975)

pierced slabs of stone filter light

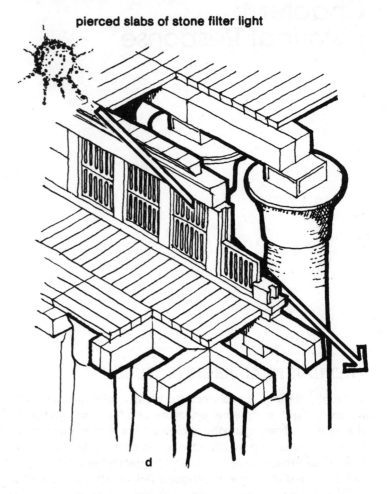

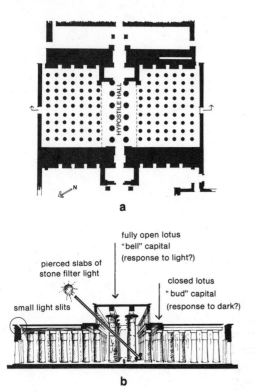

a

fully open lotus
"bell" capital
(response to light?)

pierced slabs of
stone filter light

closed lotus
"bud" capital
(response to dark?)

small light slits

b

c

d

e

ANCIENT GREECE

The climate of Greece is mild, and many public activities were conducted outdoors in ancient times. The major Greek monuments, the temples, were of post-and-beam stone construction with timber roofs. They were "object buildings" designed to be viewed from the exterior rather than inhabited. Because structural spans were limited, the extensive use of columns on the exterior (as well as the interior) created colonnades and porticoes for protection from the warm summer sun and sudden winter showers. The carved stone decoration on the exterior was originally further embellished with gold leaf and color. While these surface colorings have long since faded away, the

4   LIGHT

strong direct and reflected sunlight still sharply articulate the carved ornamentation on the column shafts, capitals, entablatures, and friezes characteristic of the period. Another feature of Greek temples was the coffered ceilings above the colonnades; abundant reflected light was required to reveal these forms.

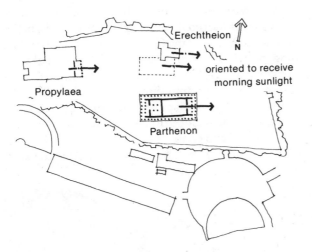

1-2. The Acropolis: plan showing east entry orientation of temples allowing morning sunlight illumination on the interior statue. (After Fletcher, 1975)

Greek temples were usually oriented to the east to illuminate the statues within through the doorways at sunrise (fig. 1-2). Although it was once thought that large roof openings provided additional direct sunlight on the statues, recent findings indicate that the timber-supported roofs were solid and that door openings were the sole source of interior illumination. Because of the relatively small opening spans, this illumination was characterized by narrow shafts of direct sunlight at low sun angles (morning) and more diffuse sky light and reflected ground light during the remainder of the day.

The orthogonal ancient Greek town plan provided solar access to houses for lighting and heating. It is likely that this solar utilization was intentional; the Greek's use of the sundial evidences their knowledge of the sun's movement. Houses were designed for winter solar penetration through the *pastas*, a long, shallow "room" or portico that opened onto a courtyard to the south. Some houses were two-storied around a courtyard. Others, according to Socrates, were one-storied on the south so as not to block sunlight to the two-storied north section. The court was typically surrounded on three or four sides by a colonnaded peristyle.

1-3. Olynthian Villa. (Based on a reconstructed model, Royal Ontario Museum, after photograph, Butti and Perlin, 1980)

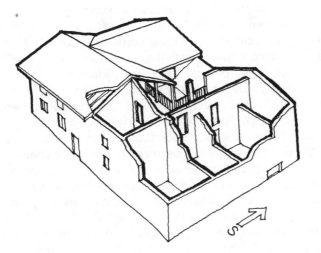

5

ANCIENT ROME

A number of Roman architectural developments allowed the use of daylighting and passive solar heating to increase substantially. The development of the round arch, barrel vault, and dome allowed masonry materials (inherently weak in bending) to be used in compression for large spans. In addition to allowing larger uncolumned interiors, this created the potential for large wall openings that could admit great sheets of light (in contrast to the narrow shafts characteristic of the Greeks). Glazing materials were available for the first time, principally in the form of small panes of glass and thin sheets of transparent stone (mica). Some researchers conclude that these were used to glaze large openings to admit light while sealing the interior from cold winds and rain. Others have disputed this conclusion, based on lack of evidence of glazing stops in existing archeological remains.

Unlike the Greeks (who conducted most public gatherings outside), the Romans built many monumental public buildings and developed a variety of strategies for daylight illumination.

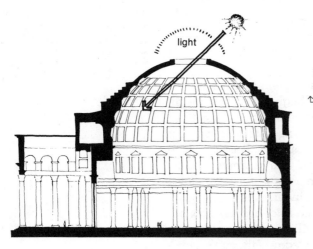
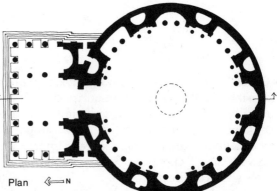

1-4. The Pantheon, Rome, A.D. 120–124. Section and plan, showing the unglazed skylight. (After Fletcher, 1975)

The "Golden" house of the Emperor Nero (fig. 1-5) employed not only the occulus skylight to illuminate the central octagonal hall, but also a series of concealed clerestories to light the surrounding chambers.

Basilicas, the halls of justice and commercial exchange, occupied a central position in ancient Rome indicative of the importance of law and business. The usual plan was rectilinear, elongated east and west to provide greater exposure to the south. The roof above the center east-west nave was raised above the adjacent lower side aisles. The structure over these side aisles consisted of concrete vaults running north-south covered by a flat roof. This flat side-aisle roof, together with the raised center roof permitted the use of very large clerestory openings (or perhaps windows) to illuminate deep into the vast interior, which typically exceeded 200 feet across the smallest dimension. Glazed or not, such large expanses of daylight openings were not to reappear until the Gothic period, nearly 800 years later.

Although firewood was abundant on the Italian peninsula in the earlier days of the empire, by the first century B.C. timber was being imported from regions up to 1000 miles from Rome. The need for energy conservation forced many wealthy Romans to build solar tempered houses and public buildings. As Vitruvius advocated, "The site for the baths must be as warm as possible and turned away from the north. . . . They should look toward the winter sunset because when the setting sun faces us with all its splendor, it radiates heat, rendering this aspect warmer in the late afternoon." From the first century A.D., most Roman baths, especially the hot bath (*caldarium*), faced toward the winter sunset to receive heat at the time of greatest use (Butti and Perlin, 1980).

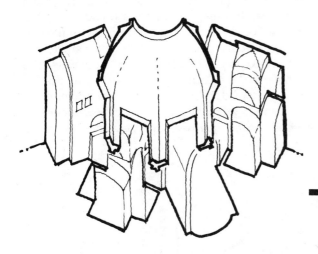

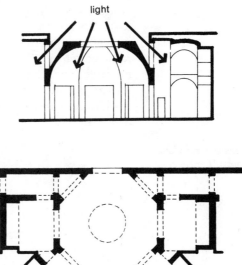

light

1-5. Nero's Golden House, Rome, A.D. 64–68 Axonometric from below: section and plan, showing occulus and concealed clerestories. (After Boethius and Ward-Perkins, 1970)

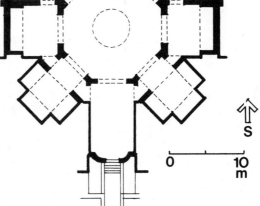

0   10 m

S

1-6. Basilica of Constantine, Rome, A.D. 310–313: (a) plan; (b) longitudinal section; (c) transverse section. (After Fletcher, 1975)

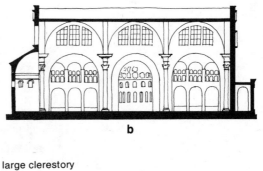

b

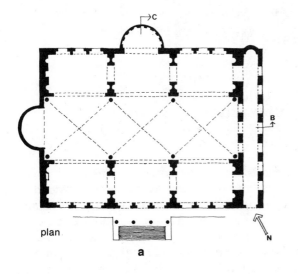

plan

a

large clerestory admitted great sheets of light

low side aisle roof allowed large clerestory

c

EARLY CHRISTIAN (A.D. 313–800)

The basilica building type, used previously for court and commercial trade functions, was adopted with little change for religious services following the decline of imperial Rome. Timber trusses replaced the Roman concrete vaulting, resulting in sloped side-aisle roofs that reduced the wall area available for clerestory windows. As a result of new technology, clerestories, as well as side-aisle windows, became smaller and more numerous. The reduced interior illumination served to enhance the mystical nature of the new religious functions. It also reinforced the linear perspective convergence toward the altar. The apse, containing the altar, was typically semicircular in plan and surrounded by windows that gave even greater visual emphasis to this area.

1-7. Saint Apollinare in Classe, Ravenna, A.D. 534–539, exterior and interior. (After Fletcher, 1975)

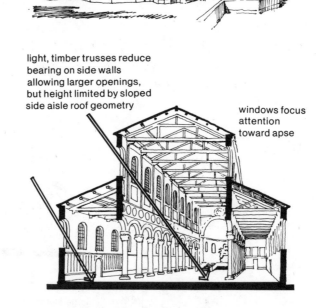

light, timber trusses reduce bearing on side walls allowing larger openings, but height limited by sloped side aisle roof geometry

windows focus attention toward apse

BYZANTINE (A.D. 330–1453)

The most distinguishing characteristic of Byzantine architecture is the use of the dome supported at four points to cover rectangular plan forms (instead of the continuously supported dome of the Roman period) (fig. 1-8). This extensive use of domes is in contrast to the Roman use of vaulting and Early Christian timber trusses to cover comparatively long, narrow plans. The resulting Byzantine plan was centralized around a primary dome, surrounded by secondary spaces covered with half domes intersecting below the main dome. Light was admitted through many small stained-glass windows piercing the base of the dome, creating the illusion of the dome floating above the supporting structure.

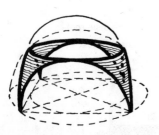

1-8. Dome construction over rectangular plan using supporting pendentives. (After Fletcher, 1975)

ring of 40 windows made
dome appear to float

1-9. St. Sophia, Constantinople, A.D. 532–537. (After Fletcher, 1975)

pendentive allowed
support of dome
at 4 points over
rectangular space

ROMANESQUE (800–1100)

The Romanesque period was characterized by a return to the round masonry vaults and arches of the Roman period, replacing the lighter wood trusses of the Early Christian period. The linear basilican church plan evolved into a cross plan with an elevated dome at the intersection. Groined vaults (resulting from the intersection of two vaults) developed, but lacked the sophistication of those in the Gothic period to follow. Windows in the bearing side walls remained relatively small (with clear glass) in Italy and southern France, becoming slightly larger in northern Europe.

Nonbearing end walls could sustain larger openings, and rose windows began to appear.

1-10. St. Michele, Pavia, Italy, c. 1100–1160: (a) plan; (b) section. (After Fletcher, 1975)

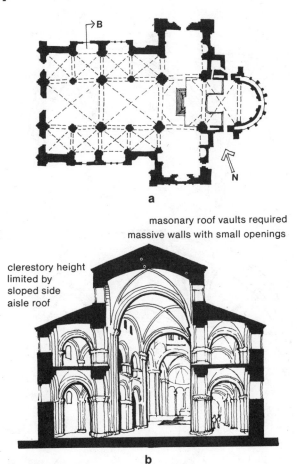

a

masonary roof vaults required
massive walls with small openings

clerestory height
limited by
sloped side
aisle roof

b

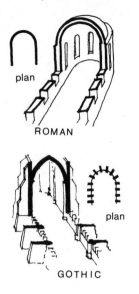

1-11. Comparison of Roman and Gothic window/wall systems. (After Fletcher, 1975)

plan

ROMAN

plan

GOTHIC

GOTHIC (1100–1600)

The Gothic period elevated stone masonry to its highest level of structural sophistication. The development of the pointed arch and vault allowed the intersection of roof vaults of different widths, which was difficult to achieve with semicircular Roman and Romanesque vaults. The ribs at the vault intersections transmitted the roof loads laterally to point locations on the walls. The flying buttress evolved to transmit the vertical loads to the ground while resisting the outward lateral loads resulting from the arch action. For the first time the wall was freed from its historic role as the primary roof-bearing element, allowing the opening of vast expanses of stained glass, with the buttresses extending beyond like fins.

The elongated basilican plan continued throughout the Gothic period. The cruciform plan also continued, usually with a spire at the intersection. The primary, twin-towered facade faced west for religious reasons. This resulted in the east-west plan orientation of virtually every major Gothic cathedral, exposing the windowed south facade to maximum daylighting.

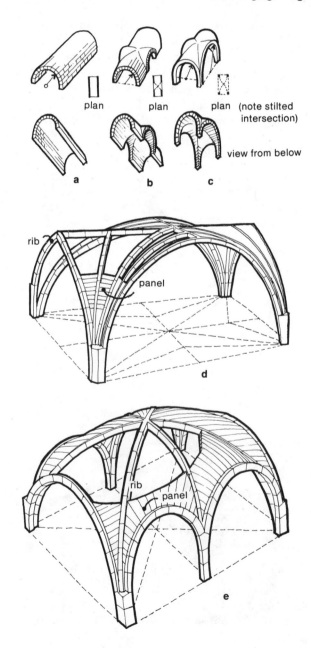

plan   plan   plan (note stilted intersection)

view from below

a   b   c

rib   panel

d

rib   panel

e

1-12. Evolution of masonry vaulting: (a) simple circular vault (Roman); (b) intersection of circular vaults of equal width (Roman); (c) intersection of circular vaults of unequal width (Romanesque) (note that the intersections are stilted in plan); (d) intersection of pointed vault and circular vault of unequal width (Gothic); (e) "sexpartite" vault intersection (Gothic). (After Fletcher, 1975)

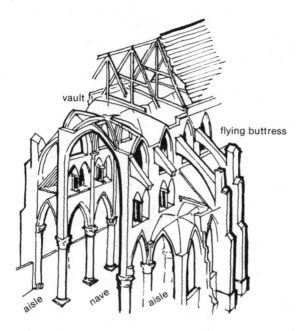

vault

flying buttress

aisle   nave   aisle

RENAISSANCE (1400–1830)

The structural innovation and expression that characterized the Gothic period gave way, in the Renaissance period, to a revival of interest in visual harmony and proportion. Classical elements were reintroduced. Daylight illumination techniques became more subtle, sophisticated, and innovative. Daylight was typically used to emphasize architectural form and dramatize internal spaces.

An important development of the Renaissance was the thick or poché wall shaped on each side in direct response to the spatial and decorative requirements of the respective rooms. In a sense, the wall became what was left over after the room spaces were "hollowed out"—a significant reversal of previous periods, particularly the Gothic period in which interior space was determined by the structural system. In the Renaissance, servicing functions (such as servants' stairs) were often housed in the thicker wall portions. In section, ceiling shapes responded similarly to the spatial needs of the room below and not at all to the exterior roof form. The thick walls and ceilings required deeply recessed daylight openings (often hidden from direct view as in figure 1-14), allowing a playfulness with lighting not previously seen.

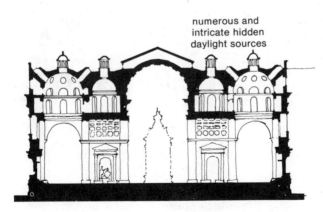

numerous and
intricate hidden
daylight sources

1-14. St. Peter, Rome, 1506–1626. Section through nave bay showing hidden daylight apertures. (After Fletcher, 1975)

Renaissance domes were typically supported on "drums" which were pierced by large windows and surrounded by columns. Often the exterior and interior domes were separate structures, requiring a complex path for admitting daylight to the upper portion of the dome.

In northern Europe, commercial buildings, especially large manors, were characterized by very large windows for direct daylighting, seemingly to occupy the majority of the wall area (figure 1-17).

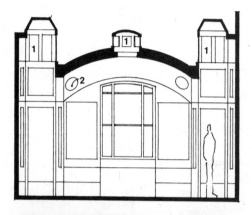

1-15. S. Lorenzo, Turin, c. 1690, G. Guarini. (After Fletcher, 1975)

1-16. Soane Museum, London, 1812–1813, John Soane. (Section after Hopkinson and Kay, 1969; photo courtesy of R. Seibenaller): (1) clerestory windows; (2) mirrors.

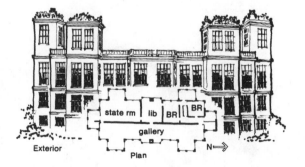

1-17. Hardwick Hall, "more window than wall," Derbyshire, England, 1590–1597, Robert Smithson. Elevation and plan. (After Fletcher, 1975)

LIGHT

INDUSTRIAL ARCHITECTURE

Prior to the 1800s, architects had to utilize the building envelope as the principal mediator between exterior and interior environmental conditions. Illumination was provided principally by daylighting and was determined by climate, window size and placement, and activity location. Supplemental illumination was in the form of candles and oil lamps; activities requiring illumination were primarily limited to daytime hours. Similarly the building envelope was the principal means of controlling the thermal environment, with the fireplace providing supplemental heat. Architects simply could not afford to ignore the existing conditions of the site and, by necessity, depended on the building envelope to admit light and control other environmental conditions. The industrial revolution changed all of that. With the innovations developed during that period, the designer was offered the means to free his buildings from the constraints that had forever determined their forms. The temptation was too great. Designers eagerly took the bait, and the direction of architecture was fundamentally and drastically changed.

Previously (with the notable exception of Gothic church architecture), bearing-wall construction was the most widely used vertical structural support system. Exterior masonry walls were thick, massive, and relatively continuous in order to support the weight of the entire structure above. The development of the structural frame and the availability of economical, high-strength steel members allowed the building to be supported solely by columns. The exterior wall was now supported by the frame at each floor. Its role was reduced to that of a skin to exclude wind and water, and its thickness and mass were reduced to minimize its weight on the columns. The larger openings permitted by the use of a structural frame were filled by great windows, utilizing the newly available larger glass sizes. The advantage of increased access to daylight illumination around the perimeter of the building was accompanied by the potential for increased glare, winter heat loss, and summer solar gain.

The thermal qualities of the earlier, more massive construction were lost, and this function was replaced by mechanical heating and cooling systems. The invention of the gas mantel, then the incandescent lamp, and later the fluorescent lamp, allowed buildings to have greater depth. These devices replaced windows, clerestories, and skylights as primary sources of illumination. No longer was lighting dependent on proximity to the exterior. Previously, the width of the building plan was limited to a maximum of about eighty feet so that no location was more than forty feet from exterior illumination. Greater building depth was previously restricted by the necessity of natural ventilation as well. The invention of forced ventilation, and later air conditioning, changed that. Operable windows became unnecessary and, in fact, even interfered with mechanical operation. It is important to recognize that it was the twin developments of the fluorescent lamp and mechanical air conditioning that made the deep, lower ceilinged office building possible. Either development alone would not have sufficed.

The structural frame and the elevator allowed buildings to exceed the height limitations previously imposed by bearing walls and stairs. The sanitary requirements of the higher buildings were adequately served by developments in water pumps, central plumbing, and waste treatment systems.

As transportation systems developed during this period (first rail and later truck), construction materials were no longer economically limited to those available locally. Mechanical cranes and excavation equipment minimized the design constraints of natural site topography.

The effects of these changes in building technology first became evident in larger buildings, where the costs of engineering, tool-up, and custom fabrication of equipment could be justified. Later, as a result of mass production, many of these developments were used in smaller buildings and residences.

THE MODERN MOVEMENT

The pioneers of the modern movement, reacting to the ornamental excesses of the late Renaissance, used the freedom allowed by the technical developments of the industrial revolution to explore new building forms.

Some (notably Frank Lloyd Wright, Le Corbusier, and Alvar Aalto) retained many of the historical principles of site orientation, natural ventilation, and daylight illumination, while selectively incorporating the new technology as a *means*.

Others, ignoring climate, used the new building technology as an *end*, directly generating the building form. This latter movement became dominant early in the twentieth century during the rebuilding of post–World War I Europe. Because the components were mass produced in a variety of distant locations, and because these architects allowed (even encouraged) the ignoring of the influence of climate and customs, this *international style* reflected none of the localized elements characteristic of traditional architecture. The movement quickly spread to the United States, partially due to the immigration of several of the leading European proponents (Walter Gropius, Eliel Saarinen, and Ludwig Mies van der Rohe) who established successful practices and began teaching and writing. The resulting simple geometric building forms were also influenced by the contemporary Cubist and de Stijl movements in painting and sculpture and were a reaction to the overornamentation of the classic revival architecture of the previous century. In general, the international style became widely accepted in America once the students of these early advocates graduated and entered the profession. As the interrelationships of these technical developments became established and matured, there emerged an identifiable, industrially based, energy-dependent architectural style that fundamentally differed from previous, shelter-oriented styles.

Economy of structure, space, ornament, labor, and construction cost was characteristic of the new international style. This concern for economy did not extend to energy, however. On the contrary, virtually every technical development that characterized the movement was possible only through a greater use of energy in every phase of the life of the building, including component manufacturing, transportation, construction, and particularly operation. The electric lamp, the structural frame, the light-weight envelope materials (especially aluminum), the large glass areas, waterproofing materials, the elevator, the electronic sound amplification and communication systems—all increased energy usage. This was the price of these devices that freed architecture from the constraints of climate and site.

The new direction of architecture was not alone in encouraging energy-intensive solutions. The very way in which architecture was practiced changed organizationally in a way that fostered energy-intensive solutions. Prior to the industrial revolution, building technology was relatively uncomplicated. The architect was sufficiently knowledgeable in all major technical areas to make overall design decisions in a holistic and integrated way. In contrast, the technology of the modern movement developed so rapidly and was so complex that it became impossible for a single individual to be sufficiently knowledgeable to make conceptual design decisions in the areas of mechanical, electrical, and structural systems.

Specialists emerged in each technical area, and the architect became dependent on them during the critical conceptual design phase regarding environmental control. He lost the capacity to evaluate independently the various technical choices in terms of their effect on the overall design.

As specialists have established independent consulting firms, design decisions have become even more fragmented, and integration more difficult. For example, the thermal implications of a certain type of wall construction might not be appreciated by an architect with a limited understanding of heat transfer and the energy and equipment costs associated with this design decision. Because the architect's rationale for the choice of this type of construction is obscure to the consulting mechanical engineer, his (the engineer's) primary concern is to provide a heating and cooling system large enough to maintain thermal comfort. Under such an organizational arrangement, there is no incentive for the consulting engineer to integrate his efforts with those of the architect in order to reduce equipment size or energy usage. On the contrary, such coordination not only requires considerably greater effort, it is discouraged by currently prevailing contractual arrangements between architects and consultants under which the consultant's fees are a percentage of the cost of equipment specified.

POSTINDUSTRIAL ARCHITECTURE

As long as energy was abundant and cheap, these excesses of the international style were of little concern. Predictions and evidence of the consequences of the prevailing direction of architecture (depletion of nonrenewable energy resources and the accompanying ecological implications) were largely ignored by architects and clients alike. The inertia of these attitudes has been considerable. The architectural profession and the construction industry (including trade union jurisdictions) have evolved and flourished in an era that favored specialization and compartmentalization at the expense of energy consumption.

The oil embargo of 1973 was a rude awakening. The combination of the economic impact of escalating energy costs (with no evidence of a long-term solution) and the personal indignity of waiting in long gasoline lines began to accomplish what environmental concerns could not: namely, an awakening of professional and public consciousness to the environmental (and economic) consequences that the modern movement had wrought.

Most professional, industrial, financial, and client decision makers were educated prior to 1970 in a protechnology, energy-abundant era. It is relatively easy for the clients and the lending institutions to change their posture to one supportive of energy conservation; it requires only a look beyond construction costs and visual aspects to life cycle cost/benefit analyses.

For the architect, the task is more formidable and requires the rethinking of previously accepted design methods and strategies developed over the last one hundred years. It requires acquisition of the fundamental technical knowledge necessary to reclaim the lost role of an integrative designer.

POSTMODERNISM

It is interesting to note that, just at the time when an energy-conscious design movement has begun to emerge, another unrelated architectural movement has surfaced. The *postmodern style* is a reaction to the visual austerity of the modern movement. It heralds a revival of the color, ornament, and spatial organization characteristic of premodern styles. Postmodernism offers a richness and variety that are a welcome relief from the sterility of the international style.

The postmodernists are currently receiving extensive acclaim in both the public and professional press. Perhaps this is because the style's prominent visual aspects are inherently suited to dramatic presentation in the drawings and photographs of printed media. It is symptomatic that postmodern architectural drawings are currently in demand as *objets d'art* and exhibited as such in galleries and museums.

It is unfortunate that the beauty of most postmodern architecture is only cosmetic. Remove the applied ornamentation and the style of the remaining building is fundamentally identical to the international style it seeks to replace. Perhaps it is precisely because the essential elements of postmodernism are inherently cosmetic that the style is gaining such rapid acceptance by the architectural profession. It is, after all, easier for a modernist to reclothe old design strategies with new facades than it is to re-examine the way that buildings are designed.

It is possible, even likely, that the future direction of architecture will emerge to combine the visual richness of postmodernism with a more responsible concern for energy usage. The applied surface ornament and poché wall may emerge to become a climatically responsive envelope. Contextual responses may extend beyond aesthetics to include materials and climate. This would require that designers acquire (1) a greater understanding of how buildings use energy for heating, cooling, and lighting, and (2) strategies for passively utilizing the building envelope for these purposes. The following chapters will, hopefully, contribute to that understanding in the area of daylighting, beginning with an introduction to the basic principles of illumination.

REFERENCES

Banham, R. *The Architecture of the Well-Tempered Environment.* Chicago: University of Chicago Press, 1969.

Boethius, A., and Ward-Perkins, J. B. *Etruscan and Roman Architecture.* Baltimore: Penguin, 1970.

Butti, K., and Perlin, J. *A Golden Thread: 2500 Years of Solar Architecture and Technology.* New York: Van Nostrand Reinhold, 1980.

Fletcher, B. *A History of Architecture,* 18th ed. New York: Charles Scribner's Sons, 1975.

Hopkinson, R. G., and Kay, J. D. *The Lighting of Buildings.* London: Faber and Faber, 1969.

Ternoey, S., Bickle, L., Robbins, C., Busch, R., and McCord, K. *The Design of Energy-Responsive Commercial Buildings.* Golden, CO: Solar Energy Research Institute, 1983.

Ternoey, S., Carlsberg, D., Dwyer, L., Mueller, H., Nash, K., and Robbins, C. "Energy-Responsive Commercial Buildings: The Effect of Environmental Systems on Architectural Form." In *Proceedings of the 5th National Passive Solar Conference,* edited by Hayes, J., and Snyder, R., pp. 35–43. Boulder, CO: American Solar Energy Society, 1980.

Chapter 2
Basic Principles

While a complete knowledge of photometry (the science of the measurement of light) is not essential as a basis for good daylighting design, certain principles and definitions provide an important foundation upon which creative design decisions can be based. If even these seem unnecessarily theoretical at first, it is hoped that their importance will become more obvious in Part II when their design implications are considered.

RADIATION

When the molecules on the surface of a substance vibrate, they give off (emit) energy in the form of electromagnetic waves (fig. 2-1). Each vibration of the surface molecules initiates a wave that travels away from the surface at the speed of light. Because this speed is constant, the frequency of vibration determines the frequency (and thus the length) of the wave.

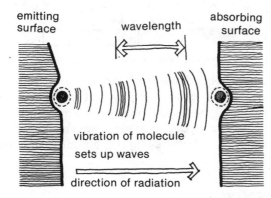

2-1. *Radiant energy transfer between surface molecules.*

The movement of these surface molecules is the result of the energy contained in the substance. For practical purposes, the level of this energy is evidenced by the substance temperature. The frequency of vibration is a function of surface temperature, with shorter wavelengths being generated by higher temperatures.

When radiation strikes a substance, it is reflected, absorbed, or (in the case of transparent materials) transmitted. As radiant energy is absorbed, surface molecules increase their vibration, thus converting radiant energy to thermal energy. The molecules on the absorbing surface are also emitting radiation at a frequency that is dependent on surface temperature.

In figure 2-2, notice that the extraterrestrial solar radiation spectrum begins at about 0.25 microns, peaks at about 0.5 microns, and then tapers back to end at about 2.5 microns. However, the atmosphere absorbs some of this spectrum, particularly the shorter wavelengths below 0.4 microns and above 0.7 microns. In particular, water vapor in the atmosphere is responsible for absorption in the infrared region between 0.7 and 2.0 microns (notice these water vapor absorption bands in figure 2-2 at 0.7, 0.9, and 1.5 microns).

Once incident solar radiation (insolation) passes through the atmosphere, most of it is absorbed by opaque terrestrial surfaces, which, in turn, emit their own radiation. Because wavelengths are dependent on surface temperature,

2-2. *The electromagnetic spectrum (with enlargements showing the thermal, solar, and visible spectrums).*

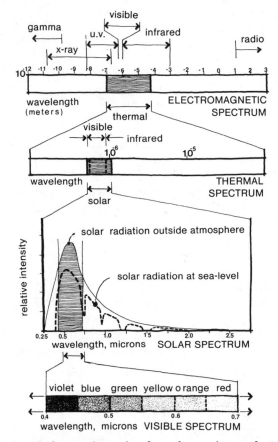

those from extremely hot surfaces (such as the sun) are relatively short. Terrestrial surfaces are much cooler, and they emit longer wavelength (infrared) radiation. The familiar "greenhouse" effect of the atmosphere is the result of the atmosphere's high transparency to short wavelength solar radiation and its opacity to outgoing longer wavelength (infrared) radiation from terrestrial surfaces.

LUMINOUS FLUX

The photometric term for the time rate of light flow is *luminous flux*. It is analogous to the rate of flow of water from a sprinkler head (measured in gallons per minute). The unit of measurement of luminous flux is the *lumen*. (See Glossary for complete definitions of *lumen, candela,* and *steradian.*)

2-3. *(a) Luminous flux; (b) luminous intensity (with water analogy).*

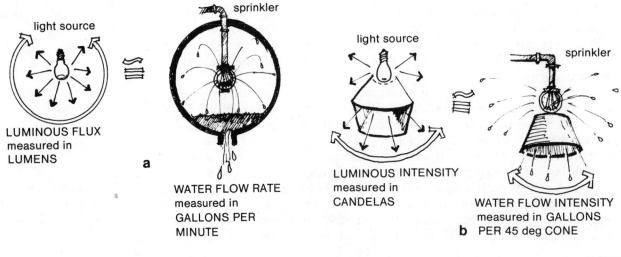

LIGHT

LUMINOUS INTENSITY

A light source emits luminous flux in various directions away from its surface. The amount emitted in each direction may vary. *Luminous intensity* is the amount of luminous flux in a given direction measured in lumens per solid angle. It is analogous to the gallons of water per minute sprayed with a 15-degree cone. Luminous intensity is measured in *candelas* (or *lumens per steradian*).

ILLUMINANCE

When luminous flux strikes a surface, that surface is said to be illuminated. *Illuminance* is the density (concentration) of luminous flux incident on a surface. It is analogous to the gallons of water per minute sprayed onto a one-square-foot surface area (fig. 2-4). The unit of measurement of illuminance is the *footcandle* (lumens per square foot) or *lux* (lumens per square meter).

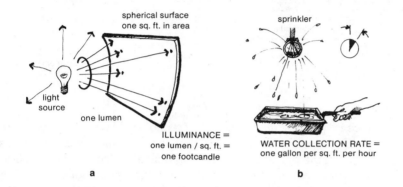

2-4. (a) Illuminance; (b) water analogy.

Like all radiation, the direction of luminous flux is always divergent away from the light source. Because the direction is not parallel, luminous flux is spread over an ever-larger area as it travels further from the source (that is, the flux within a solid angle remains constant at all distances). Because of this, illuminance is an *inverse square function* of the distance from the source. For example, when the distance from a source is doubled, the same amount of light flux is spread over an area four times as large (because the dimension of the receiving surface is doubled in each of two directions), and the illuminance (footcandles = lumens per square foot) is reduced to 25 percent. Similarly, when the distance is tripled, the illuminance is reduced to one-ninth (fig. 2-5).

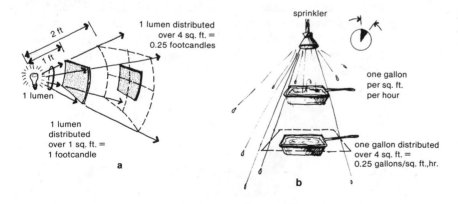

2-5. (a) The inverse square effect— illuminance as a function of distance; (b) water analogy.

If a surface is oriented perpendicular to the direction of the light, it receives (intercepts) the greatest amount of light flux possible for its area. However, if the surface is tilted relative to the direction of light, the area exposed to the source is less, fewer lumens are intercepted, and illuminance is reduced. If the surface is further tilted until it is parallel to the light direction, no light flux is intercepted, and illuminance is zero. For surfaces that are not normal (perpendicular) to the source (i.e., where the angle of incidence is greater than 0), illuminance is reduced by the cosine of the angle of incidence (fig. 2-6). This *cosine effect* is analogous to a glass used to collect rainwater; the greatest amount of water is collected when the opening is perpendicular to the path of the raindrops.

2-6. *(a) The cosine effect — illuminance as a function of angle of incidence; (b) water analogy.*

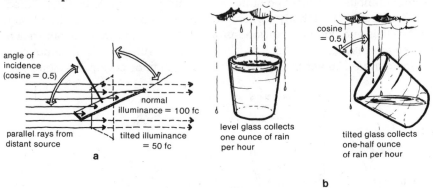

a

b

Illuminance is typically measured using a photocell housed behind a flat translucent diffusing disk. The device, called a *footcandle meter*, measures the illuminance in the plane of the diffusing disk in footcandles. Two characteristics of the footcandle meter are of particular interest for daylighting applications. First, it must be *color corrected* in order to duplicate the sensitivity of the eye in the radiation spectrum. Second, it must be *cosine corrected* so that it measures the illuminance in a flat plane and accurately responds to the cosine reduction at high incidence angles. (It should be noted that incident-type photographic light meters, which typically have a hemispheric diffuser, are not cosine corrected, and are thus not suitable for illuminance measurement.)

REFLECTANCE, LUMINANCE, AND SUBJECTIVE BRIGHTNESS

When luminous flux strikes an opaque surface, it is either reflected or absorbed. *Reflectance* is the ratio of reflected flux to incident flux. *Absorptance*, conversely, is the ratio of absorbed flux to incident flux. In cases where the surface is not opaque (i.e., transparent or translucent), some of the incident flux is transmitted through the material. *Transmittance* is the ratio of transmitted flux to incident flux.

2-7. *Light absorption, reflection, and transmission.*

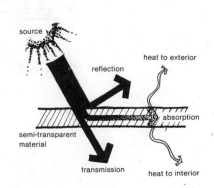

Reflected luminance is the photometric measure of "brightness" of an illuminated opaque surface and is the product of illuminance and reflectance. It is analogous to the water bounced off a sponge (fig. 2-8). *Subjective brightness* is the visual sensation equivalent of luminance and is influenced by such factors as the state of adaptation of the eye as well as by actual luminance. (While the term "brightness" is often used when referring informally to measurable luminance, the preferable term for photometric quantity is luminance, thus reserving brightness for the subjective visual sensation.)

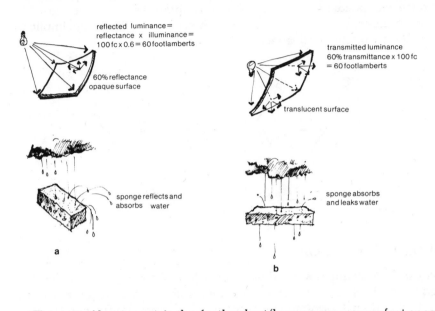

2-8. (a) Reflected luminance;
(b) transmitted luminance as functions of illumination, reflectance, and transmittance (with water analogy).

The unit of luminance is the *footlambert* (lumens per square foot or candelas per square meter). Reflected surface luminance is a function of the illuminance on the surface as well as the surface reflectance. For example, a gray surface having a reflectance of 50 percent and illuminated by 500 footcandles would have a luminance of 250 footlamberts (500fc × .50 = 250fl).

Surface texture affects the direction of reflected light and ranges from *matte* (light reflected equally in all directions) to *specular* (light reflected in one direction only). Real surfaces are not perfect diffusers and reflect light unequally in different directions (as a result of surface imperfections). The reflectance (and thus the luminance) of such a surface is dependent on the angles of incidence and reflectance and the surface's diffusion characteristics. Glossy surfaces reflect light specularly (like a mirror) and thus exhibit qualities similar to the original source (fig. 2-9). For example, the specular reflection of a point light source (such as a candle) retains the appearance, directionality, and size of the original source.

2-9. Comparison of: (a) specular; (b) diffuse; and (c) semidiffuse reflection.

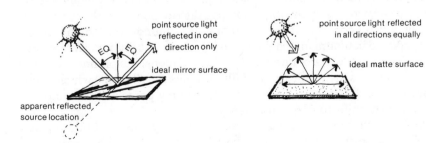

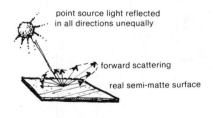

TRANSMITTANCE

Non-opaque surfaces can transmit light either specularly (e.g., clear, transparent glass) or diffusely (e.g., frosted, translucent glass) (fig. 2-10). *Light transmittance* is the ratio of transmitted light to incident light (less than 1.0). *Transmitted luminance* is the product of illumination on the reverse side of a surface (measured in footcandles) and surface transmittance. As with reflecting surfaces, the unit of transmitted luminance is the footlambert. For real translucent surfaces (which are not perfect diffusers), transmitted luminance is dependent on the angle of transmittance and the surface's diffusing qualities. See chapter 11 for further discussion of the design implications of transmittance and reflectance.

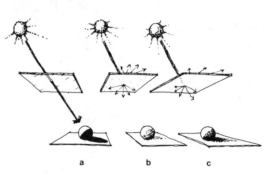

2-10. Comparison of: (a) specular; (b) diffuse; and (c) semidiffuse transmission.

DAYLIGHT FACTOR

Because interior illuminance due to daylight changes as a function of sky conditions, absolute measurements of illuminance are not directly indicative of actual building performance. The *daylight factor* is a ratio of interior to exterior illuminance under an overcast, unobstructed sky (measured in a horizontal plane at both locations and expressed as a percentage) and remains constant regardless of changes in absolute sky luminance. This is so because the relative luminance distribution of an overcast sky is constant and does not change with time. A daylight factor of 10 percent at a given interior location, for example, means that the location receives 10 percent of the illuminance that would be received under an unobstructed sky. (The constancy of the daylight factor for a building applies only to overcast sky conditions; under clear sky conditions, the daylight factor can vary as the sky luminance distribution changes with the position of the sun.)

GRAPHIC REPRESENTATION OF ILLUMINANCE

Daylight factor data from physical model studies, calculations, or building surveys can be presented graphically in the form of contours of equal daylight factors plotted over a building floor plan (fig. 2-11). This *isolux contour method* allows for ready assessment of illuminance distribution throughout an area. (Closely spaced contours represent a strong illuminance gradient, while widely spaced contours indicate a relatively even distribution.) While daylight factors can be interpolated for specific locations, the primary value of isolux contours is their indication of illuminance distribution, which is the quantitative factor most representative of visually perceived illumination quality in an architectural environment.

Graphs of illuminance levels are also frequently used for building sections. This is particularly useful for comparing data from physical model studies of alternative window configurations (fig. 2-12).

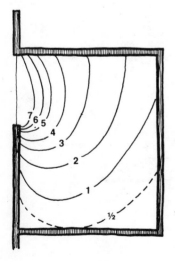

2-11. Floor plan with daylight factor isolux contours. The contours represent lines of equal illuminance, measured in a horizontal plane 30' above the floor. Widely spaced contours represent a relatively uniform illuminance distribution.

LIGHT

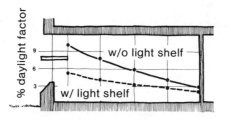

2-12. *Section with daylight factor curves resulting from physical model studies of alternative window configurations. Flat curves represent relatively uniform illuminance in the horizontal workplane at various distances from the window; steep curve slopes denote an abrupt illuminance gradient.*

MEASUREMENT OF LUMINANCE

Luminance is typically measured using a color-corrected photocell that is shielded to receive light only within a very narrow angle of acceptance (typically one degree or less). The device is aimed at the subject surface from the approximate direction and is calibrated to measure surface luminance in footlamberts (or candelas per square meter).

Chapter 3
Visual Perception and Comfort

Architecture is experienced primarily through vision. Vision is the eye's ability to sense that portion of the radiation spectrum that is defined as light. Because most of human evolution has occurred with daylight and sunlight as the primary sources of terrestrial radiation, it is not surprising that the limits of eye sensitivity approximate the limits of the solar spectrum (fig. 3-1). Vision is particularly vital because of its role in most functions requiring perception of both spatial relationships and detail.

3-1. Spectral sensitivity of the human eye compared with the spectral distribution of solar energy.

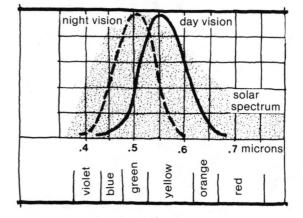

The initial stage of any visual experience includes a process of orientation and the formation of spatial impressions. This is followed by the scanning of various information cues, the making of comparisons, and the ordering of mental priorities. Visual experience can also include the process of communication, involving both the visual identification of meaningful information sources and the subsequent gathering and processing of detailed quantitative and qualitative information. Lastly, vision interprets movement and rates of change in the surrounding environment and therefore contributes to spatial orientation and safe movement within an enclosure.

VISION AND THE EYE

Light enters the eye through the *pupil*, an opening in the *iris* that varies in diameter to control the amount of light admitted. The *cornea* and the *lens* focus the light by refraction onto the *retina*, which is the light-sensitive surface on the rear of the eye. The retina is composed of two types of cells: rod cells and cone cells. The *fovea* is the small portion of the retina (opposite the iris) that constitutes our center of vision. This foveal region contains a high proportion of "cone" retinal cells, which are very sensitive to detail and color, but less sensitive to light and movement. As such, the foveal region of the retina is analogous to a slow-speed, fine-grain, color film.

The larger surrounding portion, the *parafovea*, is responsible for our peripheral vision. This parafoveal region contains an increasingly large proportion of "rod" retinal cells, which are extremely light sensitive (they can sense light 1/10,000 as bright as that sensed by cone cells) and motion sensitive, but lack color and detail sensitivity. This accounts for poor color per-

24

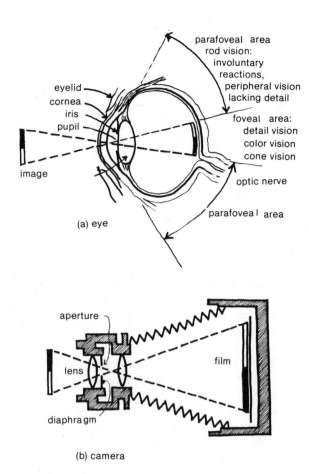

(a) eye

parafoveal area
rod vision:
involuntary
reactions,
peripheral vision
lacking detail

foveal area:
detail vision
color vision
cone vision

optic nerve

parafoveal area

eyelid
cornea
iris
pupil

image

3-2. *Comparison of the human eye with a camera. In the eye, depth focusing is accomplished by changing the shape of the lens; in a camera, the lens-to-film distance is changed. (After McGuiness, et al., 1980)*

aperture

lens

diaphragm

film

(b) camera

ception at low light levels, when "rod" vision predominates. The parafoveal region of the retina is analoguous to a high-speed, coarse-grain, black-and-white film.

Humans have binocular vision with both eyes focusing on the same center of vision. The slight difference in image that each eye receives provides three-dimensional depth cues. The total visual field of both eyes is about 180 degrees wide. However, facial features (eyebrows, cheeks, and nose) obstruct portions of the field of each eye (figs. 3-3, 3-4).

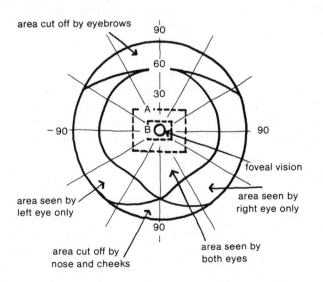

area cut off by eyebrows

foveal vision

area seen by
left eye only

area seen by
right eye only

area cut off by
nose and cheeks

area seen by
both eyes

3-3. *Human field of view, showing the relative size of (a) a magazine; and (b) a small book, as seen at normal viewing distance. (After McGuiness, et al., 1980)*

3-4. *Range of normal adult centers-of-vision angles.*

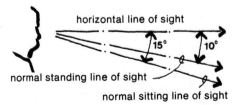

horizontal line of sight

normal standing line of sight

normal sitting line of sight

15°   10°

VISUAL PERCEPTION AND COMFORT

VISUAL ADAPTATION

The human eye is remarkable in its adaptability to various lighting conditions. All visual experience (of brightness, color, distance, perspective, and so on) is measured against some reference experience. This experience may be present (in the form of the surrounding luminous environment), or past (in the form of expectations based on prior experience—an effect known as *constancy*). There are two visual effects of one's present environment that are particularly relevant to daylight illumination: general adaptation and local brightness contrast.

GENERAL ADAPTATION

At night, electric lighting is totally under the control of the designer and the occupant(s). The quantity and quality of illumination are completely controllable and usually constant. The resulting illumination is predictable in terms of absolute quantity (footcandles). During the day, because of changing sky and sun conditions, absolute illumination levels are not predictable. The designer, by determining the size and position of windows, can determine the *proportion* of the available daylight that will be admitted, but cannot determine the *absolute amount*.

This inability to predict absolute amounts is a source of concern for some illumination engineers who are accustomed to the predictability of electric sources, and for this reason the utilization of daylight for illumination is sometimes discouraged. This is unfortunate. The eye does not perceive light in the absolute terms of the photometer. The large variations inherent in daylight do not result in correspondingly large perceived changes in the interior. This is because of the wide range of adaptation of the eye to changing overall levels of illumination. On an overcast day, it is virtually impossible to estimate illumination levels visually. Even experienced photographers must rely on meters under these conditions. Interior daylight illumination is usually expressed in terms of daylight factor. The daylight factor is thus a measure of the *proportion* of the total daylight that is available indoors and not the absolute illumination. Because of the adaptability of the eye, the daylight factor is a better measure of visibility than footcandles. As the sky brightens, the eye adapts to the resulting increase in interior illumination so that the perceived effect is more closely related to the proportion of available light (the daylight factor) than to the measurable level. The converse (darkening of the sky) is also true, provided the change is relatively gradual.

The physiological process of adaptation is a combination of rapid changing of the pupil diameter (controlling the amount of light admitted) and a slower change in retinal sensitivity. Generally, changes in sky brightness conditions occur slowly enough to allow comfortable adaptation of the eye. However, visual discomfort occurs when the eye is required to adapt to repeated and abrupt changes in overall brightness. A typical example occurs when the visual field must be shifted back and forth between a large area of high brightness (such as the sky) and an interior object (such as a book or machine).

LOCAL BRIGHTNESS CONTRAST

The eye generally adapts to the average of the various brightnesses within the field of view, being affected most by brightnesses nearest the center of vision. If an area of high brightness is seen next to an area of much lower brightness, the eye tends to adapt to the average, making it difficult to discern detail in either area, especially in the low brightness area. While the eye could adapt to either of these brightness levels alone, the adjacency of the two levels in the field of view is the source of discomfort and reduced visual acuity.

Local brightness contrast can be reduced by the use of similar reflectances on adjacent surfaces and (in the case of windows and other daylighting apertures) by ensuring that surfaces surrounding the opening have a relatively high luminance (that is, receive light and are of high reflectance).

To achieve a comfortable brightness balance, it is desirable and practical to limit brightness ratios between areas of appreciable size (from normal viewpoints) as follows:

3 to 1	Between task and adjacent surroundings.
10 to 1	Between task and more remote darker surfaces.
1/10 to 1	Between task and more remote lighter surfaces.
20 to 1	Between fenestration (or luminaires) and adjacent surfaces.
40 to 1	Anywhere in the field of view.

BRIGHTNESS CONSTANCY

Constancy is the visual tendency to perceive the environment as it is known to be, rather than on the basis of appearance alone. There are many types of constancy. An example of "size constancy" is that which occurs when viewing drawings of three persons on a grid of converging lines (which is interpreted in western cultures as a perspective grid leading to a point at infinity). The three figures, drawn the same size on the paper, appear to be of greatly different sizes—a result of size constancy.

Although rarely noticed, brightness constancy is always present in a lighted interior. For example, the amount of light reaching a white ceiling from side windows may be, at the back of the room, only one twentieth of the light on the ceiling at the front of the room. Yet the eye sees the ceiling as white all over, rather than as white near the window and dark gray near the back of the room. It is possible to demonstrate that the measured luminance of a dark gray card placed on the ceiling near the window may be as great as the white ceiling at the back, but it is not perceived as such by the eye. The observer knows from experience that the ceiling is uniformly white and thus discounts the fact that not all areas of the ceiling receive the same degree of illumination. This is reinforced by the awareness of the location of the window light source. From experience, the observer knows that objects near a light source appear brighter than those further away. Thus, the observer unconsciously concludes that, because the location of the source is consistent with the appearance of brightness gradation, the ceiling is uniformly white.

If the ceiling was viewed only through a small hole in a box, it would be impossible for the observer to determine whether the ceiling was brightly-illuminated gray or dimly-lit white. Brightness constancy is only effective if the observer is able to survey the entire surrounding environment, including the source and the surface receiving light. This information is necessary to perceptually separate the illumination component from the reflectance component of a bright surface.

VISUAL PERFORMANCE AND COMFORT

Visual acuity is the ability of the observer to distinguish fine details. (This is what is measured by the familiar optician's chart of letters of decreasing size.) Up to a point, visual acuity increases with increased illuminance of the task surface.

Contrast sensitivity is the ability of the eye to distinguish differences in luminance and is also a function of task illumination. Under poor illumination, it may not be possible to distinguish between a black card and an adjacent dark gray card; under better illumination, the difference is obvious.

While the high brightness that accompanies high levels of illumination usually improves vision, unwanted high brightness (glare) can reduce both visual acuity and contrast sensitivity. Glare can be categorized on the basis of its effect on the observer as *disability glare* or *discomfort glare*.

DISABILITY GLARE

Disability glare results from areas in the field of view of such brilliance that they cause a scattering of light within optical matter of the eye, causing a *veiling effect*. This veiling effect reduces visual contrast to such a degree that seeing is reduced. A familiar example of disability glare occurs when driving at night. In the absence of other vehicles, the road ahead is visible under headlight illumination because the light surfaces reflect more light (and appear brighter) than the dark surfaces. When oncoming headlights are encountered, the light scattered within the eye exceeds the light reflected from both light and dark road surfaces, resulting in a temporary loss of useful vision. With some extreme exceptions (e.g., the sky seen through a window at the end of a dark corridor, or reflections from a glossy work surface), disability glare is seldom a major building design consideration.

DISCOMFORT GLARE

Glare that produces discomfort, but does not necessarily interfere with visibility or visual performance, is termed discomfort glare. It may result from bright sources within the field of view that are not inherently distressing, but are seen in much darker surroundings.

The most widely used measure of discomfort glare in daylighting is the *glare index*. While the calculation of the glare index is complex, the important variables are:

■ the luminance of the sky as seen through the window (the larger the window, the higher the index);

■ the apparent size of the visible area of sky (the larger the area, the higher the index);

■ the position of the visible sky within the field of view (the closer to the center of vision, the higher the index); and

■ the average luminance of the room excluding the visible sky (the darker the room, the higher the index).

Hopkinson, Petherbridge, and Longmore (1966) describe the calculation of the glare index for daylighting applications and present various tables and nomographs to simplify its computation.

In the United States, the *Index of Sensation* is used to assess discomfort glare (primarily for electric lighting applications). It is defined by the Illuminating Engineering Society (1981) as "a number which expresses (for a single source) the effects of source luminance, solid angle factor, position index, and the field luminance on discomfort glare rating . . ." The discomfort glare rating is a summation of the effects of several sources in the field of view.

DIRECT AND REFLECTED GLARE

Glare can also be categorized on the basis of the path of the light. Direct glare is caused by sources directly visible within the field of view. Reflected glare is glare from a glossy surface that reflects an image of the light source. (Discomfort and disability glare can be caused by either direct or reflected light.)

VEILING REFLECTIONS

A *veiling reflection* is a form of reflected glare that occurs when the source of illumination is reflected by a specular task surface. A familiar example is the image of an overhead skylight or electric lighting fixture reflected on the surface of a glossy magazine. Veiling reflections reduce visibility because the brightness of the reflected image causes an increase in the brightness of both the light and dark features of the task surface. (For example, if the brightness of both the black lettering and the white surrounding page are increased to very high levels, the contrast between the two will be eliminated.) Because veiling reflections are specular, they can be anticipated whenever concentrated light sources occur within the reflected field of view of the task surface. In other words, if the task surface is a mirror, any source within the area seen in the reflection is a potential source of veiling reflections.

Veiling reflections can be controlled by:

■ locating all relatively concentrated light sources outside of the reflected field of view;

■ reducing source luminance by distributing the light source over a larger area. (For comparable illumination at the workplane, a luminous ceiling minimizes the effect of veiling reflections compared with a concentrated source in the reflected field of view.)

EQUIVALENT SPHERE ILLUMINATION (E.S.I.)

Veiling reflections reduce the effectiveness of illumination for visual task purposes. *Sphere illumination* is a standard reference condition in which the light source is a uniformly luminous sphere surrounding the task. Sphere illumination minimizes veiling reflections but does not eliminate them entirely because some portions of the sphere are in the reflected field of view. Most real lighting conditions require a greater amount of task illuminance than would be required by sphere illumination for comparable visibility. *Equivalent sphere illumination* is the reference "effective" illumination equivalent for a real lighting condition. For example, to achieve 50 E.S.I. footcandles, 45 to 250 "real" footcandles might be required, depending on the position of the source and the resultant veiling reflections.

REFERENCES

Hopkinson, R. G., et al. *Daylighting.* London: William Heinemann, Ltd., 1966.

Kaufman, J., ed. *Lighting Handbook 1981 Reference Volume.* New York: Illuminating Engineering Society of North America, 1981.

McGuiness, W., Stein, B., and Reynolds, J. *Mechanical and Electrical Equipment for Buildings,* 6th ed. New York: John Wiley and Sons, 1980.

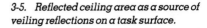
3-5. *Reflected ceiling area as a source of veiling reflections on a task surface.*

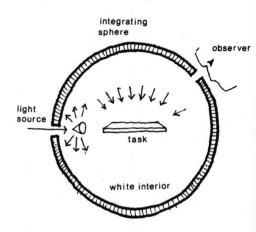

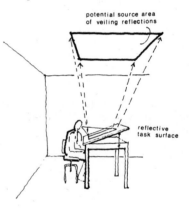
3-6. *Sphere illumination of a task.*

Chapter 4
Natural Sources

For design purposes, daylight sources can be characterized as *direct* (direct sunlight and diffuse sky light) and *indirect* (light from reflective or translucent diffusers that were originally illuminated by primary or other secondary sources).

DIRECT SUNLIGHT

Direct sunlight illuminates normal (perpendicular) surfaces with 6,000 to 10,000 footcandles. As such, it is too intense to be used directly for task illumination. Because of this, most illuminating engineers prefer to exclude direct sunlight completely from interiors. This is unfortunate, because the movement and sparkle associated with controlled shafts of sunlight add considerably to the visual variety and excitement of a space. Even where visual tasks are fixed in location and subject to direct glare, occupant controls, such as shades and blinds, are preferable to permanent exclusion of direct sunlight. In addition, when the glazing is south-facing and vertical, direct sunlight contributes favorably in the winter to psychological as well as thermal comfort.

4-1. Efficacy of various forms of daylight and electric lamps (sources: (a) Hopkinson et al., 1966; (b) I.E.S., 1981).

LIGHT SOURCE	EFFICACY (lumens/watt)	SOURCE
Sun (altitude = 7.5 degrees)	90 lm/w	(a)
Sun (altitude > 25 degrees)	117 lm/w	(a)
Sun (suggested mean altitude)	100 lm/w	(a)
Sky (clear)	150 lm/w	(a)
Sky (average)	125 lm/w	(a)
Global (average of sky and sun)	115 lm/w	(a)
Incandescent (150 w)	16–40 lm/w	(b)
Fluorescent (40 w, CWX)	50–80 lm/w	(b)
High Pressure Sodium	40–140 lm/w	(b)

Because of its importance to passive solar heating, direct solar radiation is often considered undesirable for illumination purposes due to its associated thermal content. This is a misconception. As can be seen from figure 4-1, the luminous efficacy of direct sunlight, while less than that of clear sky light, is still considerably greater than that of commonly used electric alternatives. Virtually all of the energy from each source is ultimately converted to heat within the building (at the rate of 3.4 BTUs per watt). Thus, direct sunlight introduces less heat per lumen into a building than do most electric alternatives. This even makes direct sunlight an attractive strategy for reducing cooling loads in buildings due to lighting, *assuming that it can be effectively distributed and fully utilized for illumination.* Strategies for achieving this distribution will be considered in subsequent chapters. Since most sunlight entering a building is ultimately absorbed and converted to heat, it also contributes favorably to winter heating performance if the glazing is oriented in such a way that solar gain exceeds glazing heat loss (i.e., vertical, south-facing). This is particularly true for buildings whose thermal load is dominated by convective and conductive envelope losses.

Because of the importance of the contribution of direct sunlight to illumination and solar heating, a method for visualizing the sun's position in the sky is valuable to the designer. The movement of the sun across the sky at a given site latitude can be visualized as a path on an imaginary overhead skydome. This dome can be represented two-dimensionally as a plan of a dome with concentric circles for vertical (altitude) angles, and radial lines for horizontal (azimuth) angles. The path of the sun on various days of the year is shown in such a sun path diagram in figure 4-2. Similar diagrams for other U.S. latitudes in 4-degree increments are provided in Appendix B.

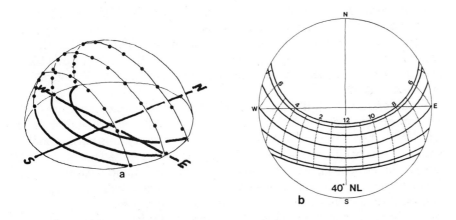

4-2. (a) Typical skydome with sun paths; (b) corresponding plan diagram for 40° north latitude.

DIRECT SKY LIGHT

Sky light is diffuse light resulting from the refraction and reflection of sunlight as it passes through the atmosphere. Under clear skies, the very small size of the atmospheric particles causes only the wavelengths of light in the blue portion of the spectrum to be refracted, imparting a blue color to the sky. Under such clear conditions, the sky is darkest 90 degrees from the sun and brightest near the sun (fig. 4-3).

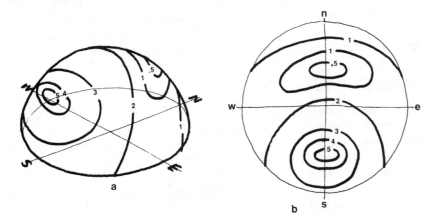

4-3. (a) Typical clear skydome; (b) plan with isoluminance contours showing 10 to 1 distribution ratio (greatest luminance near sun, least ninety degrees from sun).

Under overcast skies, the relatively larger water particles diffusely refract/reflect all wavelengths equally in all directions. This results in a white-colored sky, about three times brighter at the zenith (directly overhead) than at the horizon (fig. 4-4).

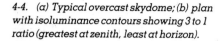

4-4. (a) Typical overcast skydome; (b) plan with isoluminance contours showing 3 to 1 ratio (greatest at zenith, least at horizon).

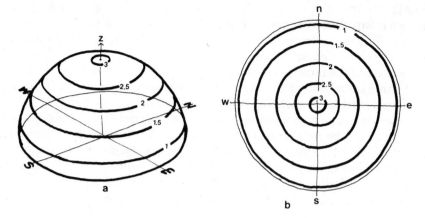

While sunlight is a point source of illumination, sky light (from either a clear or overcast sky) is a distributed (area) light source. It produces a soft, nondirectional, relatively shadow-free illumination. The resulting illuminance levels are considerably less than those from sunlight; typically 500 to 2,000 footcandles for an overcast sky compared to 6,000 to 10,000 footcandles for direct sunlight.

Traditionally, daylighting has been achieved by employing large north window areas to receive diffuse north sky light while excluding direct sunlight. With the recent interest in passive solar heating, this north-oriented approach has been criticized because of the large associated net winter heat losses. This criticism is valid for buildings with skin-dominant thermal loads. These typically include residences and small commercial buildings with large surface-to-volume ratios and small internal gains from equipment and electric lighting in colder climates. All of these tend to favor south orientations with the associated increased winter solar heat gain.

For larger buildings with smaller surface-to-volume ratios, daytime occupancy, and large internal heat gains (from equipment, people, and lighting), the choice between dominant south and north orientation is less obvious. In such buildings, where winter heating requirements are minimal and cooling loads dominate, north sky light may be preferable. Furthermore, such buildings are subject to utility charges for peak power demand as well as total power consumption. Under such rate structures, reduced power consumption does not necessarily translate into lower energy costs. It is thus important to recognize that optimizing energy costs in such buildings becomes much more complex than the south-dominated passive solar heating strategies that have proven so successful for residences.

INDIRECT SOURCES

When a matte reflective (i.e., flat white) surface is illuminated by a primary source (sunlight or sky light), its resulting luminance makes it an indirect source of illumination (fig. 4-5). Because it is a distributed source, the quality and distribution of its light is virtually identical to direct sky light admitted through a similar-sized opening. If directly sunlit, white reflector luminance can be as high as 5,000 to 10,000 footlamberts, substantially more than the luminance of the skydome (500 to 2,000 footlamberts).

In a similar manner, translucent glazing materials can be used as indirect sources (fig. 4-6).

LIGHT

4-5. White reflector "light scoop" used to illuminate exhibition indirectly, Rovaniemi Library, Finland (Alvar Aalto, Architect).

4-6. Translucent drapes provide soft, diffuse, secondary source illumination. Lecture room, Museum of Fine Arts, Miami University, Oxford, Ohio (Skidmore, Owings, and Merrill, Architects; Walter Netsche, partner-in-charge).

REFERENCES

Hopkinson, R. G., et al. *Daylighting.* London: William Heinemann, Ltd., 1966.

Kaufman, J., ed. *Lighting Handbook 1981 Reference Volume,* New York: Illuminating Engineering Society of North America, 1981.

Chapter 5
A Conceptual Model for Design

SOURCE—PATH—TARGET

In order to understand lighting, it is necessary for the designer to have a conceptual frame of reference.

One such approach is to consider light in the sequential terms of *source—path—target*. The location of the light source and the target are determined, and a direct or reflected path between the two is planned. As arrows can be used to represent light direction, this is an obvious, simple, and convenient method of visualization for designers (fig. 5-1).

5-1. Source-path-target conceptual model (clear path).

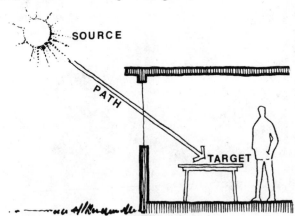

However, this source—path—target concept provides an accurate basis for intuitive understanding *only* when the light emanates from a *point source* (sun, incandescent lamp) and the path is specular (clear glazing or mirror reflectors). These conditions are typical of those associated with solar heating and shading design. However, it is difficult to extend this convention to include *distributed sources* (such as the diffuse sky vault or a luminous surface) or *diffusing path* elements (such as translucent glazing or matte, white reflectors). This diffusion results in such a confusion of "arrows" (either mental or graphic) that the method becomes ineffective as a conceptual model for design (fig. 5-2).

5-2. Source-path-target conceptual model (diffuse path).

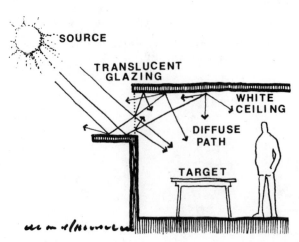

LUMINANCE × APPARENT SIZE

In order to develop a workable alternative, first consider illumination as a function of areas of brightness that can be "seen" by the target or *receiver*. The basis for this approach is that the amount of light at the target is the result of exposure to all of the bright and dim surfaces within the view of that target. More precisely, the light contributed to (the illuminance of) the target is the product of the luminance of a particular source multiplied by its apparent size as viewed from the receiver (fig. 5-3). For simplicity, the effect of cosine reduction is ignored here, but will be considered later.

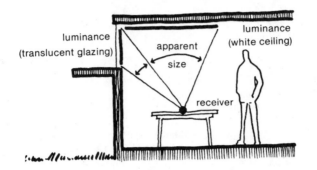

5-3. Luminance × apparent size *conceptual model.*

This concept does not differentiate between various sources; e.g., a cloudy sky "seen" through a clerestory window contributes the same quality and quantity of light to a receiver as an illuminated white wall surface (assuming equal luminance, color, and apparent size).

The apparent size of the source as seen from the receiver is a function of source *size*, object-to-reflector *distance*, and source *tilt* relative to the receiver. In figure 5-4, it can be seen how these three variables affect apparent size.

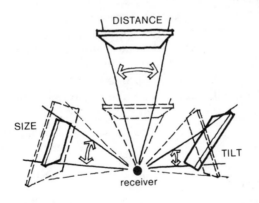

5-4. *Apparent size of distributed source as a function of size, tilt, and distance.*

REFLECTING DIFFUSERS

If the distributed source is a white reflector, the tilt of the reflector relative to the receiver does not affect reflector luminance (assuming an ideal matte finish). This reflector-receiver tilt does, however, affect the apparent size (exposure decreases as tilt increases). Thus for a given reflector location, the apparent size is maximized when the reflector is tilted normal to the receiver. This tilt is invariably different from the tilt that maximizes reflector luminance (reflector normal to source). The optimum tilt to provide maximum receiver illuminance becomes a compromise between these two tilts (just as if the reflector were a mirror) (fig. 5-5). Note that this optimum tilt is not a function of specular focusing (as a mirror would be) but is instead the result of compromising the reflector area projected to both the source and receiver. Because of this (and unlike a specular reflector), considerable design deviation from this optimum is possible with little effect on the illumination of the receiver.

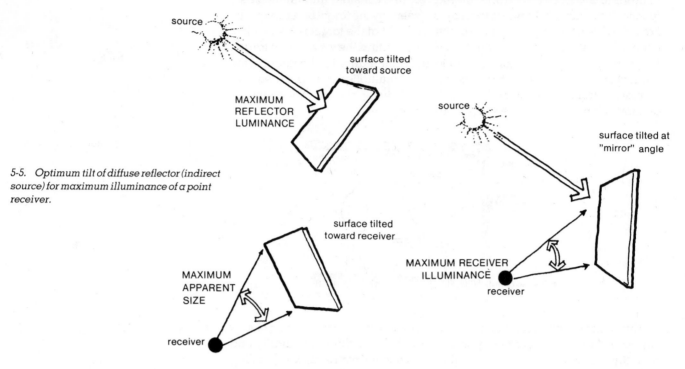

5-5. *Optimum tilt of diffuse reflector (indirect source) for maximum illuminance of a point receiver.*

TRANSLUCENT DIFFUSERS

Translucent diffusers, such as patterned glass or white fabric, become indirect sources when illuminated from behind. While the resulting luminous surface is distributed (similar to white reflectors), translucent diffusers are of particular value in lighting building areas away from the direct source (i.e., when located between the target and the direct source). Perfectly diffuse glazing has many qualities analogous to white reflectors. It has the greatest luminance when oriented normal to the direct source and contributes the greatest apparent size when the opposite side is oriented normal to the target point. The optimum tilt for maximum illumination of the target is between these two (fig. 5-6).

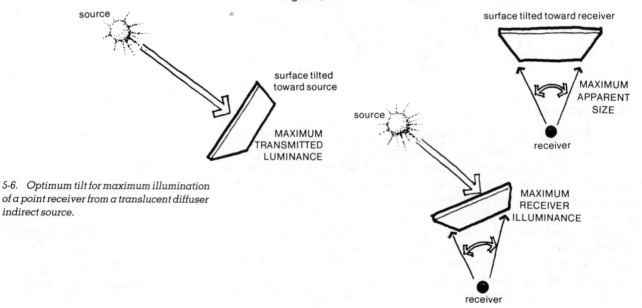

5-6. *Optimum tilt for maximum illumination of a point receiver from a translucent diffuser indirect source.*

LIGHT

Like white reflectors, translucent diffusers permit considerable design freedom in deviating from this optimum, with little effect on illuminating performance. However, if the translucent diffuser is also used as exterior glazing, thermal performance becomes an important consideration. The need for reducing transmitted solar gain in the summer usually makes a vertical, south-facing tilt most desirable.

The high reflectance of high-diffusion, opalescent material can be used advantageously on the interior to diffuse light in both directions. Suspended white fabric banners behind south-facing clerestories reflect light back to south building areas, while diffusely transmitting light to north areas (fig. 5-7).

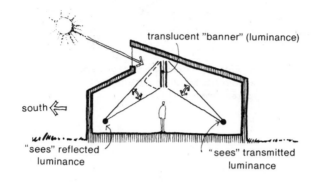

5-7. *Illumination by a transmitting/reflecting diffuser.*

SOURCE POSITION (COSINE EFFECT)

This luminance × apparent size concept, as stated so far, is an oversimplification. If the target is a two-dimensional surface (i.e., a workplane) then the position of the source relative to the receiving surface becomes a consideration because of the cosine effect. As discussed in chapter 3, light that is normal to the reference plane contributes more illumination than does light that is oblique to the reference plane. If the reference plane is horizontal (e.g., a table surface) an overhead reflector location would maximize illumination. If the reference plane is vertical (e.g., an artist's easel, bookshelves, or vertical exhibits), a reflector level with the reference plane would provide maximum illumination. However, other considerations, such as veiling reflections and the user's shadow, tend to favor oblique lighting over normal-incidence lighting. A 45-degree angle of incidence from above only reduces illumination by 30 percent (due to the cosine effect) for either vertical or horizontal reference planes, while minimizing ceiling reflections and source glare in the occupant's field of view (fig. 5-8).

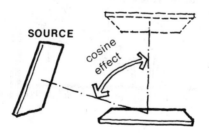

5-8. *Cosine effect of distributed source position on reference plane illuminance.*

Therefore, the conceptual model for reference plane illuminance becomes *luminance × apparent size × source position* (figs. 5-9, 5-10).

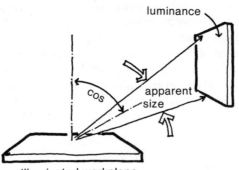

5-9. *Illuminance of a reference plane as a function of* distributed source luminance × apparent size × position.

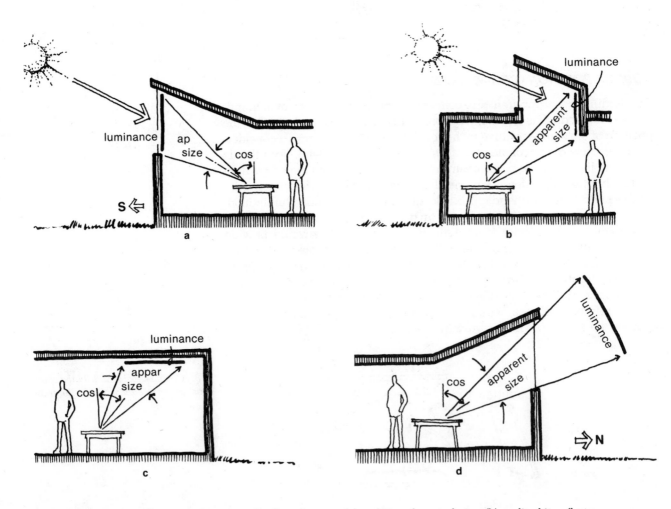

5-10. *Reference plane illuminance by various distributed sources: (a) sunlit translucent glazing; (b) sunlit white reflector; (c) fluorescent fixture; and (d) diffuse skydome.*

EXAMPLES FROM AALTO'S LIBRARIES

Daylighting was a primary design determinant for most of the buildings designed by the Finnish architect, Alvar Aalto (1898–1976). Aalto's libraries are particularly rich in examples of the application of the luminance × apparent size × position conceptual model.

The main reading room of the Seinäjoki Library has four visual task areas: the reading counter (between the columns), the sunken reading area, the stacks, and the charging desk.

a

5-11. Seinäjoki Library (1963): (a) northeast exterior; (b) south exterior.

b

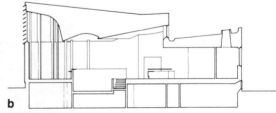

The large, high, south window has clear glazing with horizontal, diagonal exterior louvers. The louvers are white on both sides with a cut-off angle of 45 degrees. At angles higher than 45 degrees, no sunlight or sky light penetrates directly, but is reflected twice by the parallel louvers. As a result, the high window acts like a translucent diffuser to high light sources. Its large area

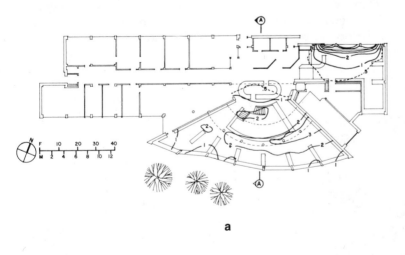

a

5-12. Seinäjoki Library: (a) isolux plan (as a percentage of exterior horizontal illumination, excluding direct sun); (b) section.

b

adequately illuminates the reading areas from above the field of view of the reader. The result is generous illumination evenly distributed, little cosine reduction, and minimal glare because of the high source location.

5-13.   Seinäjoki Library. Exploded axonometric.

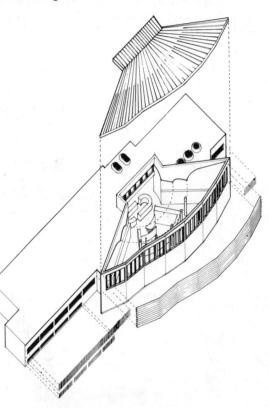

At angles below the 45-degree cut-off angle, direct sky light (and in the winter, direct sunlight) enters directly. Most of the direct sunlight strikes the lower part of the large, curved, reflective "light scoop." The lower portion of this scoop has a high luminance level (due to its orientation relative to the window). This bright surface becomes the principle light source for the vertical book stacks along the exterior wall. Note, in figure 5-14b, the large apparent size of the scoop as "seen" from the stacks. It is not as obvious from the section that the stacks perpendicular to the wall receive diagonal illumination from the scoop as well as directly from the window (due to the fan-shaped wall curvature in plan).

5-14.   Seinäjoki Library: (a) interior showing light scoop; (b) explanation.

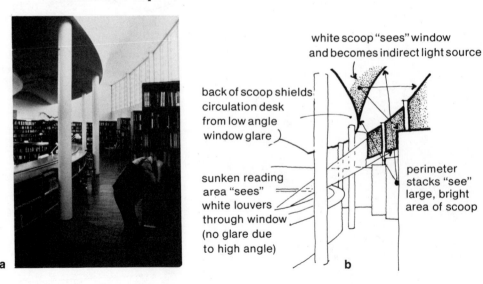

white scoop "sees" window and becomes indirect light source

back of scoop shields circulation desk from low angle window glare

sunken reading area "sees" white louvers through window (no glare due to high angle)

perimeter stacks "see" large, bright area of scoop

a

b

LIGHT

The top of the scoop receives light reflected from both the lower part of the scoop as well as the top of the louvers and exterior ground. The exterior wall (below the window and above the stacks) receives light from the lower part of the scoop. While both the upper scoop and this wall portion in turn contribute to the general illumination of the room, their luminance is important in reducing the brightness contrast around the window.

The opposite side of the scoop serves as an "eyebrow" to screen the circulation desk librarian from most of the low-angle glare from the high south window. The charging desk has poor daylight illumination because most of the south window is obstructed by this "eyebrow," and the north clerestory is directly overhead. This results in a small apparent size of each source from this location. It appears that the structural requirements of the building prevented placing the north clerestory even further to the north (which would have increased its apparent size, and thus the illumination, in this area). However, the sloped ceiling receives light reflected from the snow on the adjacent roof, and, to a lesser extent, directly from the sky.

The sunken reading area "sees" two large, bright secondary sources: the high, south window and the north clerestory. The sunken location places both sources high, reducing the cosine reduction from both sources onto a horizontal reading plane, while keeping them above the reader's field of view to reduce glare.

In addition to a fan-shaped plan (such as that at Seinäjoki), most Aalto libraries employ a sunken study area located in the center of the main library space. This creates a strong spatial focus. It also allows stacks to be located in the center without blocking visual control from the circulation desk. In those libraries where light is admitted only from the perimeter, the sunken floor configuration keeps the high side light above the field of view of the reader, while reducing the cosine reduction of illumination on reading tables.

The library in the Wolfsburg, Germany cultural center (figs. 5-15 to 5-18) also has a fan-shaped plan. However, the library is only one of several units

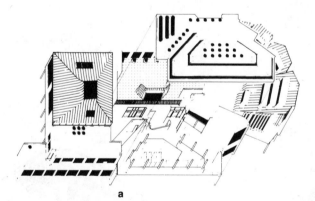

a

5-15. Library, Cultural Center, Wolfsburg, Germany (1959): (a) exploded axonometric; (b) section.

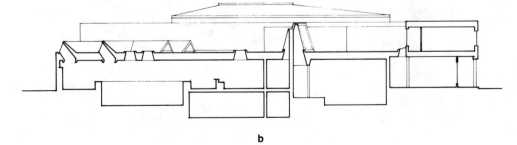

b

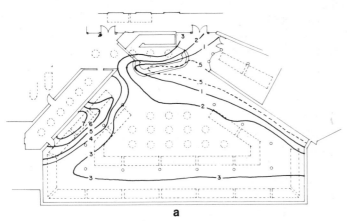

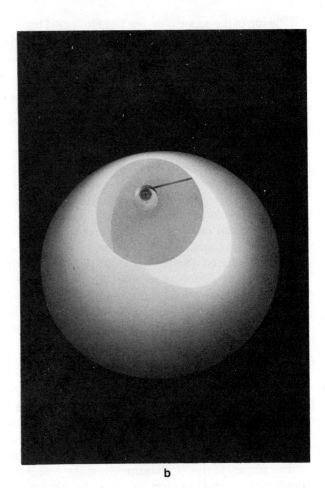

5-16. Wolfsburg Library: (a) plan with isolux contours; (b) conical skylight from below.

5-17. Wolfsburg Library. Roof showing skylights and monitors.

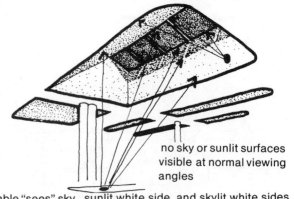

white side "sees" sky, opposite reflector and possibly direct sun

no sky or sunlit surfaces visible at normal viewing angles

table "sees" sky, sunlit white side, and skylit white sides

5-18. Wolfsburg Library: (a) reference reading room skylight; (b) explanation.

LIGHT

in the larger building. Greater design emphasis was given to the five lecture rooms (dramatic exterior forms and interior spaces) with relatively less emphasis on the library. Aalto used smaller roof monitors with "scoops" to illuminate the perimeter stack area. These are oriented east, southwest, and northwest with 70-degree clear glazing. There are no exterior louvers for sun control. This multiple orientation of monitors of the same design is presumably a result of the predominantly overcast local climate. Penetration of direct sunlight is minimized on clear days by the pronounced curvature of the scoop. Thus, the backs of the scoops receive either direct sunlight or diffuse sky light, and in turn become secondary sources for illuminating the adjacent perimeter stacks.

At Wolfsburg, due to the low ceiling height and the small, shielded configuration of the perimeter scoop, central illumination is supplemented by a field of small, round skylights with clear, horizontal glazing. The ceiling thickness forms a well to minimize direct sunlight penetration. The well is conically shaped, with smooth, white plaster sides. Diffuse light from the skydome is admitted directly. On clear days, however, only the upper part of the well is sunlit. This bright surface, in turn, illuminates the space below, as well as the remaining white surfaces within the well. Because sunlight typically strikes only the uppermost part of the well (unseen at normal viewing angles), and because the lower part of the well is smoothly curved, matte white plaster that appears evenly bright (due to the diffuse interreflections within the cone), these wells have the appearance of horizontal luminous disks in the plane of the ceiling. Their true shape is apparent only when the occupant intentionally looks up (fig. 5-16b). This same device is found in many Aalto buildings, usually in a single line (such as above a corridor), reinforcing a linear spatial emphasis.

At Wolfsburg, in a separate, smaller reference/periodical reading room, a similar but much larger skylight configuration is used above the reading tables (fig. 5-18). In order to reduce direct sunlight penetration in these larger variations, the section profile is asymmetrical with the north surface nearly vertical and a shallow sloping south surface. The larger recess serves to spatially define the reading area while providing a wider, more even distribution of light.

Aalto's largest public library is located in Rovaniemi, Finland. The fan-shaped plan is segmented with separated sunken reading areas. Each is

a

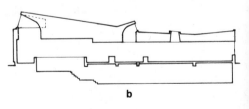

b

5-19. *Rovaniemi Library (1965): (a) northwest exterior; (b) section. The large, high glazing surrounding each segment of the fan-shaped plan illuminates the adjacent interior reading areas.*

defined and illuminated by a light scoop and a high window on three sides. Considering the location (virtually on the Arctic Circle), the glass area is surprisingly large. The north orientation results in excessive winter heat loss, but this exposure and high window placement admits large amounts of diffuse daylight to illuminate these reading areas. The backs of the light scoops

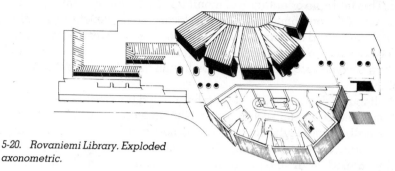

5-20. Rovaniemi Library. Exploded axonometric.

a

"sees" more sky

"sees" more ground

bottom of scoop forms "eyebrow" to shield circulation desk from direct low-angle sky glare

lower desk "sees" sky

upper desk "sees" sky and white scoop

stack "sees" scoop and sky through end window

b

5-21. Rovaniemi Library: (a) interior; (b) explanation, showing typical bay with sunken reading area, high window, and light scoop.

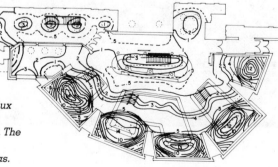

5-22. Rovaniemi Library. Plan with isolux contours (percent of exterior horizontal illumination, excluding direct sunlight). The levels of greatest illumination are concentrated in the sunken reading areas.

LIGHT

also receive diffuse daylight as well as low-angle, direct morning sunlight in summer. The result is a relatively uneven distribution of illumination with the greatest amounts occurring at each sunken reading area. Like the Seinäjoki library, the bottom of the scoops in the Rovaniemi library act as eyebrows, preventing glare (i.e., large amounts of bright sky visible at low viewing angles) at the centralized circulation desk. This is achieved at the expense of deep light penetration from the high perimeter windows.

Elsewhere in the building, deeply configured smaller scoops are used for perimeter, secondary-source illumination of wall-hung exhibits. These scoops project above the flat ceiling/roof in the form of long monitors. These face north, east, and south and are sloped at about 75 degrees, with clear glazing and no overhang. It is interesting that, even at this extreme northern latitude, reflective film has been added to reduce summer solar heat gain on the east and south glazing.

The main library at Otaniemi Technical University, near Helsinki, is larger than the other libraries designed by Aalto, all of which are for community use (figs. 5-23 to 5-27). Most of the stacks are closed and located on basement

5-23. Main Library, Otaniemi Technical University (1965). Northwest exterior. Ends of the two northeast-facing roof monitors are visible.

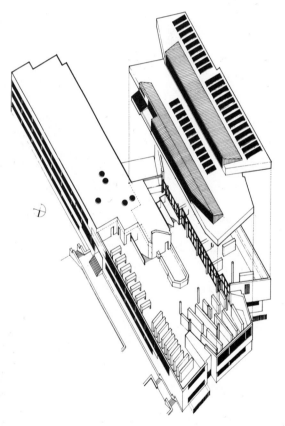

5-25. Otaniemi Library. Exploded axonometric.

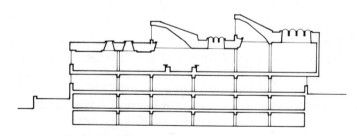

5-24. Otaniemi Library. Section.

levels. The reading area is on the top floor to allow the use of skylights and large northeast-facing roof monitors for illumination. This required the use of stairs for access from the lower entry level.

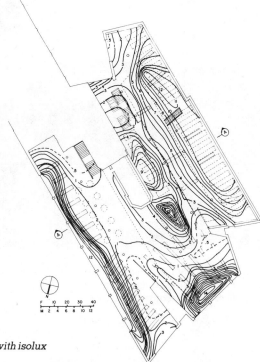

A "sees" larger sky than B, but receives less illumination due to cosine reduction

"sees" scoop only

desk is closer to clerestory but "sees" only white scoop and reflector below clerestory

"sees" large sky through window and overhead skylight

a

b

5-26. Otaniemi Library: (a) interior; (b) explanation.

5-27. Otaniemi Library. Plan with isolux contours.

The two large monitors provide generous, even, diagonal illumination. Notice from the isolux contours in the plan (fig. 5-27) that the areas of highest illumination occur, not directly below the "scoops" behind the monitors (as might be expected), but in adjacent areas to the southwest. This is due to the larger apparent size of the vertical glazing from this location. Additional light is provided by the many long, horizontally glazed skylights located directly above these areas of greatest luminance (where the apparent size of the horizontal glazing is largest).

The Nordic House Library in Reykjavik, Iceland (fig. 5-28) employs a simple but effective strategy for daylight illumination. Large vertical clerestories are located along each side of the reading room. Their high location allows effective illumination to the opposite side of the relatively narrow plan. In addition, the roof of the lower, surrounding rooms below the clerestory is usually snow-covered and thus effective in reflecting light onto the reading room ceiling. In another climate, the use of such large unprotected areas of glass would admit unacceptable amounts of direct sunlight. Presumably, this is less of a problem in the overcast Icelandic climate.

5-28. Nordic House, Reykjavik, Iceland (1965): (a) north exterior; (b) interior, showing library.

a

b

The small sunken reading area receives additional overhead illumination from the large, clear, prism-shaped skylight directly above. The rationale behind this tall prismatic configuration lies not in an increased ability to transmit low-angle sunlight (horizontal glazing would transmit an equal amount of light with less heat loss), but in the ability to penetrate thick snow cover. The snow-covered lower portion acts as a white reflector, in the manner of the conical skylight well.

The last library to be designed by Aalto is located at Mount Angel Abbey, a Benedictine monastery near Portland, Oregon (figs. 5-29 to 5-32). Using the

a

5-29. Mount Angel Library (1967): (a) south exterior; (b) north exterior.

b

familiar fan-shaped plan, light is introduced over the center reading area by a north-facing, crescent-shaped roof monitor, with a white scoop behind clear glazing sloped at about 60 degrees. The sectional profile is shallow, allowing

A CONCEPTUAL MODEL FOR DESIGN   47

5-30. Mount Angel Library: (a) interior; (b) explanation.

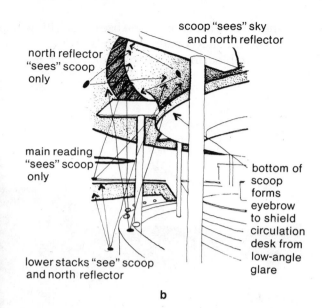

scoop "sees" sky
and north reflector

north reflector
"sees" scoop
only

main reading
"sees" scoop
only

bottom of
scoop
forms
eyebrow
to shield
circulation
desk from
low-angle
glare

lower stacks "see" scoop
and north reflector

b

a

5-31. Mount Angel Library: (a) high north window; (b) explanation. Both the sloped soffit and the perpendicular wall receive end light directly from the north sky vault. Their brightness reduces contrast with the sky visible through the window. In addition, the soffit illuminates the carrels below (which receive little direct sky light) and the wall below the window (again to reduce brightness contrast with the sky).

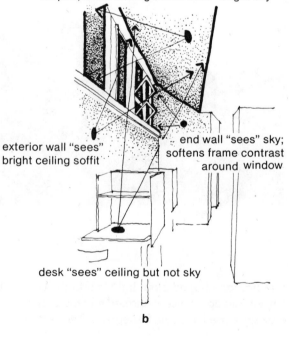

sloped, white ceiling soffit "sees" bright sky

exterior wall "sees"
bright ceiling soffit

end wall "sees" sky;
softens frame contrast
around window

desk "sees" ceiling but not sky

a

b

48

direct sky illumination in one direction and reflection from the scoop in the opposite direction. This provides generous illumination to the reading stations surrounding the sunken mezzanine crescent and the mezzanine level itself. In addition, adequate light penetrates down past the mezzanine into the open stack area in the basement to allow selection of books.

On the main level, stacks radiate out from this center light chamber, allowing visual control from the circulation desk. At the perimeter of the main level, open carrels are illuminated from above by high window light that is reflected from the sloped ceiling. This straight scoop also washes the wall below the window to reduce the brightness contrast of the sky seen through the windows. A similar sloped ceiling is positioned above corner windows in the small lecture room. In addition to light reflected by the sloped ceiling, each lower wall is washed from the adjacent perpendicular window.

5-32. Mount Angel Library. Roof monitor.

AALTO BUILDINGS IN PERSPECTIVE

After visiting numerous Aalto buildings and making detailed illuminance measurements in the six major libraries, I remain impressed with the breadth and richness of Aalto's architectural and illumination vocabulary. In most cases, the two are inseparable. It is easy to be awed by his buildings (and his reputation) and to dismiss them as somewhat mystical creations of a gifted genius. There is also a temptation to transpose Aalto's strategies directly to the design of contemporary buildings.

This is unwise. Not only were most of Aalto's solutions heavily influenced by local (typically overcast, northerly) daylight environments, they were designed during a time of abundant energy. Little regard seems to have been given to problems of excessive heat loss or gain. For contemporary architects designing in an environment of clearer skies and much higher relative energy costs, perhaps the single most valuable principle to be gleaned from Aalto is the use of white surfaces as diffuse, secondary illumination sources. This principle must now be adapted to the preferred use of sunlight (instead of diffuse sky light) to allow smaller glazing areas. The south-facing roof monitor (with suitable reflective baffles) for top lighting, and the light shelf for side lighting are two feasible adaptations of secondary-source reflective diffusers to the relatively high sun angles and present energy costs in the U.S.

PART II: BUILDINGS

Chapter 6
Siting

Access to daylight in cities has long been a concern of lawmakers. Bryan, et al. (1981) have described the following historical examples. The ancient Greeks and Romans mandated minimum lighting standards for their cities. The British Law of Ancient Lights (which dates to 1189) and its later embodiment into statute law, The Prescription Act of 1832, provided that if a window enjoyed uninterrupted access to daylight for a twenty year period, right to that

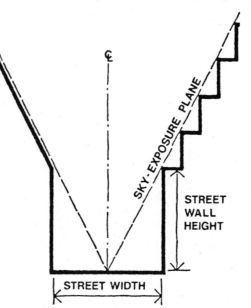

6-1. Section through typical street showing maximum allowable building envelope under Atkinson's 1912 proposal for limiting building height to ensure daylight at street level. (Reprinted, by permission, from Bryan, et al., 1981)

access became permanent. In 1912, William Atkinson proposed a geometry for limiting building heights in urban areas that ensured daylight exposure to the street by defining the allowable limit to the building envelope (fig. 6-1). Based on similar geometry, the New York 1916 zoning ordinance was the first

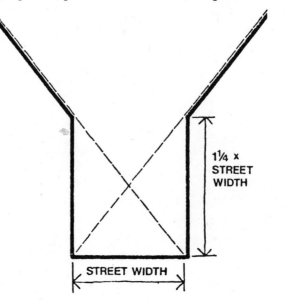

6-2. Section through typical street showing building set-backs required under New York 1916 Zoning Ordinance. (Reprinted, by permission, from Bryan, et al., 1981)

comprehensive municipal attempt to ensure minimum street-level standards for daylight (New York Planning Commission, 1945; fig. 6-2). The city was divided into five "height districts" that attempted to recognize the perceived activities of the area, neighborhood character, and the need for "pedestrian amenities" (fig. 6-3). A 1980 proposed New York zoning revision provides for graphic evaluation of the amount of the sky obstructed by a proposed building (fig. 6-4).

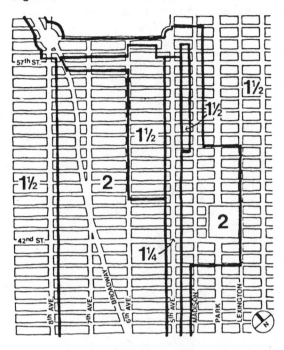

6-4. Proposed New York daylighting evaluation diagram. (Reprinted, by permission, from Bryan, et al., 1981)

6-3. New York 1916 height district plan showing maximum allowable ratios of street wall height to street width, as defined by figure 6-2. (Reprinted, by permission, from Bryan, et al., 1981)

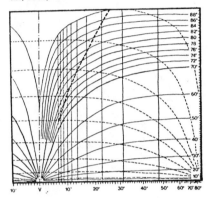

SOLAR GEOMETRY AND SITE SELECTION

If daylighting is to be utilized in a proposed building, it is necessary to determine its availability at the site. Surrounding objects such as other buildings, trees, and land forms all act as daylight obstructions by blocking either direct sunlight or portions of the skydome that are visible from the building location. Because of its potentially large contribution to illumination, and because of its directionality, the position of the sun is of particular interest to the designer. In addition to its effect on illumination, solar position is important because of its effect on winter sun penetration for passive heating and on the design of summer shading devices.

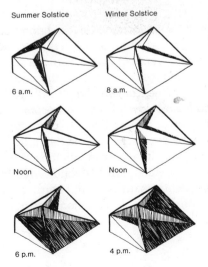

Summer Solstice   Winter Solstice

6 a.m.   8 a.m.

Noon   Noon

6 p.m.   4 p.m.

6-5. "Solar Envelope"; the upper edges of the vertical planes define the maximum volume that can be built on a sloped site without shading beyond the site during critical hours. (After Knowles, 1977)

Under clear sky conditions, because skydome luminance is greatest near the sun, obstruction of the sun also means obstruction of the brightest portion of the skydome. Under overcast sky conditions, because skydome luminance is greatest at the zenith, low obstructions are less costly in terms of loss of daylight. Furthermore, the contribution of low-angle sources to horizontal illuminance is relative small due to cosine reduction.

The position of the sun in the sky can be described by its *altitude angle* (vertical angle above the horizon) and its *azimuth angle* (horizontal angle east or west of south) (fig. 6-6).

6-6. *Solar azimuth and altitude angles. Azimuth angles are measured in each direction from south (e.g., northeast = 135° east). Altitude angles are measured vertically from the horizon.*

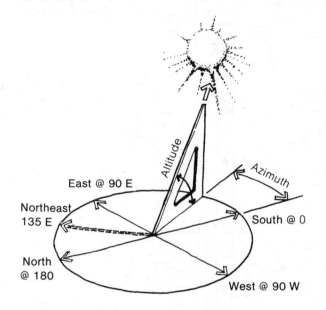

Solar azimuth and altitude angles are a function of site latitude, day of the year, and solar time of day. While azimuth and altitude angles can be determined by a formula or from tables in standard reference books (e.g., *ASHRAE Handbook of Fundamentals,* 1981), these numerical values are not as visually meaningful in the architectural design process as are more graphic representations.

Two graphic methods are available that are particularly applicable in daylighting, passive solar design, shading, and reflector design. These are the sundial and sun path diagrams.

SUNDIAL

The sundial is a diagram of the locations of the shadow of the tip of a *gnomon* (vertical pointer) cast on a horizontal plane. It is constructed using polar coordinates where the gnomon is assumed to be at the center. The polar angles are the azimuth angles, and the distance from the center out to the end of the shadow (radius) is equal to the tangent of the height of the pointer. Since the sundial is flat, the shadows of low sun angles become long, and sunrise and sunset positions cannot be accommodated. In practical use this limitation is not serious and is offset by the simplicity and flexibility of the method.

A complete set of sundials for northern latitudes 28 through 56 is provided in Appendix A. (Sundials for comparable southern latitudes are mirror images of these with the compass arrow being north instead of south.) The 4-degree latitude increments provide sufficient accuracy for most building design applications.

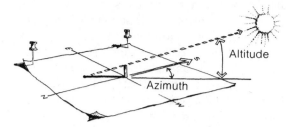

6-7. *Shadow location on a sundial at 2 P.M.
December 21, 40° north latitude.*

6-8. *Shadow path for December 21, 40° north
latitude. The dotted lines represent lines of
sight from sun, through tip of gnomon, to
shadow location on sundial.*

6-9. *Completed sundial for 40° north latitude.
Arrow indicates south direction. Cut out
dashed triangle at top, and glue along dotted
line to form gnomon.*

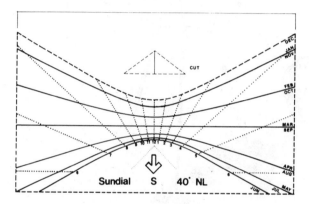

PRELIMINARY SITE OBSTRUCTION SURVEY

Numerous commercial devices are available for determining solar obstructions to a site. The sundial allows a quick and accurate identification of those
obstructions during the critical December period (when the sun is lowest in
the sky). Make a copy of the sundial (from Appendix A) for the latitude nearest
the site. Cut out the pointer. Glue the copy of the sundial onto a piece of stiff
flat board. Cut along the outside dotted "cut" line. Fold the pointer down the
center to form two triangles and glue it where shown on the sundial so that the
folded edge is vertical. Next, where each of the "hour lines" meets the curved
edge of the dial (i.e., the December sun path), place a black mark on the edge
of the mounting board. The sundial is now complete. When the base is horizontal and oriented toward true south, a line from any time point on the dial
to the tip of the pointer will point to the position of the sun at that time (true
solar time) and date. Conversely, the time points on the dial show the location
of the shadow of the pointer at that time. The sundial is used typically to
predict the sun's position (and corresponding shadows) at selected times of
the day and year; thus it is usually unnecessary to convert solar time to local
time.

At the site, hold the sundial horizontal and oriented south (fig. 6-10). (A camera tripod can be used by cutting a small hole in the sundial to receive the mounting screw.) With your eye slightly below (and to the north of) the sundial, sight over the curved edge so that the top of the pointer is just visible and aligned with an hour mark previously made on the curved edge. This line of sight corresponds to the sun's location on December 21 at that time. If there is an obstruction in that line of sight, it will obscure the December sun at that time. By moving your eye along the curved edge in alignment with the pointer, all December solar obstructions can be identified.

6-10. Use of sundial for preliminary obstruction survey. Sundial is level and oriented south. Sight from north edge, over pointer, to December sun location.

This same sundial can be used for model studies later in the design process (fig. 6-11). Attach the sundial to the model base, oriented toward south on the model. In direct sunlight, tilt the model base so that the shadow of the pointer touches the time and month of interest. The resulting shadows allow detailed study of overhang shading, site shading by the building, and sunlight penetration throughout the year. The use of tilted models to measure interior daylight illuminance will be discussed in detail in chapter 14.

6-11. Model shadow studies using the sundial.

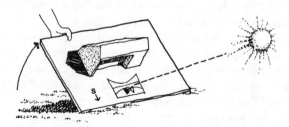

If direct sunlight is not available, the sundial can be used with a distant incandescent lamp (distance should be large relative to the dimensions of the model). The lamp should be positioned to cast a gnomon shadow on the desired time position. An alternative to studying cast shadows directly is to view (or photograph) the model under diffuse light from the sun's position by using the sundial on the model base as a "sighting" device. With the eye (camera) in the sun's location, all visible surfaces will be sunlit. Conversely, all hidden surfaces will be in shadow (fig. 6-12).

SITE SHADOW PLAN

Another valuable site analysis tool is a site plan showing the shadows of solar obstructions (fig. 6-13). A shadow plan is prepared over a site plan with topographic contours (with the location and height of all potential obstructions shown). Because sunlight illumination is minimal when solar altitude angles are below 10 degrees, it is recommended that shadows be plotted only for hours when the sun is above 10 degrees. Differentiate between obstructions that are permanent (e.g., buildings, land forms, evergreen trees) and those that are seasonal (e.g., deciduous trees).

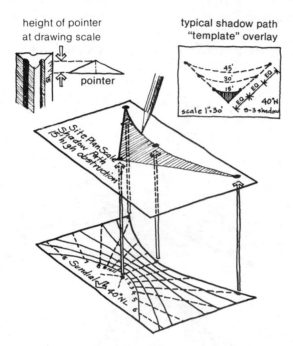

6-12. Viewing (photographing) the model from the sun's position, using the sundial as a sighting device.

6-13. Construction of a site shadow template overlay.

Using the sundial base for the latitude nearest that of the site, note the December 21 hours that fall within the 10-degree altitude circle. For example, at 40 degrees latitude these hours include 9 A.M. to 3 P.M. standard time (10 A.M. to 4 P.M. daylight savings time).

On a tracing overlay, draw a line from the pointer base straight to the December 21, 3 P.M. point. Then trace along the curved December 21 line from 3 P.M. to 9 A.M. and draw a straight line back to the pointer. Next, measure the height of the pointer at the scale of the site plan. For example, if the pointer height is fifteen feet, then the traced outline represents the area path of the shadow of a fifteen-foot-tall vertical pole on a flat site. Enlarge or reduce this shape proportionally for other heights. On sloped terrain, change the shadow length to compensate for differences in contours between the obstruction and the end of the shadow.

For daylighting or solar collection purposes, window shading is more critical than ground shading. Therefore, to evaluate window shading, deduct six feet from the height of all obstructions to define areas subject to shading six feet above the existing grade. (Six feet is the assumed height of the center of the window.) Using the outline as a template, sketch the shadows on a tracing over the site plan. Similar templates and site overlays may be prepared for March/September (these are the same because the sun's location is identical on March 21 and September 21) and June.

SUN PATH DIAGRAMS

As discussed previously, the path of the sun across the sky can be visualized as a path traced on the overhead skydome. This three-dimensional representation must be translated into two dimensions in order to be useful in the design process. One way of doing this is based on a plan projection of the skydome (fig. 6-14). The plan is constructed so that altitude angles are projected as equal distances in plan (to avoid foreshortened distortion near the horizon). This equidistant plan projection is the basis for two widely used methods. Olgyay and Olgyay (1957) present a detailed method of shading device analysis using this plan projection. The Libbey-Owens-Ford sun angle calculator (1981) includes a complete set of sun path charts for north latitudes from 24 to 52 degrees. Because of the widespread use of this format and the availability of the L.O.F. calculator, this latter method will be the basis for the discussion and charts presented in subsequent chapters. All charts herein are compatible with the L.O.F. calculator.

6-14. Skydome, with equidistant plan projection showing azimuth and altitude coordinates.

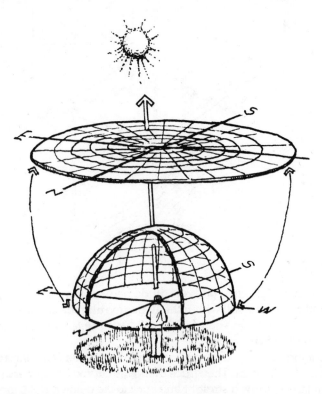

A complete set of sun path charts for northern latitudes 24 through 52 is provided in Appendix B. (Charts for comparable southern latitudes are mirror images of these, with the north and south designations reversed.) Charts for other latitudes can be constructed from local solar angle data.

BUILDINGS

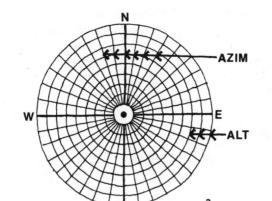

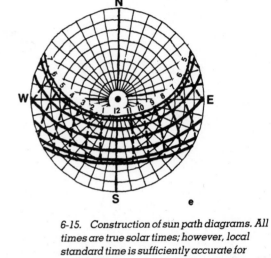

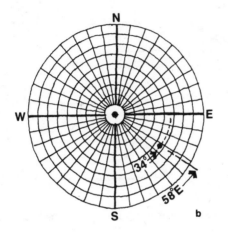

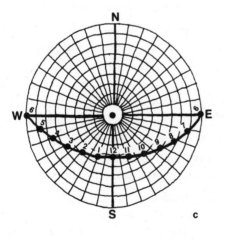

6-15. Construction of sun path diagrams. All times are true solar times; however, local standard time is sufficiently accurate for design applications. (a) The coordinates of the sun chart represent the altitude (vertical) and azimuth (horizontal) angles of the skydome; (b) the sun's position for 9 A.M. March 21, 40° north latitude (58° east azimuth, 34° altitude); (c) plotting the sun's position for various hours on a particular day results in the sun path for that day; (d) plotting the sun path for the 21st day of each month provides monthly sun paths. (Note that except for the extreme solstice dates of June 21 and December 21, each sun path is the path for two days. For example, the sun paths for March 21 and September 21 are identical.); (e) dotted lines indicate the sun's position at a particular hour throughout the year.

DETAILED SITE OBSTRUCTION SURVEY

While the sundial allows identification of obstructions to sunlight at the lowest sun angles (most critical for winter solar heating), a more detailed analysis may be desirable for building design. The sun path diagram can be used to plot a profile of all site obstructions. This provides a graphic representation of obstructions at all sun angles and forms the basis for later calculation of illuminance at window locations (due to beam, sky, and/or ground components), shading and reflector device design, and interior illuminance due to the sky component (daylight illuminance from the skyvault only, excluding direct sunlight and interior and exterior reflecting surfaces).

In order to measure altitude angles at the site, a surveyor's transit is desirable. However, because a high degree of accuracy is unnecessary for preliminary design purposes, a simple protractor with a plumb bob can be substituted. In addition, a magnetic compass for measuring azimuth angles is required.

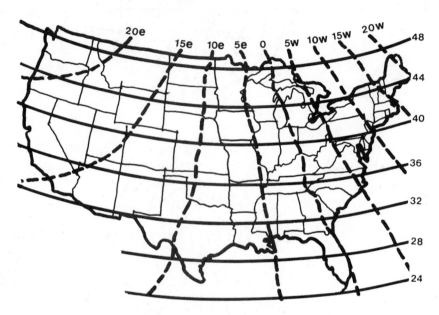

6-16. U.S. latitudes and magnetic deviations; an easterly deviation means that a magnetic compass needle will be deviated to the east of true north.

The altitude of the skyline can be determined as follows:

1. Determine which direction (bearing) is true south.

2. Aiming the level toward true south, determine the altitude (angle above the horizon) of the skyline. Plot this point on the sun chart above 0 degrees true south.

3. Similarly, find and record the altitudes of the skyline for each 10 degrees azimuth both east and west of south. Plot these readings for the respective azimuth angles on the sky chart and connect them.

4. For isolated tall objects that block the sun, such as tall evergreen trees, find both the bearing angle and the altitude for each object and record them at the appropriate point on the chart.

5. Finally, plot the deciduous trees in the skyline with a dotted line. These must be treated separately because they will block the sun during spring through fall and let most of the sun pass through when their leaves are gone (late fall through early spring). This completes the skyline. The open areas on the completed chart represent those times when sunlight will reach this specific location.

6. Plot charts for several locations around the perimeter of the anticipated location. If possible, use a ladder to survey higher locations for multistory buildings.

BUILDINGS

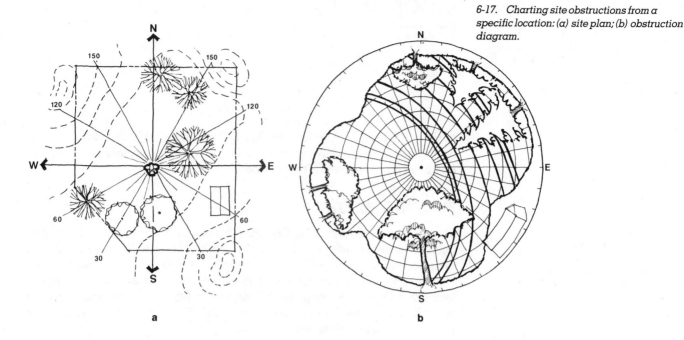

6-17. *Charting site obstructions from a specific location: (a) site plan; (b) obstruction diagram.*

a

b

REFERENCES

American Society of Heating, Air Conditioning, and Refrigerating Engineers. *ASHRAE Handbook, Fundamentals Volume.* New York: American Society of Heating, Air Conditioning, and Refrigerating Engineers, Inc., 1981.

Atkinson, W. *The Orientation of Buildings or Planning for Sunlight.* New York: John Wiley and Sons, 1912.

Bryan, H., Moore, J., Kwartler, M., and Jones, T. "The Utilization of Daylighting as an Urban Design Strategy." In *Daylighting Resourcebook,* edited by Kroner, W., Bryan, H., and Leslie, R. Washington, DC: Association of Collegiate Schools of Architecture, 1981.

Knowles, R. *Energy and Form.* Cambridge: M.I.T. Press, 1974.

Libbey-Owens-Ford. *Sun Angle Calculator.* Merchandising Department, 811 Madison Avenue, Toledo, OH.

New York City Planning Commission. *1916 Zoning Resolution* (amended to 1945). New York: City of New York, 1945.

Olgyay, V., and Olgyay, A. *Solar Control and Shading Devices.* Princeton: Princeton University Press, 1957.

Chapter 7
Form

In the early stages of design, building shape has a primary effect on day-lighting performance. As a general rule, daylighting is a function of the exposure of interior space to the skydome.

BUILDING HEIGHT

Single-story structures (and the top story of multistory structures) are particularly suited for daylighting because of the accessibility of virtually all interior areas to the skydome. Furthermore, overhead light sources are more efficient for illuminating horizontal task surfaces (such as tables and desks) than are side sources, because the cosine reduction is less. Because overhead sources tend to occur above the normal field of view of the occupants, the potential for direct glare is also reduced.

7-1. Floor area available for top lighting is a function of roof area (and thus inversely of the number of floors).

BUILDING WIDTH AND ORIENTATION

If, as a result of nondaylight considerations, multiple stories are to be used, exposure to the skydome becomes a function of the narrowness of the plan. The "15/30" rule of thumb is a useful guide in the schematic design phase: with careful fenestration design, a fifteen-foot perimeter zone can be task-lighted primarily by daylight, the next fifteen feet partially daylighted with supplemental electric lighting, with the remainder requiring entirely electric illumination. (This guide is based on high windows and a ten-foot floor to ceiling height.)

Prior to the widespread use of air conditioning, office building plans tended to be narrow (about sixty-five to seventy feet wide), to provide adequate ventilation. With a center circulation zone, all of the work areas were within about thirty feet of the exterior (fig. 7-2). With the increased availability of air conditioning, plans became deeper, leading to the present dependence on fluorescent lighting due to the average increased distances to the exterior wall.

7-2. Typical pre-1950 office building (half section) allowed side light and ventilation penetration through transparent partitions and open transoms.

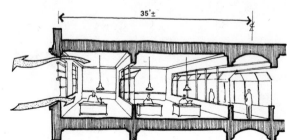

To utilize daylighting effectively in multistory buildings, narrow plans must be used to keep work areas within thirty feet of the exterior. "Finger" plans (wings of the building extend like fingers) can be used where other conditions make a straight plan undesirable (fig. 7-3). However, if the structure is tall and the space between wings is narrow, each wing becomes a skydome obstruction to the adjacent wings. This effect can be minimized by the use of light-colored exterior surfaces.

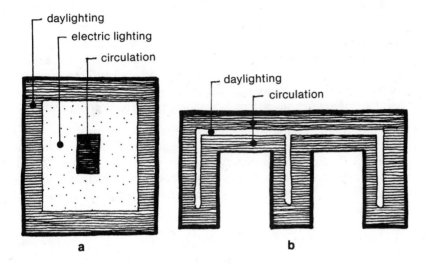

7-3. Typical multistory office building plans: (a) 1970; (b) 1940.

In designing small-scale buildings (such as residences) the desirability of southern exposure for passive solar heat gain must be balanced against the need to minimize perimeter area to reduce heat loss. In larger daylit buildings, heat loss is less of a concern (because of greater internal loads), and the need for exposure to relatively uniform lighting levels predominates.

Because light on the south facade is most abundant and relatively uniform, and because excess solar gain in the summer can be controlled with overhangs, this is the most desirable facade for admitting daylight; its dimension should be maximized.

The north facade, because of its exposure to less abundant, but more uniform diffuse sky light, is the next most desirable. The large net heat loss through north glazing is still a disadvantage, but not to the degree associated with smaller buildings (with minimum internal gains).

Both east and west orientations afford only half-day exposure to sunlight, making optimum fenestration design more difficult. Both orientations (especially the west) experience large summer heat gains at unwanted times, while providing little passive solar contribution in winter. For these reasons the east and west facade dimensions should be minimized.

Early energy studies for the Tennessee Valley Authority (TVA) Chattanooga Office Complex made by Van der Ryn, Calthorpe, and Partners and the Berkeley Solar Group (Ternoey, et al., 1983) provide examples of the combined effects of building width and orientation on energy usage. Detailed computer analyses were performed on a prototypical medium-rise office building, changing the parameters of width and orientation while holding all other parameters constant. The five plan configurations had aspect ratios (N/S dimension to E/W dimension) of 0.2, 0.36, 1.0, 2.8, and 4.5 (45-N, 60-N, square, 60-E, and 45-E respectively (fig. 7-4a). The design team concluded that east-west elevations were a liability and that narrow forms with broad north and south elevations had a distinct advantage. More specifically they found that:

■ The annual need for lighting energy was reduced as the building massing became thinner north to south. Thin buildings with broad east/west elevations required more energy for lighting since they required more extensive shading devices to block the low morning and afternoon sun. While orientation may not be significant in a building where a cube form and identical elevations are used, the design team found that a substantial difference in energy usage was possible when shading strategies and facade treatments were varied and climate adaptation was central to the proposed design.

■ Heating requirements increased as the building became thinner. Two variables influenced this fact. First, a narrow building has a larger building skin. Second, a narrow building has a greater daylit proportion than a deeper building and, therefore, a reduced heating contribution from electric lights. However, this liability was small since the need for heating energy was much less than that required for lighting and cooling.

■ Cooling energy needs were consistent in all configurations. The only significant pattern seemed to be a slight decrease in cooling energy needed in configurations with smaller external surface areas. The impact of this variation was small and counteracted by reduction in the heat of electric lights due to the larger daylighting potential of the shallow buildings.

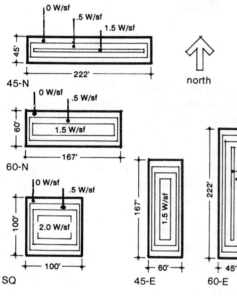

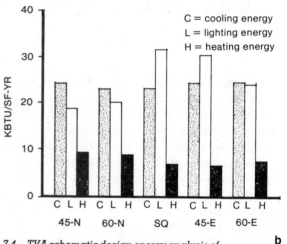

7-4. TVA schematic design energy analysis of the effects of width and orientation: (a) alternative plan configurations; (b) source energy comparisons for the configurations. (After Ternoey, et al., 1983)

COURTYARDS AND ATRIA

The courtyard plan is the most compact variation of the finger plan and thus creates the most self-obstruction of the skydome. It does, however, provide some daylight access to the center of an otherwise deep plan. Because interior locations are typically unable to "see" the sky in a courtyard configuration, the impact of exterior wall illuminance is increased. A horizontal light shelf or scoop is particularly effective in such a structure. There is one advantage inherent in the geometry of courtyards: while the opposite wall obstructs the skydome, it also obstructs low-angle direct sunlight, reducing glare problems and the need for wide overhangs.

The lighting performance of an atrium is very similar to that of a courtyard of similar dimensions because the same skydome obstructions are present. A clear atrium roof glazing simply replaces courtyard window glazing. There

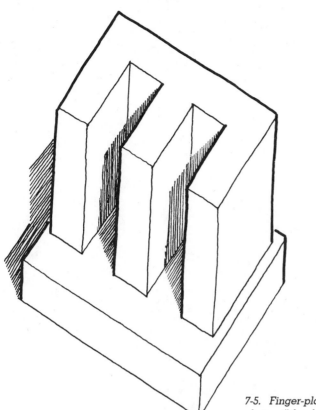

7-5. Finger-plan buildings tend to "self-obstruct" the skydome.

are, however, major thermal differences. In cold climates, the atrium remains habitable in the winter, at the expense of considerable summer heat gain. If an opaque roof with clerestories is used to cover the atrium, skydome obstruction is increased and illuminance is reduced accordingly. Based on the monitored performance of a small number of atrium office buildings, it is not clear if life-cycle costs are lower for buildings with an atrium than for comparable courtyard buildings.

BORROWED LIGHT

Side light through windows, because of its inherently low angle, is particularly subject to interior obstructions. These include furnishings (such as filing cabinets) as well as interior partitions. As a general rule, work surfaces that cannot "see" a window directly will receive reduced illuminance. This poses a particular problem for the designer who is unable to control the placement of movable obstructions during the life of the building. When the architect does not control the interior design directly, considerable collaboration with interior designers and occupants is required to avoid decisions that reduce daylight penetration.

REFERENCES

Ternoey, S., Bickle, L., Robbins, C., Rusch, R., and McCord, K. *The Design of Energy-Responsive Commercial Buildings.* Golden, CO: Solar Energy Research Institute, 1983.

7-6. "Borrowed" light through translucent partitions of study carrel to stack area, Mount Angel Library, Oregon (Alvar Aalto, architect).

PART III: FENESTRATION

Chapter 8
General Design Considerations

DESIGN OBJECTIVES

Fenestration may be defined as: "any opening or arrangement of openings (normally filled with media for control) for the admission of daylight." (Kaufman, 1981.)

For the purpose of illumination on a horizontal plane, fenestration should:

- maximize light transmission per unit area of glazing;

- control direct sunlight penetration onto the workplane;

- control brightness contrast within the occupant's visual field, especially between fenestration and surrounding room surfaces;

- minimize cosine reduction of workplane illuminance resulting from low fenestration placement;

- minimize veiling glare on workplane surfaces, resulting from high fenestration placement;

- minimize heat gain during overheated periods;

- minimize conductive heat loss and gain.

These objectives are sometimes contradictory, and their individual importance varies with orientation, season, time of day, latitude, building thermal load, and occupant usage. This complexity requires that both glazing type and fenestration geometry (glazing slope and orientation, sunlight shielding, and reflectors) be selected and designed specifically for each project. In particular, the objectives of direct sunlight control and solar heat gain control imply a different configuration for each orientation because of the seasonal and daily movement of the sun.

The following five chapters will introduce the principles of fenestration at a depth sufficient to permit the design of successfully daylighted buildings. The theory presented in these chapters is fundamental to a level of understanding that will enable the designer to respond to unique project requirements with imagination and confidence. In the chapter on fenestration strategies, for example, comparative performance data are presented to illustrate how changes in fenestration geometry affect interior illumination levels and distribution. In the chapter on glazing, considerable emphasis is placed on transmission in certain regions of the radiation spectrum. (A basic understanding of these important differences is essential to selecting glazing to maximize light, to minimize or maximize heat gain, to reduce heat loss, to control glare, and so on.)

INTERIOR LOCATION

The interior location (relative to the horizontal) of fenestration affects illumination quality and quantity in a number of ways:

COSINE REDUCTION

As discussed in chapter 3, illuminance on a plane is reduced by the cosine of the angle of incidence. For a horizontal workplane, this means that overhead fenestration produces more illuminance than a comparable side window the same distance away.

VEILING REFLECTIONS

While overhead sources produce greater illuminance than side sources, they are also more likely to produce veiling reflections. These can so seriously reduce contrast within the boundaries of the task surface that user visual performance is reduced. Griffith (1963) concluded that, since 10 to 15 percent more illuminance is required to make up for each 1 percent loss of contrast, most tasks require two or three times as much illuminance from overhead sources as from sidewall lighting. Thus, the reduced veiling reflections from side windows tend to offset the accompanying cosine reduction (see chapter 3).

SOURCE BRIGHTNESS

Large, high window areas appear very bright because of the relatively high luminance of the exterior environment (i.e., the skydome or sunlit exterior surfaces). If the window position is low in the field of view, this can be a source of direct glare. Direct glare results from high luminances or insufficiently shielded light sources in the field of view. In the case of low window positions, the offending source is usually not direct sunlight (which does not penetrate deeply through low windows), but bright exterior areas. Positioning window areas as high as possible (preferably 45 degrees or more above the horizontal) locates the offending brightness above the field of view. This is the rationale behind the design of conventional fluorescent luminaires with egg-crate diffusers, which effectively shield the bare tubes from direct view at angles less than 45 degrees.

Note that, while high window locations reduce glare from high-brightness exterior areas, they increase the potential of deep sunlight penetration, which can result in glare on interior surfaces. (At high angles, direct view of the sun is not a problem.)

ILLUMINANCE DISTRIBUTION

Because illuminance is a function of both apparent size and cosine reduction, higher fenestration provides more uniform distribution than comparable lower locations.

SKYDOME LUMINANCE AND EXTERIOR OBSTRUCTIONS

Fenestration exposed to the upper part of the skydome (i.e., a high window or roof) "sees" the brightest part of an overcast sky (zenith luminance is three times that at the horizon) and is less subject to obstruction from surrounding trees and buildings. For these reasons, the preferred interior location for fenestration is about 45 degrees above the horizontal. This controls veiling reflections while affording most of the advantages related to overhead placement. In addition, it illuminates vertical surfaces effectively.

SIZE

Assuming that the total quantity of light admitted remains the same, distributing the interior fenestration over a larger area will (1) reduce shadows, contrast, and texture definition, (2) provide more uniform light distribution, and (3) reduce veiling reflections.

SHADOWS, CONTRAST, AND TEXTURE

Light sources cast shadows, the sharpness of which are inversely related to the apparent size of the source. Concentrated light sources (such as direct sunlight or unfrosted incandescent lamps) create sharp, dark, directional shadows. As the size of the light source is increased, shadows become softer at the edges and less directional. An extreme example of a distributed light source is exterior overcast sky light, under which shadows virtually disappear. It should be emphasized that apparent size (rather than physical size) is the primary determinant of shadow sharpness and directionality. A translucent skylight four feet in diameter acts as a point source in a tall room (particularly if the room surfaces are dark to reduce reflections), but as a distributed source if located five feet above a desk.

Of less importance for architectural applications is the effect on shadow definition of the distance between the edge casting the shadow and the shadow itself. The greater this distance, the softer the shadows. For example, a hand casts a very sharp shadow in direct sunlight one foot from a surface; this shadow becomes less distinct as the hand moves further away from the surface.

Directly related to shadow definition is the effect of contrast between surfaces that are directly illuminated and those that are not. Under point source illumination, this effect is exaggerated so that shadows appear extremely dark and opaque. This is due to the adaptation of the eye to the brightness levels of the illuminated areas.

Surface textures are accentuated by point source lighting at low-incidence angles. However, a larger, unidirectional source is usually preferred to reveal large three-dimensional forms (such as sculpture) more softly. Point-source lighting emphasizes shape, while a large source size allows a gradual transition from light to shade on curved surfaces. Portrait photographers, for example, often use large diffusers to soften skin textures while retaining the modeling of general facial features.

DISTRIBUTION

Large-area sources provide relatively uniform illumination. Because illuminance is reduced as the target's distance from the source increases (inverse square effect), the use of a large, distributed source tends to equalize the effective distance to the various receiving locations in the room. The effect is similar to dividing a single point source into several distributed smaller sources.

Conversely, the uneven distribution characteristic of point sources can contribute to visual emphasis and variety. "Places" can be formed with pools of light. The theater has greatly refined this technique to create intimacy and containment on stage without the use of physical props.

VEILING REFLECTIONS

Glossy surfaces, such as magazine paper, can result in veiling reflections if the light source is positioned within the reflected field of view of the observer. This effect is most pronounced for point sources. In the case of a magazine page, the print is visible as a function of illuminance on the page (from sources in any direction). The strength of the veiling reflection image of the source is a direct function of source luminance. Therefore, while a distributed source might provide the same page illumination as a comparable concentrated source, veiling reflections would be reduced (because source luminance would be less) to a level where they would no longer compete with the contrast between the letters and background.

SOFT FRAMES

The brightness contrast between fenestration and surrounding room surfaces can be great if those adjacent surfaces are not daylit. This contrast is most extreme when an opening is placed in the middle of a thin wall or roof, away from any perpendicular surfaces that can serve as reflectors. Under these conditions, the surrounding wall or roof surface is left very dark, and contrast with the bright opening is extreme.

Deep windows with splayed reveals form a "soft frame" to soften this transition. Locating the window at the corner illuminates the endwall directly by daylight. The window becomes a secondary source, reducing contrast with the adjacent window. This, in turn, reflects light back onto the wall surrounding the window. This effect is further enhanced if the window is wrapped around the corner, allowing both walls to be directly illuminated (fig. 8-1).

8-1. (a) Corner windows cross-illuminate the adjacent wall surfaces to reduce brightness; (b) explanation.

sloped soffit "sees" sky and sunlit ground

south wall "sees" sky (through west window) and sloped soffit

west wall "sees" sky (through south window) and sloped soffit

a   b

VIEW WINDOWS

Because view windows are usually located at or below eye level, they are especially subject to brightness contrast. The strategy of providing surrounding soft frames reduces the contrast here as well as for other fenestrations. However, exterior brightness levels may still exceed those of the interior by a factor of ten or more. The low placement of view windows results in so much cosine reduction that workplane illuminance is minimal. For this reason it may be advantageous to separate the function of seeing from that of illumination. This can be achieved by locating view windows without regard to illumination and utilizing gray glass (as well as soft frames) to reduce brightness contrast. Conversely, illumination windows can be placed high with clear glazing. Egan (1983) cautions that if the exterior is simultaneously visible through adjacent areas of clear and tinted glass, a feeling of "gloom" (resulting from confusion and anxiety) results from the contradictory expectations the occupant has from the different interior illuminance levels. Others feel that the visual comfort advantages of this arrangement outweigh such disadvantages.

REFERENCES

Egan, J. *Concepts of Architectural Lighting.* New York: McGraw-Hill, Inc., 1983.

Kaufman, J. E., ed. *IES Lighting Handbook: 1981 Reference Volume.* New York: Illuminating Engineering Society of North America, 1981.

Chapter 9
Geometry

The sun path diagrams introduced in chapter 6 (and available in Appendix B or with the L.O.F. sun angle calculator) can be used to determine both the seasonal shading of glass due to shadows cast by overhangs (important for thermal analysis) and daylight penetration into the building.

OBSTRUCTION MASKS

Using the plan projection format, it is possible to construct a diagram that defines that portion of the sky that is masked out by surrounding obstructions (and, conversely, that portion that can be "seen"). When used together with the appropriate sun path chart, the hours of direct sun penetration and shading can be determined.

HORIZONTAL EDGES

Imagine a series of parallel, horizontal, overhead "bars" as viewed from a reference point on the ground. If these bars were projected as lines on the skydome, they would form an "orange-segment" pattern, with the lines converging to a point on the horizon in the direction of the bars. This pattern would project in plan as a series of converging curved lines (except for the trace of a bar directly overhead, which would project as a straight line through the center: figs. 9-1 and 9-2).

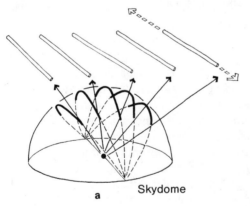

a   Skydome

9-1. *Plan projection of horizontal bar projections (profiles): (a) on skydome; (b) in plan.*

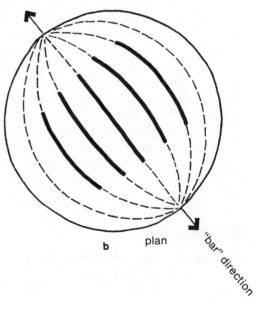

b   plan

"bar" direction

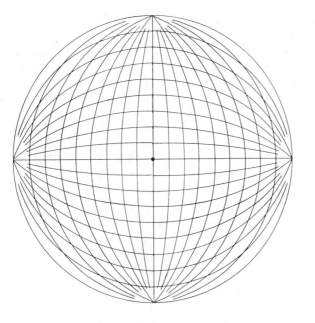

This chart can be used to construct a mask showing, for example, the portion of the skydome obscured by a long horizontal overhang from a window (fig. 9-3). The critical angle is the profile (or cut-off) angle—the vertical angle between the horizon and the obstruction, measured in the vertical plane perpendicular to the glazing. None of the sky above this angle is visible from any point on the window.

9-3. *Obstruction mask of a long overhang with a ninety-degree profile angle (measured from window sill).*

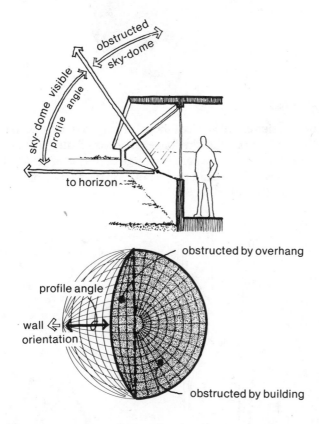

If the overhang extends a certain length on each side of the window, the mask should be modified to show the portion of the skydome "visible" under each end. Because each end of the overhang is also horizontal (though perpendicular to the window opening), the same profile angle chart can be used to further define the mask (indicating that the overhang has a finite width instead of extending infinitely to the horizon). In a similar manner, a mask can be constructed for a long sloped skylight. The relevant profile angle defines the portion of the sky visible from the opening.

9-4. Modified obstruction mask for a short overhang.

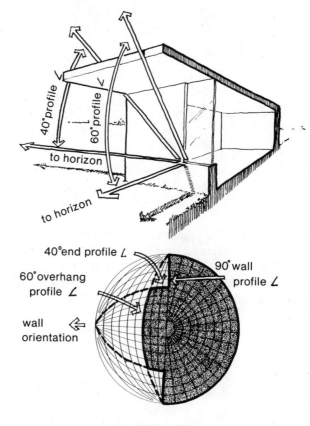

VERTICAL EDGES

Next, imagine a series of tall vertical "bars" arranged in a circle. If these bars were projected as lines on the skydome, they would also trace an orange-segment pattern, but the lines would converge at the top of the skydome (i.e., at the zenith). This pattern would project in plan as a series of straight lines radiating out from the center (fig. 9-5).

9-5. Plan projection of vertical bar traces on skydome.

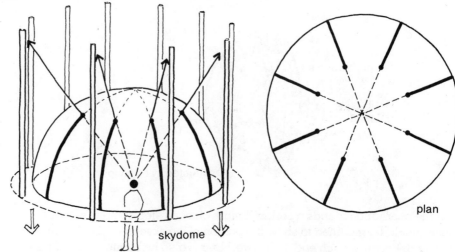

FENESTRATION

This chart can be used to construct a mask showing the portion of the skydome obscured by a vertical side fin from a given reference location (fig. 9-7). The critical angle here is the horizontal cut-off angle. None of the sky beyond this angle is visible from any point on the window. Figures 9-7 through 9-10 show examples of obstruction masks for various shading devices. Obstruction masks can be used to assess the extent of shading on glass (fig. 9-11). Masks can also represent sky exposure from various building locations (fig. 9-12).

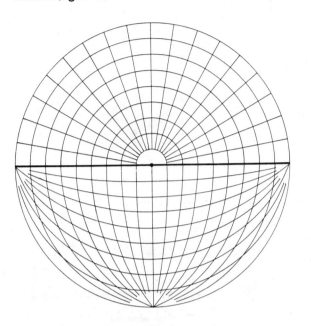

9-6. Combination chart for vertical and horizontal masks. (A full-size vertical/ horizontal mask chart, sized to match the L.O.F. sun angle calculator, is provided in Appendix B.)

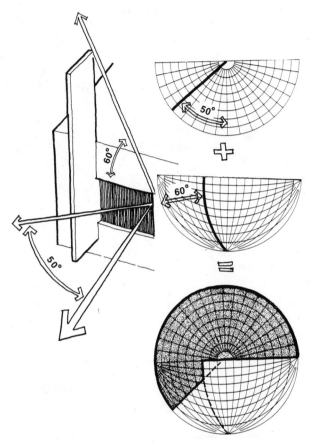

9-7. Glazing shading mask for vertical fin.

9-8. Glazing shading mask for overhang with vertical fins.

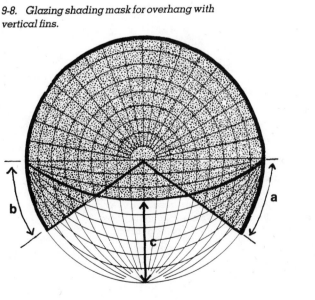

GEOMETRY

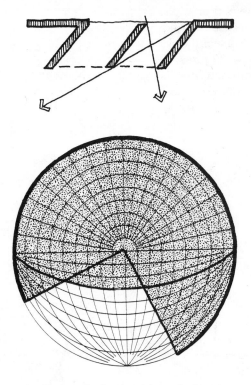

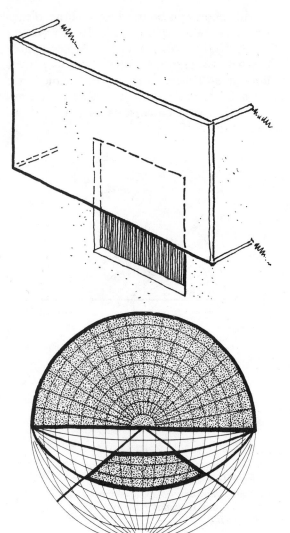

9-9. Glazing shading mask for vertical louvers (plan).

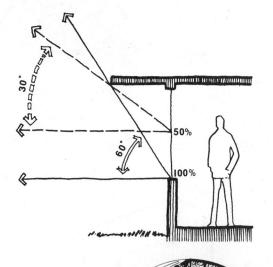

9-10. Glazing shading mask for freestanding panel (parallel to glazing).

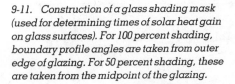

9-11. Construction of a glass shading mask (used for determining times of solar heat gain on glass surfaces). For 100 percent shading, boundary profile angles are taken from outer edge of glazing. For 50 percent shading, these are taken from the midpoint of the glazing.

FENESTRATION

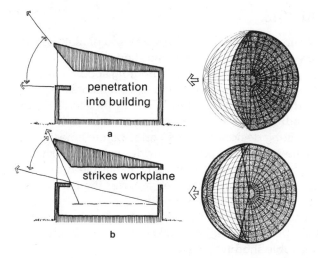

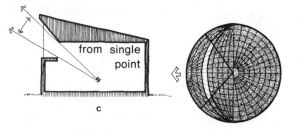

penetration into building

a

strikes workplane

b

from single point

c

9-12. *Construction of sunlight penetration mask, used to determine when direct sunlight will penetrate to any given portion of the building interior, regardless of glass location: (a) for any penetration into the building; (b) for any penetration to the horizontal workplane thirty inches above the floor; (c) for any penetration to a single point location.*

It should be noted that the obstruction mask itself is dependent only on the building configuration and not on compass orientation or latitude (i.e., a given overhang geometry has only one obstruction mask regardless of wall direction or site location.) Moreover, angular geometry (not physical size) determines an obstruction mask. A single large overhang and a series of small blind louvers with the same cut-off angles will generate the same mask (fig. 9-13).

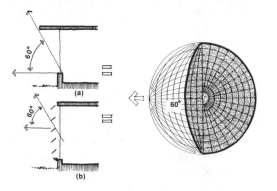

9-13. *Cut-off angles determine the obstruction mask. A large, single overhang (a) produces the same mask as several smaller blinds (b).*

OBSTRUCTIONS AND SUN POSITION

While an obstruction mask is not dependent on orientation, it is constructed using the same coordinate system as the sun path charts. Because of this, the mask can be overlaid on the appropriate chart to determine the times of shading or sunlight penetration. The mask can be rotated so that its orientation arrow points to the correct compass direction on the sun chart (fig. 9-14). Those times on the sun chart visible through the unshaded portions of the mask indicate sun exposure.

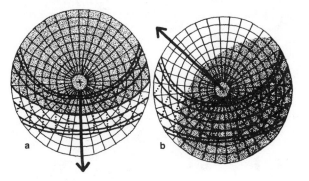

9-14. *Overhang oriented (a) south; (b) northwest.*

BIOCLIMATIC ANALYSIS

Olgyay and Olgyay (1957) have proposed a detailed method of plotting the overheated portion of the year (i.e., that portion when shading is required to maintain human comfort) on the sun charts and evaluating shading device effectiveness based on how closely the mask covers this overheated period. Figure 9-15 shows the overheated period for New York City plotted on a sun chart. Because climate conditions are hotter after June 21 than before, two periods result. A fixed overhang designed for the period before June (i.e., a mask that roughly covers the overheated period) provides insufficient shade in the hot August and September period. Conversely, desirable April and May solar gains are lost if the mask is configured to cover the hotter late summer period. This graphically illustrates the dilemma of designing a single shading device for conditions in which temperatures typically lag a month or more behind solar position. This also makes clear the advantages of awnings and other adjustable shading devices.

9-15.   *Overheated period for New York City.*
(After Olgyay and Olgyay, 1957)

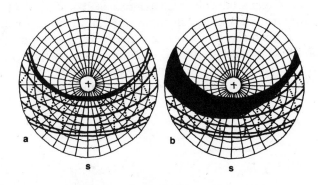

To construct a chart of overheated times for a specific site, hourly temperature and humidity data are required. Furthermore, in Olgyay's system, the need for shading is the criterion used for defining the ambient temperatures required to construct the overheated period. This will vary considerably depending on the internal building heat loads (people, equipment, lighting). For this reason, the literal application of the method appears better suited to "skin-loaded" buildings (such as residences) than for "internally-loaded" buildings (such as commercial structures).

REFERENCES

Libbey-Owens-Ford, *Sun Angle Calculator*, Merchandising Department, 811 Madison Avenue, Toledo, OH.

Olgyay, V., and Olgyay, A. *Solar Control and Shading Devices.* Princeton: Princeton University Press, 1957.

Chapter 10
Design Strategies

Building surface exposure to sunlight and sky light is strongly dependent on orientation and slope (fig. 10-1). This chapter will consider the effectiveness of various fenestration strategies for different wall and roof orientations. The performance of alternative strategies will be discussed comparatively.

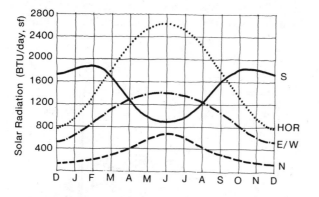

10-1. Comparison of total solar energy incident on various building surfaces by month. (S = south vertical, HOR = horizontal, E/W = east or west vertical, N = north vertical.) (After Mazria, 1979)

While the basis for the following discussion is a large number of physical model studies, it would be a mistake for the reader to assume that the data presented represent absolute performance and can be directly applied to a specific project. It is unlikely that the model conditions tested will even approximate a particular building project.

Instead, the reader should study how relative illumination levels and distributions change with different fenestration designs. To facilitate this, each strategy is presented relative to one or more competing strategies as well as to a base reference strategy (high-diffusion translucent glazing).

Studying the comparative effects of fenestration design changes will afford the designer a grasp of the performance potential of only the specific strategies presented. The variety of fenestration strategies presented is by no means comprehensive, however, because new variations are being invented daily. Instead, they were selected on the basis of their ability to illustrate general principles of daylight manipulation.

The reader will gain the insight essential to imaginative design only by going beyond the effects (presented in the following graphs) to try to deduce the causes of the comparative differences in performance. The reader should find the *luminance × apparent size × cosine effect* conceptual model (as presented in chapter 5) helpful in developing this insight.

DAYLIGHT FACTOR

The fenestration strategies will be compared quantitatively in terms of interior illuminance of a horizontal workplane. Since interior daylight illumination is directly dependent on exterior daylight, the interior illuminances are presented not in absolute quantities, but as ratios of interior to exterior illuminances (daylight factors). More specifically, the daylight factor, as used in this book, is the ratio of interior horizontal workplane illuminance (at a height of thirty inches) to exterior illuminance in the unobstructed horizontal, expressed as a percent. (The internationally accepted Commission Internationale de l'Eclairge [C.I.E.] definition is more restrictive and only applies to the ratio of interior to exterior horizontal luminance under an unobstructed standard overcast sky.)

INTERPRETING THE GRAPHS

The daylight factor illuminances are presented here as graphic overlays on a building section cut through the fenestration. The daylight factor curve for each fenestration reveals a good deal of design information above and beyond the individual illuminances used for the plot. As shown in figure 10-2, daylight factor illuminance is plotted on the vertical axis, and the location of the point of measurement (at 30" height) relative to the south wall is plotted on the horizontal axis. The average illuminance is represented by the total area under the curve and provides a basis for comparing total illumination on the workplane.

10-2. Comparison of interior illuminances: (a) horizontal, flat skylight with high-diffusion translucent glazing; (b) same with mirror-finish reflector.

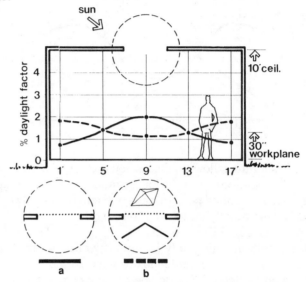

A more important criterion is the relative shape of the curve. Flatter curves imply a more uniform distribution of light but may also be a symptom of potential contrast glare in the occupant's horizontal field of view. As shown in figure 10-2, for example, one skylight design has a steep bell-shaped curve with the maximum illuminance directly below the skylight and rapid fall-off at the perimeter of the room. (This may be the result of simple cosine reduction, center exposure to the brightest part of the overcast sky through clear glazing, dark walls or ceilings, or a combination.) The predominance of the vertical illumination component, however, would increase the potential of veiling reflections. An alternative design, with a suspended reflector, produces a flatter curve. Since a stronger side component is necessary to overcome the effect of cosine reduction, the apparent size and/or luminance of the fenestration must be greater as "seen" from perimeter workplane locations compared with those directly below. This would reduce the potential for veiling reflections on the workplane under the skylight, but would also tend to cause glare in the viewing field.

The slope of the curve at any one point is a measure of the rate of illuminance change over distance, or *illuminance gradient*. Because of the eye's adaptive ability, this gradient is a better measure of perceived brightness changes than are absolute illuminance values.

Finally, changes in distances between curves (as well as slope differences) provide important clues as to which fenestration difference is responsible for a change in illuminance distribution.

FENESTRATION

THE MODEL STUDIES

The fenestration comparisons presented here are based on a total of 205 physical model experiments, performed either under direct sunlight with clear skies or under a translucent dome (to simulate overcast sky conditions). Two models (1" = 1') were used (fig. 10-3), and inserts were used to compare fenestration. Typically, ceiling or wall opening size was equal, but glazing area differed. Interior sidewall and floor reflectances were 48 percent matte gray, and ceiling and exterior reflectances were 78 percent matte white. Translucent, high-diffusion glazing was simulated with a white bond paper having an average transmittance of 46 percent and relatively uniform transmitted and reflected diffusion.

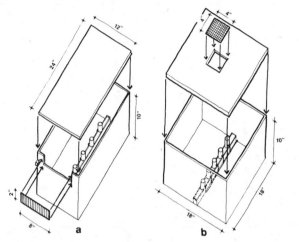

10-3. One-to-twelve scale (1" = 1') test models used for fenestration comparison experiments: (a) wall fenestration model; (b) roof fenestration model.

As a general rule in daylighting, the location of clear glazing within a given fenestration system has a negligible effect on interior illuminance distribution; its use is primarily determined by other considerations (e.g., thermal or aesthetic). For this reason, clear glazing was not used in the model studies, and apertures used to represent clear glazing were left open.

Illuminances were measured using seven remote, precision photometers (one horizontal and one vertical exterior global, and five horizontal interior global at thirty-inch (scale) workplane height). The sensors were scanned and recorded using a microcomputer-based data acquisition system (see Ensar system in Appendix F).

WALL FENESTRATION

Because different wall orientations receive different amounts of sunlight throughout the day and throughout the seasons, optimum fenestration designs for each orientation will differ. The following sections will compare strategies for south, east/west, and north wall orientations.

SOUTH WALLS

Summer solar heat gain on south-facing vertical glass is small due to the high midday altitude angle and large azimuth angles in the morning and afternoon. A simple solid overhang can be used to shade the glass completely during the summer months. However, while the solar gain from low winter sun angles may be welcome thermally, the deep penetration of direct sunlight is unacceptable for task lighting.

Projected Fenestration: Overhangs and Awnings

Extending a solid overhang far enough horizontally to shield low winter sun angles is impractical. Sloping the overhang down reduces the required width but also reduces the view to the exterior. This results in obstruction of the skydome and hence exclusion of desirable direct sky light as well as direct sunlight (figs. 10-4, 10-5).

10-4. Widths required to shield 30° profile-angle sunlight for (a) horizontal overhang; (b) 30°-sloped overhang; (c) 45°-sloped overhang.

10-5. Effect of solid overhang slope on interior illuminances: (a) reference translucent glazing; (b) horizontal overhang, clear glazing; (c) 30° slope, clear glazing; (d) 45° slope, clear glazing (30° solar altitude, noon).

The overhang can be made to "transmit" diffused light in two ways. The overhang material itself can be translucent (for example, a white fabric awning), or it can be comprised of a series of parallel, opaque white louvers that provide shielding between critical solar profile angles. All sunlight and most sky light will be diffused by double reflection before reaching the glazing plane (i.e., light will be reflected off the top of one louver onto the bottom of the one above, which will then become a secondary source of luminance "seen" by the workplane). Because the reflection is diffuse, a large amount of light will be reflected back to the exterior (fig. 10-6).

10-6. Effect of diffusing awnings on interior illuminances: (a) reference translucent glazing; (b) translucent awning, clear glazing; (c) white, horizontal slatted awning, clear glazing; (d) white, vertical slatted awning, clear glazing.

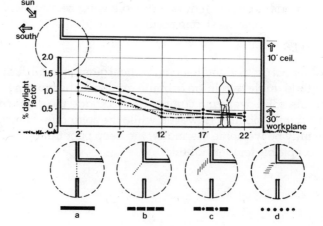

Sunlight can also be shielded and diffused on south orientations at the wall plane. The primary strategies are high-diffusion glazing and sloped white louvers.

Translucent Glazing and Sloped Louvers

The diffusion properties of translucent materials vary, but high-diffusion materials (i.e., materials through which the transmitted image of the sun is not visible), such as flashed opalescent glass and white acrylic, typically have relatively high reflectances and low transmittances (less than 50 percent). As such, both the reflected and transmitted luminance of such sunlit materials are very high (typically brighter than the skydome would appear through clear glass) and are a source of serious glare when it occurs within the field of view of the occupant.

Both sloped louvers and translucent glazing are effective in diffusing direct sunlight. However, louvers tend to direct a larger amount of sunlight toward the ceiling (due to the initial reflectance off the top of the louver). Thus the light-colored ceiling becomes an important part of the louver fenestration system. Under both sunlit and overcast conditions, high-diffusion glazing (45 percent transmittance) produces workplane illuminances comparable to horizontal louvers, but glare to the occupants is greater because higher luminances occur in the normal field of view (i.e., horizontal louvers reflect a larger proportion of light to the ceiling).

There are five main parameters in the design of horizontal louvers: cut-off angle, louver slope (angle between louver and normal to opening), reflectance (color), surface diffusion (i.e., mirror vs. matte), and louver shape.

Effect of Cut-off Angle

Compared with high-diffusion glazing, fixed white louvers transmit proportionally less light at higher summer sun angles than at lower winter angles. This occurs because the cut-off angle for fixed louvers is determined by lower sun angles. At these times sunlight strikes the entire louver and, in turn, a large portion of the reflected light strikes the underside of the louver above. At higher sun angles, only the outer portion of the louver is sunlit (the rest being shaded), and a greater proportion of the sunlight is reflected back to the exterior.

Effect of Louver Slope

For a given cut-off angle, white louvers have the highest average transmittance (about 45 degrees slope relative to the overall plane of the louver system). While the actual transmittance for each slope varies with solar altitude and receiver location, 30-degree slope louvers transmit about 80–90 percent as much light as do 45-degree louvers, while the transmittance of very steep 60-degree louvers is only about 25–35 percent of 45-degree louvers.

Effect of Adjustable Louvers

White venetian blinds (and similar exterior configurations) can be adjusted to achieve greater transmittance of reflected sunlight than fixed white louvers. Up to twice the workplane illuminance can be achieved with optimum adjustment compared with fixed designs, depending on solar altitude. In practice, this advantage is not fully realized unless relatively expensive automatic controls are installed. Even when not optimally adjusted, however, venetian blinds provide illuminance comparable to fixed louvers and high-diffusion glazing with the added advantage of allowing a view out when adjusted for high sun angles and the capability of being raised for overcast days.

Effect of Louver Color

For matte-finish opaque louvers, light from the sun and sky above the louver cut-off angle can only enter after being reflected, and its transmission is a direct function of louver reflectance. Sky light from below the cut-off angle and reflected ground light may be transmitted directly or by louver reflection. The net effect is that transmittance is strongly dependent on louver reflectance but is also affected to a lesser degree by cut-off angle and ground reflectance.

Effect of Surface Diffusion

White louvers, because they reflect diffusely, behave similarly to translucent glass in that they reflect a great deal of sunlight and sky light back to the exterior; the underside of the louver becomes a diffuse secondary source, distributing light approximately equally in all directions regardless of solar azimuth angle. Mirror-finish louvers can reflect much more light to the interior, particularly onto the ceiling. They are highly directional and reflect most sunlight (in plan) in a direction from the solar azimuth angle. Properly oriented, mirror-finish louvers reflect all direct sunlight and most sky light to the interior ceiling where it is diffusely reflected down to the workplane.

10-7. Comparison of: (a) reference translucent glazing; (b) white horizontal louvers; and (c) mirror-finish louvers (concave, mirror surface up).

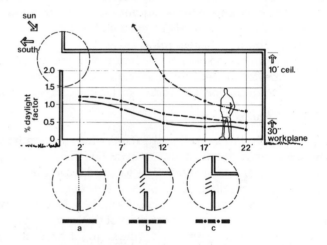

In practice, this cannot be achieved with fixed louvers because of the wide range of solar altitudes that must be accommodated. During certain times, sunlight is either reflected back to the exterior or directly down onto the workplane because of secondary reflection on the underside of the louver above. This conclusion is based on a study of conventionally shaped (planar at single-radius, curved section) mirrorlike surfaces. With the recent development of Fresnel-type reflective films (angle of reflectance is not equal to angle of incidence), such an ideal fixed louver might be achieved.

Effect of Louver Shape

For diffuse (matte-finish) louvers, shape has a negligible effect on effective transmittance and distribution. However, specular louver performance is very sensitive to shape. Flat louvers reflect direct sunlight similarly to a single flat mirror, while either a convex or concave louver shape tends to diffuse the sunlight over a larger area, reducing the potential for glare.

Solar Modulators

Adjustable mirror-finish louvers (fig. 10-8) can reflect all direct sunlight onto the ceiling for all sun angles throughout the year. Lebens (1979) has reported on the adaptation of commercially produced venetian blinds for that purpose. The slats are inverted (concave up) with the top mirror-finished. The curved profile provides a controlled diffusion of reflected sunlight onto the ceiling. The slat curvature and spacing determine the number of seasonal adjustments. It was found that a single curvature (2.9-inch radius for a 1.0-inch slat) with two spacings (0.62 inch for Boston and wider at lower latitudes) provides satisfactory control with a minimum number of adjustments per year. The above optimum radius is slightly larger than that found in most commercially available blinds, which have a radius of approximately 2 inches. However, this radius is satisfactory, requiring slightly more frequent adjustment. In practice, adjustment every two weeks is sufficient for most working hours.

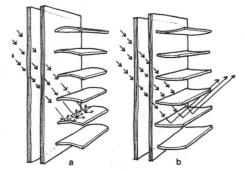

10-8. Adjustable louver reflection of sunlight: (a) white venetian blinds, concave down; (b) mirror-finish (solar modulator) venetian blinds, concave up.

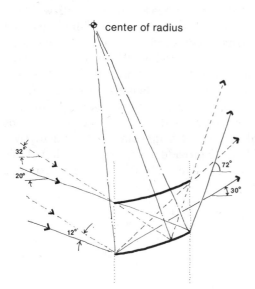

10-9. Ray diagram analysis of inverted venetian blinds with mirror-finish (solar modulator) top surface. In this configuration, 12° is the accepted profile angle range for this adjustment. Sunlight entering from below a 20° profile angle will enter directly, whereas sunlight entering from above a 32° profile angle will be reflected twice back down into the room; thus the accepted profile angle range is 32° − 20° = 12°. (After Lebens, 1979)

Lebens' studies were directed at passive solar heating applications of the solar modulator (mirror-finish blinds, concave up). In a later study, Rosen (1982) investigated the daylighting potential of solar modulators for commercial office buildings. He concluded:

■ Under overcast skies, reflective blinds outperform conventional white blinds. The reflective blinds are clearly able to reflect diffuse sky light. This results in improved daylight distribution and increased light levels at the rear of the room. With the sun higher than 25 degrees, daylight levels at the rear of the room were increased by more than 20 footcandles.

■ Under clear skies, reflective blinds greatly increase interior light levels when there is direct sun on the windows. However, when there is no direct sun on the windows, the reflective blinds have little effect on interior light levels.

■ The combination of reflective blinds and white blinds was not notably better than using all white blinds.

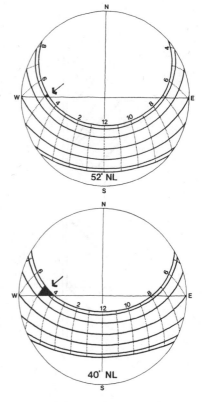

10-10. Sun path charts for 40° and 52° north latitude showing workday times when sun's position is in the northern half of the skydome (8 A.M. to 5 P.M. workday).

EAST/WEST WALLS

Like south orientations, east and west orientations must accommodate a wide range of sun profile angles. As such, south orientation shielding strategies are also effective for east and west orientations. However, east and west orientations have two solar exposure characteristics of importance to daylighting that differ from those of the south. First, sunlight exposure occurs during only half of the working day. Second, the sun's position is limited to the southern half of the skydome during most of the working day at most U.S. latitudes (fig. 10-10).

Fixed vertical white louvers, angled 45 degrees toward the north with a 90 degree cut-off angle, allow sky light to enter directly while diffusing direct sunlight by double reflection. When compared with southern exposure strategies (high-diffusion glazing and fixed horizontal white louvers), vertical louvers provide greater illuminance at locations near the window and comparable illuminance deeper into the room. This is because the northern skydome is directly visible from the locations near the window and shielded by the louvers from deeper locations (figs. 10-11, 10-12). The nearer locations are thus more subject to direct glare from the bright skydome, particularly if the window is low. The vertical louvers provide a view to the north, but this advantage may be limited to perimeter locations by the presence of partition walls perpendicular to the window.

10-11. West orientation fenestration with masks: (a) plan, vertical louvers (45° louver angle/90° cut-off angle); (b) section, horizontal louvers (45° slope/20° cut-off angle).

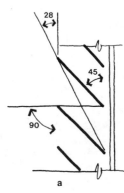
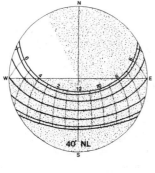
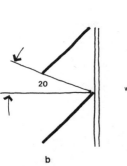
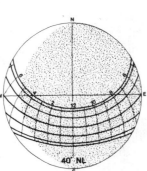

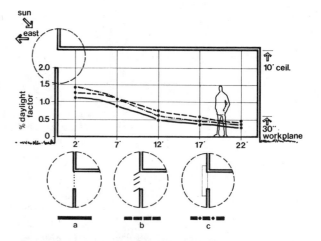

10-12. Comparison of east/west fenestration using (a) reference translucent glazing; (b) white horizontal louvers (cut-off angle = solar profile angle); (c) vertical louvers (45° slope/90° cut-off angle) in interior illuminances.

Like south exposures, east/west exposure illuminances are increased if the vertical louvers are adjustable. This effect is greater at east/west exposures because the louvers can be set perpendicular for the half day when no sunlight shielding is required; during the rest of the day, the sun is shielded by the cut-off angle resulting from this same perpendicular setting.

FENESTRATION

NORTH WALLS

During normal workday hours, no direct sunlight shielding is required for north exposures at most U.S. latitudes. Even at extreme latitudes, in practice, northern sunlight rarely penetrates deeply into the interior due to the shielding effect of interior partitions perpendicular to the window. Thus clear glazing, with no shielding fenestration, can usually be used. If shielding is required, widely spaced fixed vertical louvers will suffice.

While direct sunlight penetration is not a problem at north orientations, it should be noted that the south walls of any adjacent buildings located to the north are directly sunlit on clear days. On winter days, those south wall surfaces may receive 6000 footcandles, and if they are light in color they may become important secondary sources of illumination (and glare). For example, a light buff-colored building with a surface reflectance of 60 percent could have a midday winter luminance of 3600 footlamberts, which is about twice the typical clear sky luminance.

SHELF REFLECTORS

Illumination through all of the above-mentioned fenestration types (at all orientations) is increased with the addition of a reflective horizontal shelf below the glazing. Such a shelf has the effect of increasing the ground-reflected component. For clear glazing, with no other fenestrations (as is typical of north facades), this component is most useful when directed to the ceiling only, from where it is diffusely reflected down onto the workplane. If the shelf is used with diffusing fenestration (translucent glazing or white louvers), its reflected component will increase transmitted luminance (fig. 10-13). This is still desirable, but there is a tendency to increased glare because the increased brightness occurs lower in the field of view.

The location of the light shelf relative to the exterior building plane affects its exposure to the sky (and thus its reflection of light onto the ceiling). As a general rule, the smaller the overhang above the shelf, the greater its contribution to interior illuminance (fig. 10-14).

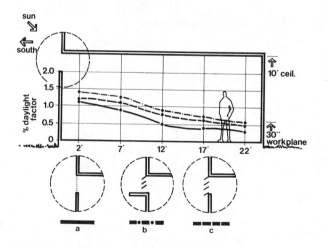

10-13. Comparison of high-diffusion glazing and white horizontal louvers in daylight factor: (a) reference translucent glazing; (b) with exterior white horizontal reflector (width = glazing height); (c) without reflector. Solar altitude = 45°; relative azimuth (direction of sun relative to wall) = 0°.

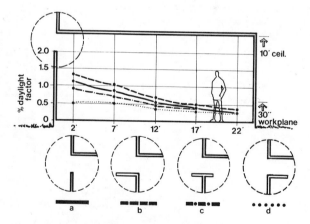

10-14. Comparison of effect of white light shelf position on interior illuminance (clear glazing, overcast sky); (a) no shelf; (b) white shelf outside; (c) white shelf half out/half in; (d) interior white shelf.

The contribution of light shelves to interior illuminance is directly affected by ceiling reflectance. Backwall reflectance also affects interior illuminance, but its contribution is limited by its exposure to direct sky light and, to a lesser degree, to light reflected from the ceiling; direct exposure of the back wall to the horizontal reflector is negligible (fig. 10-15).

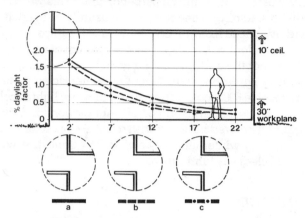

10-15. Effect of ceiling and wall reflectance with white light shelf (overcast sky, clear glazing): (a) white ceiling, white back wall; (b) white ceiling, black back wall; (c) black ceiling, white back wall.

If the top surface of the shelf is mirror finish, illuminances will be further increased. If used with diffusing glazing, this increase will be relatively constant throughout the year, because the principal effect will be to increase transmitted glazing luminance. However, if used with sloped white louvers, much of the reflected component from the shelf will be reflected to the ceiling near the window at higher sun profile angles and further back on the ceiling at lower sun profile angles. If the louvers are mirror finish on the bottom, this high-profile reflected component will be directed further back on the ceiling without affecting low-profile distribution. If a mirrored surface is used on the bottom surface of the louver, care should be taken to assure that the lower slope is at least 45 degrees, to preclude any direct reflections down onto the workplane.

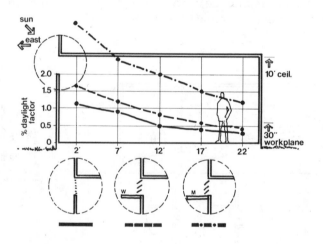

10-16. Effect of light shelf finish with white horizontal louvers: (a) reference translucent glazing; (b) white light shelf, white louvers, clear glazing; (c) mirror-finish light shelf, white louvers, clear glazing (45° solar altitude, 0° relative azimuth).

Effect of Light Shelf Slope

Tilting light shelves beyond horizontal can increase the average amount of light reflected onto the ceiling. For white light shelves, the optimum tilt is the angle required for a mirror to reflect light from the average solar profile angle to the center of the ceiling (fig. 10-17). This is based on optimizing the exposure to the sun with exposure to the ceiling (i.e., luminance-weighted view factor; this is unrelated to mirror reflections, per se; see chapter 4). For medium depth (15′ to 25′) rooms, the following rules of thumb can be applied for white shelves:

- For south exposures: *shelf tilt = 40° − .5 × latitude.*

- For east, west, and north exposures: *shelf tilt = 15°.*

- Reduce the tilt 10 degrees if louvers or diffusing glazing are used. Increase the tilt slightly for very deep rooms, and reduce it for shallow rooms. Increase the tilt for very high sills and reduce it for lower sills. Decrease the tilt if an overhang above the shelf is used.

- For east, west, and south orientations, sunlit white shelf surfaces may be visible to occupants and the source of serious glare. It is therefore recommended that, if no other diffusing fenestration (such as louvers) is used, the above tilts be limited to prevent the reflective surface from being viewed anywhere in the room. This limitation should always apply to mirror-finish shelves.

- Rear wall reflectance becomes increasingly important as light shelf tilt is increased, because a greater area of the shelf is "seen" by the back wall.

10-17. Optimum shelf tilt angle.

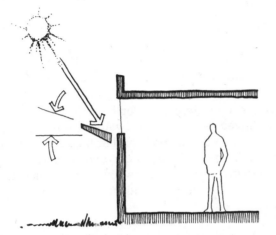

Intermediate Light Shelves

Light shelves are often used to divide upper and lower glazing. They reflect additional light through the upper glazing, while acting as an overhang for the lower glazing, shading it from direct sun and obstructing the skydome.

It is a popular misconception that this configuration actually increases illuminance deep in the room. In practice, the added reflectance onto ceiling surfaces does not make up for the direct sky light that is obstructed by the shelf. The principal advantage of intermediate light shelves lies in the reduction of glare from the skydome at locations near the window.

10-18. Daylight factor illuminances with (w) and without (wo) an intermediate light shelf (overcast sky).

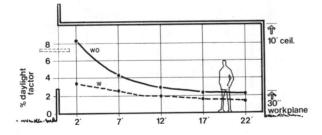

LIGHT SCOOPS

The preceding discussion has focused on strategies to increase light penetration deep into a room. At times it is desirable to increase illuminance on a work surface located adjacent to the exterior wall or on the vertical wall below

DESIGN STRATEGIES

a high window. The use of a sloped ceiling (light scoop) adjacent to the window exposes that ceiling section directly to sky light (and potentially to low-angle direct sunlight). This becomes a significant secondary source reflector to areas directly below and onto the outside wall. The addition of an exterior light shelf further enhances this effect. The increased illuminance near and on the window wall is achieved at the expense of penetration deep into the room. This is because the lower ceiling acts as an "eyebrow," reducing the apparent size of the window as seen from deep workplane locations.

10-19. *Effect of combinations of light shelves and light scoops on illuminance distribution (overcast sky): (a) no shelf, no scoop; (b) shelf only; (c) scoop only; (d) scoop and shelf.*

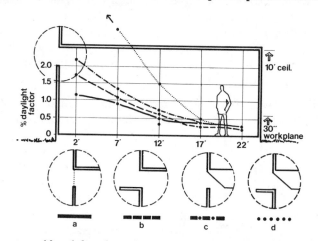

The exact profile of the sloped portion has relatively little effect on light distribution. The curved scoops favored by Aalto (see case studies, chapter 5) perform similarly to straight, sloped profiles; the curved profile (without an exterior light shelf) directs a slightly larger amount of light toward the upper part of the outside wall and slightly less downward. If an exterior light shelf is added, performance is virtually identical.

LIGHT BAFFLES

Light baffles can be used to introduce daylight into basement areas while excluding direct sunlight. All interior surfaces should be white to maximize reflections. Use a 45 degree reflector and 45 degree cut-off angles to maximize basement illuminances (fig. 10-20).

10-20. *Basement illuminance: (a) reference (above-ground) translucent glazing; (b) with reflective window well.*

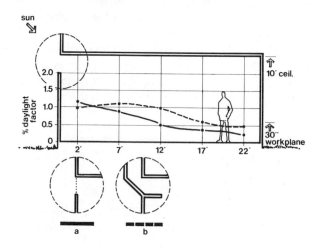

ROOF FENESTRATION

In addition to the wall fenestration strategies discussed above, single-story and the top of multistory buildings can employ skylights (horizontal and shallow-sloped glazing) and monitors (vertical and steeply-sloped glazing)

FENESTRATION

to introduce daylight. This is particularly advantageous for large-area floor plans with interior areas inaccessible to exterior walls and windows.

SKYLIGHTS

Because of the large amount of solar radiation on horizontal surfaces during the summer, skylights introduce considerable heat gain and are often avoided in order to reduce air-conditioning loads. It is important to recall that daylight (whether direct sunlight or diffuse sky light) introduces less heat per unit of light than commercially available electric lamps (approximately 125 lumens per watt for sunlight and sky light versus 65 for fluorescent lamps, 30 for incandescent lamps, and 110 for high-pressure sodium lamps). Thus, for a given amount of light, skylights introduce less cooling load than electric lights provided that all of the daylight can be effectively used and distributed.

Skylights with clear glazing leave direct sunlight concentrated in shafts, resulting in unusably high illuminance in certain small areas and the remainder underilluminated. The following are strategies for diffusing sunlight and sky light. They are compared on the basis of workplane illuminances expressed as daylight factors (described at the beginning of this chapter). The control strategy for all of the comparisons is a flat, high-diffusion, 45-percent transmittance, horizontal glazing (4' × 4').

Effect of Skylight Above Roof Plane

The shape (domed, barrel, flat, pyramid) of clear glazed skylights has little effect on transmittance and light distribution. The rationale for any such shape is thus based on condensation control, snow penetration, dirt collection, and so on.

Translucent glazing, because it changes light direction by refraction and reflection, *does* affect illuminance transmittance and distribution in the presence of direct sunlight. Convex shapes that project above the roof plane are unequally illuminated by direct sunlight, resulting in an uneven distribution of illuminance in the room below. Typically, the room areas that "see" the higher luminance portions of the dome will receive the most illumination. At low sun angles more sunlight is received by convex shapes. While some of this light is lost through the opposite side of the dome, there is a net increase in the total amount of light transmitted to the room (fig. 10-21).

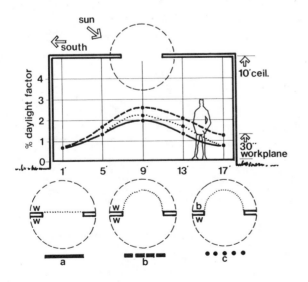

10-21. Effect of translucent skylight shape: (a) flat, horizontal; (b) half-round barrel (white opaque ends); (c) steeply-sloped A-frame (white opaque ends).

Effect of Roof Reflectance

In addition to receiving sunlight more directly, convex skylight domes "see" surrounding roof surfaces. Roof reflectance therefore contributes additional light to the interior (fig. 10-22). Roof reflectance does not affect the performance of concave or horizontal flat skylights, nor does it significantly affect clear convex glazing performance.

10-22. *Effect of roof reflectance on skylight performance: (a) flat, horizontal; (b) half-round barrel, white roof; (c) half-round barrel, black roof (all translucent).*

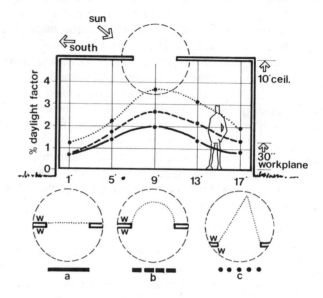

Effect of Clear, North-facing Glazing

If the convex shape of the dome is extreme, total transmittance is increased slightly, under both sunlit and overcast conditions, provided that the north-facing section is clear rather than translucent. This is a result of (1) greater transmittance of direct sky light from the north, and (2) greater transmittance of light reflected from north roof surfaces (which is then reflected down into the room by the translucent portion). These gains more than offset the increased loss of transmitted sunlight back out through the clear portion.

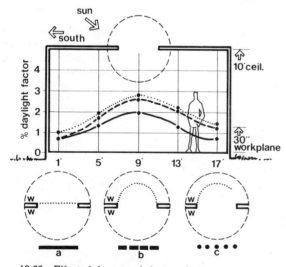

10-23. *Effect of clear, north-facing glazing; (a) flat, horizontal, translucent; (b) barrel, all translucent (white ends); (c) barrel, translucent with clear north section (white ends).*

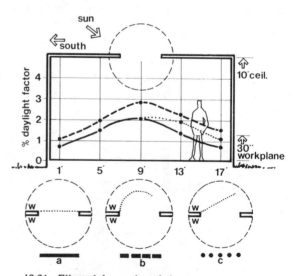

10-24. *Effect of shape of south-facing translucent section with north-facing clear section: (a) flat, horizontal, translucent; (b) barrel, translucent with clear north section; (c) flat, sloped, translucent with clear north section.*

Effect of Skylight Shape Below Ceiling

Most conventional skylight fenestration does not extend below the ceiling plane. As a result, the ceiling does not receive any direct light transmitted by the skylight and thus contributes little to daylight distribution. Projecting a translucent skylight diffuser below the ceiling line refracts light onto the ceiling directly, utilizing its reflectance. In addition, the resulting increased ceiling luminance serves to reduce brightness contrast with the skylight itself. Unless the projection is very shallow, its apparent size is larger than a flush opening as "seen" from distant workplane locations. Because concave surfaces are unequally sunlit, transmission is also greatest in the direction from which those sunlit surfaces are "seen" (fig. 10-25).

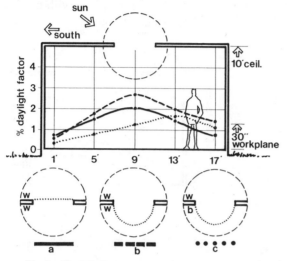

10-25. Effect of plane projection below ceiling and ceiling reflectance: (a) flat, horizontal, translucent; (b) concave, translucent barrel, white ceiling; (c) concave, translucent barrel, black ceiling.

Effect of Deep Skylight Wells

A sloped skylight well diffuses light admitted through a small roof opening over a larger area before entering the room cavity. If clear glazing is used, the sides of the well can shield sunlight from entering the room directly, diffusing it by multiple white-wall reflection. At U.S. latitudes, it is necessary to slope the center axis of the well itself toward the north in order to prevent direct sunlight penetration during summer months. Workplane illuminance is greater at locations from which the sunlit sidewall surfaces are "seen" directly. This skylight configuration, in a conical shape, is found in many buildings designed by Alvar Aalto (see fig. 10-26 and case studies, chapter 5, especially Wolfsburg Cultural Center).

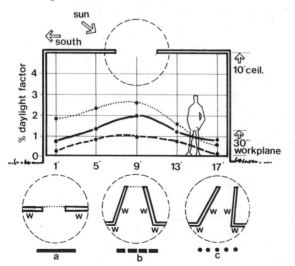

10-26. Effect of sloping light wells; (a) flat, horizontal, translucent; (b) symmetrical white well, sloped sides, translucent; (c) asymmetrical white well, sloped sides, clear (all glazed opening areas = 2' × 4'; ceiling openings for (b) and (c) = 4' × 4'.

Effect of Reflector Below

The uneven distribution of illuminance typical with flat, translucent skylights can be improved with sloped reflectors. These reflect transmitted light back onto the ceiling surrounding the opening and block out direct light to the room directly below, while allowing light to penetrate directly to the perimeter of the room. The net result is more even distribution of illuminance to the workplane (fig. 10-27). Given that the diffusion of sunlight is achieved by the translucent glazing, further diffusion (e.g., by making the reflector white) accomplishes little. A mirror-finish reflector is preferable because it reflects less light back through the glazing. The addition of a white vertical roof-mounted reflector to the north of the skylight improves performance, especially during the winter (fig. 10-28). (This is true with or without the room reflector.)

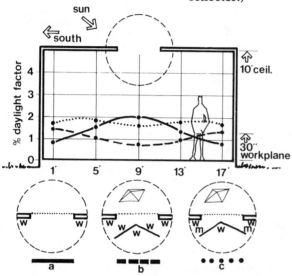

10-27. Effect of sloped (pyramid) reflectors below skylight: (a) flat, horizontal, translucent; (b) same with white room reflector; (c) same with mirror-finish room reflector.

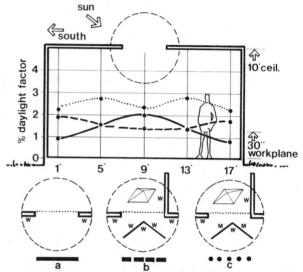

10-28. Effect of adding roof-mounted vertical white reflector: (a) flat, horizontal, translucent; (b) same with white roof and white room reflectors; (c) same with white roof and mirror-finish room reflectors.

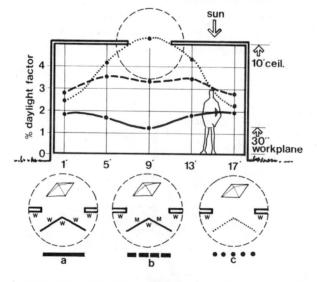

10-29. Effect of skylight reflectors for use with heliostat reflectors providing vertical sunlight only: (a) opaque white; (b) mirror-finish; (c) translucent pyramid reflectors.

If direct sunlight can be controlled so that it always enters vertically (as with a tracking, roof-mounted heliostat), clear glazing can be used, and performance increased. With the use of an opaque white ceiling reflector, the greatest illumination occurs at the room perimeter with little change in the average illuminance throughout the room (compared with a flat translucent skylight). If the ceiling reflector is mirror finish, illuminance is approximately doubled and is distributed evenly throughout the room. If the ceiling reflector is translucent, very high illuminances occur at the center of the room, with considerable fall-off at the perimeter. Reflector performance is a function of distance below the opening (as much as is practical) and reflector slope (a mirror-surface slope will reflect to the extremities of the ceiling regardless of surface finish). A slight concave curve allows a higher mounting height of mirror-finish reflectors, but otherwise has little effect on performance. The performance difference between a pyramid reflector and a conical reflector of comparable area is negligible for white and translucent reflectors and minor for those with a mirror finish (fig. 10-29).

NORTH/SOUTH ROOF MONITORS

Monitors are roof structures that utilize vertical or steeply sloped glazing. This allows for the contribution of roof-reflected light and (in the case of south-oriented glazing) more direct exposure to winter sunlight. Typically, north-facing monitors employ clear glazing for maximum transmission since diffusion is inherent in the sky light and roof-reflected sunlight. South-facing monitors must employ translucent glass or white baffles to diffuse direct sunlight.

With north-facing monitors, the combination of direct north sky light and twice-reflected sunlight (roof + monitor interior) provides about half the illumination (with similar distribution) as does the reference horizontal translucent skylight. A comparable south-facing monitor with translucent glazing transmits illuminance comparable to the horizontal skylight, but the greatest illuminance occurs slightly north of the opening (fig. 10-30).

Clear-glazed north monitors with sloped reflectors perform virtually identically to those with vertical reflectors, with the illuminances being a direct function of glazed area. The effect of several sloped monitors (i.e., sawtooth), compared with a single larger one of the same geometry, is negligible (fig. 10-31).

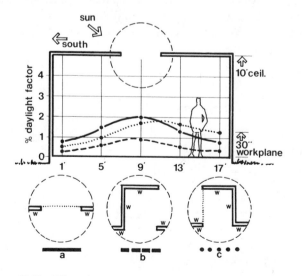

10-30. Effect of vertical-sided roof monitors: (a) reference skylight; (b) north monitor, clear glazing; (c) south monitor, translucent glazing.

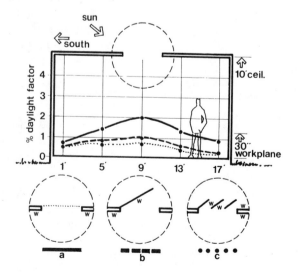

10-31. Effect of monitor spacing: (a) reference skylight; (b) single, large, sloped monitor; (c) sawtooth.

Sawtooth Roof Angle

When the sawtooth slope is greater than 45 degrees, the average illuminance is constant, in spite of the increased vertical glazing area. The location of greatest workplane illuminance is a function of monitor roof slope. At very low sawtooth slopes, the maximum illuminance is less than for steeper slopes, but distribution is very even and minimums are slightly higher (figs. 10-32, 10-33).

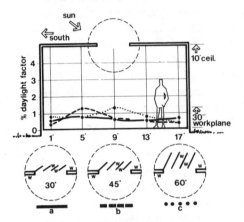

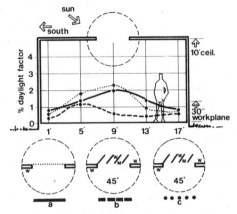

10-32. Effect of north sawtooth roof slope: (a) 30°; (b) 45°; (c) 60°.

10-33. Effect of mirror-finish underside of sawtooth: (a) reference skylight; (b) white-ceiling sawtooth; (c) mirror-ceiling sawtooth.

Translucent Glazing versus Diffusing Baffles

South-facing sloped monitors are very efficient at collecting light with small glazing area. The sloped configuration allows the use of multiple, adjacent monitors with minimum winter self-shading. Translucent-glazed south monitors provide illuminances comparable to the reference skylight with about half the glazing area. The use of white baffles (instead of diffuse glazing) increases illuminance by a factor of two.

Mazria (1981) has described a south monitor with vertical glazing combined with an overhang and interior vertical baffles spaced to shield all direct sunlight (fig. 10-34). The result is very high illumination immediately below, with a rapid fall-off at the perimeter. While illuminance distribution from a single monitor is thus limited, this results in low baffle brightness at critical viewing angles (below 45 degrees). Where even distribution is required, a series of these monitors is recommended.

10-34. Effect of overhang with vertical diffusing baffles; (a) reference skylight; (b) vertical translucent glazing; (c) vertical diffusing baffles.

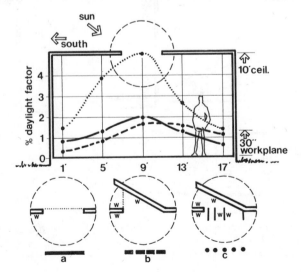

a

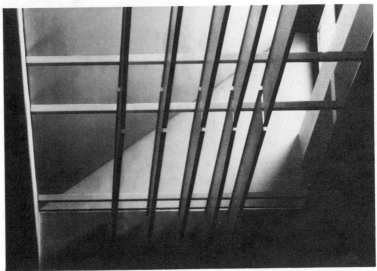

10-35.   Mount Airy Library, North Carolina (1980) (J.N. Pease, Project Architect; Mazria/ Schiff, Associate Architects, daylighting and energy consultants): (a) interior; (b) detail of baffled south monitor; (c) winter operation; and (d) summer operation. (Drawings courtesy of Edward Mazria.)

b

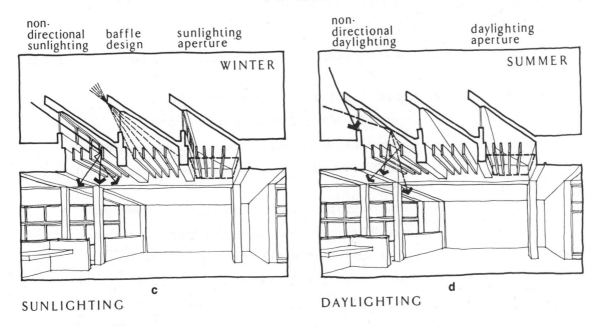

non-directional sunlighting   baffle design   sunlighting aperture   WINTER

non-directional daylighting   daylighting aperture   SUMMER

c

d

SUNLIGHTING   DAYLIGHTING

DESIGN STRATEGIES

In another variation, sloped glazing is used, with no overhang, requiring the use of sloped baffles to intercept all direct sunlight (fig. 10-36). In the configuration tested, interior illuminance was more evenly distributed than in the previous design, with a lower maximum directly under the monitor, a higher south perimeter and a comparable north perimeter.

10-36. *Effect of no overhang with sloped diffusing baffles: (a) reference skylight; (b) sloped translucent glazing; (c) sloped diffusing baffles.*

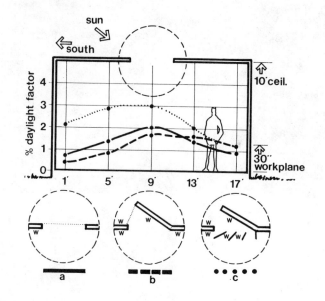

The procedure for designing a baffled, south monitor with an overhang is as follows (fig. 10-37):

10-37. *Design geometry for south monitor with overhang.*

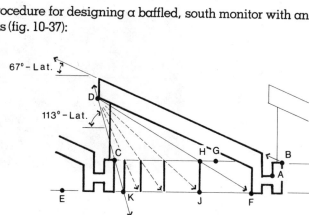

1. Beginning at flat roof plane (A), locate (B) to provide for gutter and structure.

2. Construct roof line at 67 degrees latitude from (B).

3. Locate (C) level with (B) at bay spacing distance.

4. Construct line through (C) each way at 113 degrees latitude.

5. Locate (D) along this line to provide adequate depth for structure and insulation.

6. Locate bottom plane of baffles at (E), typically at ceiling line.

7. Locate (F) on plane (E) to provide adequate room for structure.

8. Locate plane of baffles at (G), typically level with (C).

9. Construct cut-off line from (D) to (F).

10. Locate top of first baffle at (H) and bottom directly below at (J).

11. Construct next cut-off line from (D) to (J), and repeat for remaining baffles.

12. Ideally, the line extended from (D) and (C) should just touch bottom of last baffle at (K). This can be adjusted by relocating plane (G) or (E) and repeating the procedure.

The design procedure for a south monitor with variable-slope baffles, no overhang, and sloped glazing is as follows (fig. 10-38):

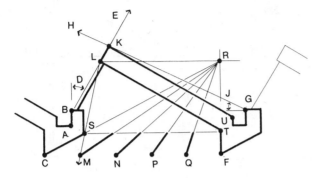

10-38. Design geometry for south monitor with variable slope baffles (using Euclidian geometry).

1. Beginning with flat roof plane (A), locate (B) to provide adequate curb height.

2. Locate (C) relative to (A) and (B) to provide adequate insulation and structure.

3. Construct line (E) at angle (D) = 67 degrees latitude.

4. Locate (F) and (G) level with (C) and (B) at selected bay spacing. Line (C–F) is the bottom plane of the baffles.

5. Construct line (H) at angle (J) = 67 degrees latitude, with (K) at intersection of lines (H) and (E).

6. Locate (L) along (E) to allow adequate insulation and structure.

7. Divide the line between (C) and (F) into equal parts (E in this example).

8. Construct line (L–R) level.

9. Locate (R) directly above (F).

10. Draw baffle slope lines from (R) to (C), (M), (N), (P), and (Q) respectively.

11. Draw cut-off line from (L) to (M).

12. Draw a level line through (S) to establish the plane of the top of the baffles. By Euclid's rule for dividing parallel lines, the cut-off line for each pair of baffles will exactly intercept at (L).

13. Construct monitor ceiling line from (L) to (T), and a parallel line from (K) to (U) to form the roof and gutter.

Perimeter Skylights and Monitors

Locating skylights and monitors adjacent to the northern wall of a room simplifies the problem of shielding the workplane from direct sunlight. It is possible to use clear glazing for skylights. The sunlit wall below the opening then becomes a very bright secondary source reflector. Adding an additional vertical, white, sunlight reflector above the roof plane exaggerates this effect (fig. 10-40). While direct sunlight is shielded, the sunlit wall may be a source of serious glare.

10-39. The mean slope of the baffles in figure 10-38 can be adjusted to direct the transmitted light in a different direction by relocating (R) relative to (L). Decreasing this distance directs light downward, but generates a greater baffle depth for a given spacing.

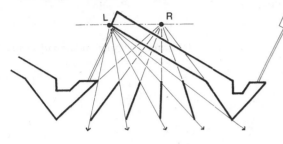

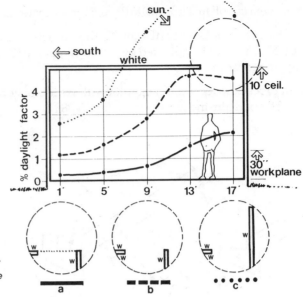

10-40. Effect of clear skylights adjacent to north wall: (a) reference translucent skylight; (b) clear skylight; (c) same with vertical white reflector.

East/West Roof Monitors

Admitting daylight through east and west monitors poses a distribution problem because of the daily sun movement. Translucent glazing admits more light through the sunlit monitor, but illuminance distribution is relatively even as a result of roof reflectance and multiple reflections within the monitor cavity. White, north-angled, vertical white louvers (90 degree cut-off) admit sunlight only after double-diffuse reflection; performance is only slightly better than translucent clerestories. Both provide about half the illuminance of a horizontal, translucent skylight (fig. 10-41).

10-41. Comparison of east/west monitors: (a) reference horizontal skylight; (b) translucent clerestory glazing; and (c) clear glazing, vertical white louvers, angled 45° toward the north, 90° cut-off angle. (Total glazing areas are identical.)

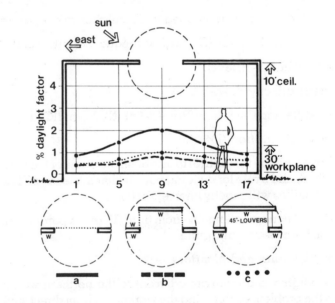

CEILING BAFFLES

An alternative to creating sunlight diffusion in the glazing plane is the use of white baffles in the lower ceiling plane (fig. 10-42). One variation combines an overhang above the clerestory with white vertical diffusing baffles. The spacing of the baffles is adjusted to compensate for changes in the cut-off angle relative to the edge of the overhang. The resulting illuminance distribution is nearly symmetrical with a two-to-one concentration near the center.

Another variation of the same strategy requires no overhang, with the increased shielding provided by sloping the baffles near the window. The spacing and the slope of the baffles is generated by cut-off angles from the top of the window and the depth of the center baffle. The resulting illuminance distribution is slightly more even because cut-off angles are optimized from both directions for all baffles.

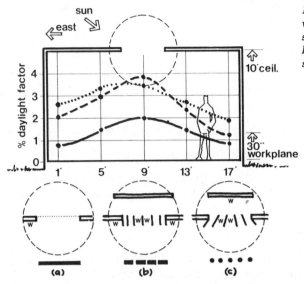

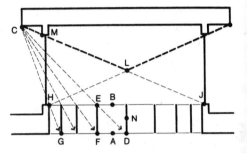

10-42. *Effect of ceiling baffle diffusers for east/west monitors: (a) reference horizontal skylight; (b) clear glazing, overhang, vertical baffles; and (c) clear glazing, no overhang, sloped baffles. (Total glazing areas are equal.)*

10-43. *Design geometry for east/west monitor with vertical baffles and overhang.*

The design procedure for an east/west monitor, with vertical baffles and an overhang is as follows (fig. 10-43):

1. Design the roof monitor at a height and width required by the project. The glazing can be any height, but higher glazing heads require more (or deeper) baffles.

2. Extend the overhang about 30 percent of the glazing height and ensure that (C), (M), and (J) are in a line.

3. Establish the bottom of the baffles at (A), usually equal to surrounding ceiling height.

4. Locate top of baffles at (B), usually at glazing sill height. Locate first louver at center of ceiling opening.

5. Draw cut-off line from (C) to (D) to locate (E), top of next baffle. Repeat for remaining louvers.

6. Bottom of last baffle should exactly match the intersection of the extension of line (C–H) and plane (A). If it does not, adjust the overhang or the baffle depth and repeat.

7. Repeat for opposite side.

8. Performance can be improved by sloping the ceiling and overhang soffit to (C–L–K).

9. The above geometry results in a louver at the center. To get a space at the center, locate (N) at the center of the opening, halfway between planes (A) and (B).

10. The intersection of (C–N) with planes (A) and (B) locates the first two baffles. The rest of the procedure is as above.

10-44. *Design geometry for east/west monitor with sloped baffles and no overhang.*

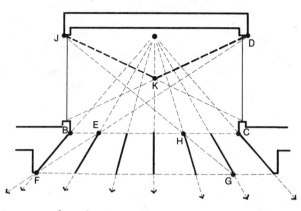

The design procedure for an east/west monitor with sloped baffles and no overhang is as follows (fig. 10-44):

1. Lay out the glazing and level monitor roof as required.

2. Locate locus of baffle slopes (A) at center, level with top of glazing.

3. Locate (B) and (C) below glass at highest location consistent with structure and insulation requirements to form plane of top of baffles.

4. Divide (B–C) into equal parts (six in this example). (E) is the first such division.

5. Locate (F) at the intersection of the extensions of lines (D–E) and (A–B) to determine the plane of bottom of the baffles.

6. Draw the baffles in at slopes radiating from (A), plane of top at (B–C) and bottom at (F). By Euclid's rule for dividing parallel lines, the cut-off line for each pair of baffles will pass through (D) and (J). Performance can be improved slightly by sloping the monitor ceiling at (J–K–D). Supplementary electric lamps can be installed between (A) and (K).

EXTERIOR VERTICAL SHIELD/REFLECTORS

Lam (1983) has described an alternative to interior ceiling baffles for diffusing direct sunlight, using exterior white vertical shield reflectors. This depends on the use of sunlight diffusely reflected through the opposite clerestory, (while direct sunlight is shielded from direct entry). Compared with ceiling baffles, illuminance distribution is more uniform, but the average is slightly

10-45. *Effect of exterior reflector shields on east/west monitors: (a) reference horizontal skylight; (b) opaque white reflector shield, clear glazing; and (c) translucent reflector shield, clear glazing. (Total glazing areas are equal.)*

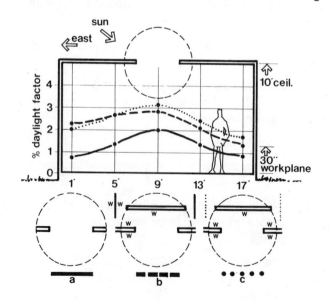

less. Construction cost is less, and clerestory window maintenance is easier. The use of translucent exterior shields (instead of opaque white) offers a slight increase in illuminance of the center and perimeter opposite the sun (fig. 10-45.)

The design procedure for exterior reflector shields on an east/west monitor is as follows (fig. 10-46):

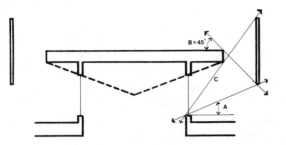

10-46.   *Required geometry of exterior reflector shields on east/west monitor.*

1. Construct angle (A) equal to the solar profile angle of the critical morning (or afternoon) hour.

2. Construct angle (B) equal to 45 degrees.

3. Construct line (C) so as to touch the top of the shield, the edge of the overhang, and the bottom of the clerestory glazing. Illumination is slightly improved by sloping monitor ceiling at dotted line. (This permits the use of an inverted truss or top-hinged insulating shutters.)

REFERENCES

Lam, W.E. "Sunlighting as a Formgiver for Architecture." In *Proceedings, International Daylighting Conference,* edited by Vonier, T., pp. 77–84. Washington, DC: American Institute of Architects Service Corporation, 1983.

Lebens, R.M. "Determining the Optimum Design for the Solar Modulator." *Proceedings, Third National Passive Solar Conference,* edited by Miller, et al., pp. 100–106. Boulder, CO: American Solar Energy Society, 1979.

Mazria, E. "Case Study: Mount Airy Public Library." In *Daylighting Resourcebook,* edited by Kroner, W., et al., pp. 8.35–57. Washington, DC: Association of Collegiate Schools of Architecture, 1981.

Robbins, C.L., and Hunter, K.C. "A Method for Predicting Energy Savings Attributed to Daylighting." SERI report TR-254-1664. Golden, CO: Solar Energy Research Institute, 1982.

Rosen, J.E. "Natural Daylighting and Energy Conservation: Innovative Solutions For Office Buildings." Master of Architecture thesis, M.I.T., 1981.

Chapter 11
Glazings and Reflectors

Glazings are used in buildings for a variety of radiation control purposes including admitting light, admitting solar heat, allowing views in and out, and blocking or allowing radiant losses from the interior. In addition to radiation control, glazings are used as a barrier to convection. (Glazing materials have a relatively high conductance and do not contribute directly to reducing conductive losses.) While other materials are equally effective in controlling convection, glazings are unique in their capability to control radiation.

THREE REGIONS OF THE RADIATION SPECTRUM

As discussed in chapter 2, when radiation strikes a surface it is either transmitted, reflected, or absorbed. It is obvious that different glazings vary in their capacities to transmit, reflect, and absorb radiation. It is not as obvious (but very important in daylighting) that for a given glazing material, transmittance, reflectance, and absorptance vary considerably depending on the radiation wavelength.

There are three regions of the radiation spectrum that are of particular interest in building design. These may be characterized as the *visible, solar IR* (near infrared), and *room IR* (far infrared) regions of the spectrum. The visible region is that part of the total solar spectrum that is visible to the eye and thus useful for lighting (0.4 to 0.7 microns). The solar IR region is the invisible portion of the solar spectrum (0.7 to 4.0 microns). The small ultraviolet solar region (0.3 to 0.4 microns) is also invisible but architecturally significant only for its effect on the fading of interior finishes and plant growth. The room IR region is the invisible portion of the spectrum emitted from warm (0° to 150° F) room surfaces (greater than 8.0 microns). The distinction between the solar IR and room IR regions is particularly important architecturally because of the different behavior of glazing materials in these regions.

Radiation (in either of these regions) that is transmitted or reflected retains similar wavelength characteristics. However, absorbed radiation is converted to heat which is then conducted, convected, or reradiated. This reradiation occurs only in the room IR region and should thus not be confused with transmitted or reflected radiation. In glazings, this absorbed energy is transferred (by radiation and convection) to both the room interior and the exterior depending on their temperature relative to the glass. Thus, in the summer, absorbed heat tends to flow to the cooler room interior, while in the winter more heat is radiated to the exterior.

GLAZING SPECTRAL RESPONSE

There are seven basic types of glazings that are important to daylighting and solar heating/cooling applications because of their distinctly different behavior in the three regions of the radiation spectrum. These are:

1. clear glass

2. gray/bronze glass

3. "heat-absorbing" green glass

4. light reflecting film

5. room IR reflecting film

6. solar IR reflecting film

7. IR transparent plastic

The spectral response (in other words, the relative transmittance, reflectance, and absorptance in the various wavelengths of the radiation spectrum) of various "ideal" glazing materials are described in figures 11-1 through 11-7. This behavior is represented graphically in two ways: (1) spectral response curves for transmittance, absorptance, and reflectance in the visible, solar IR, and room IR regions, and (2) a section through the glazing diagramming the reflection, transmission, and absorption in each of these three regions. In figure 11-1a, for example, we see that in ordinary glass, most of the visible and solar IR radiation is transmitted in the visible and solar IR regions while very little is transmitted in the room IR region (solid line). The absorptance (dotted line) is negligible in the visible and solar IR regions but very high in the room IR region, while the reflectance (dashed line) is negligible in all regions. In figure 11-1b, a section through the glazing shows that, under typical circumstances, most of the visible and solar IR is transmitted from the outside to the inside, while the room IR from the inside is absorbed as heat and dissipated (via convection and radiation) to the outside and inside. (For clarity, these types will first be considered as single layers even though some, such as mirror finishes, are usually applied to a different layer. The combined effects of multiple layers will be considered subsequently).

CLEAR GLAZING

Clear glass is highly transparent in both the visible and solar IR regions, highly absorptive in the room IR region, and reflective in none of the regions (fig. 11-1). It is most suited for solar heat collection, for viewing from light to dark areas (such as through display windows), and for best color rendition. Even standard "clear" glazing typically contains iron oxide, which imparts a greenish color to the edge. "Water white" glass contains less iron oxide and thus has slightly greater visible and solar IR transmittance.

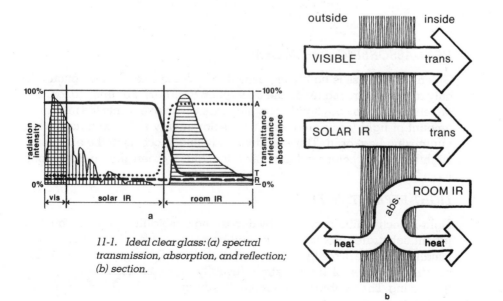

11-1. Ideal clear glass: (a) spectral transmission, absorption, and reflection; (b) section.

GRAY/BRONZE GLASS

Gray (and "bronze") glass is pigmented to increase visible and solar IR absorption (and thus decrease transmittance). Like clear glass, it is also highly absorptive in the room IR region and reflective in none of the regions (fig. 11-2). It is best suited for viewing from dark to light areas (such as view windows to the exterior) because it reduces the brightness contrast between the view and surrounding interior surfaces. It is also used for reducing solar heat gain, but is less effective than "mirror" glass because energy not transmitted is absorbed as heat, much of which is ultimately transmitted to the interior in the summer. Because of its neutral tint, gray glass is preferred to bronze where color rendition is important.

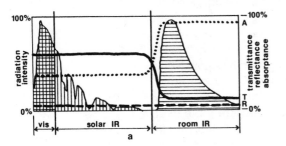

11-2. *Ideal gray glass: (a) spectral transmission, absorption, and reflection; (b) section.*

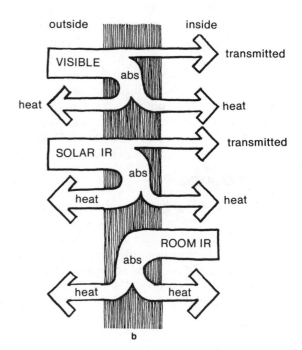

HEAT-ABSORBING GREEN GLASS

Green-tinted glass is lightly pigmented to increase solar IR absorption with only a small increase in visible absorption (fig. 11-3). For this reason, it is preferred for many daylighting applications where one wants the maximum amount of light (compared with total solar energy to be admitted) while minimizing heat gain. This selectivity advantage occurs at the expense of slightly reduced color rendition. Like clear glass, green glass absorbs most room IR.

LIGHT-REFLECTIVE FILM

Light-reflective film is created by depositing a metallic coating on a transparent substrate, producing a mirrorlike appearance. This type of film is usually reflective in the IR regions as well as the visible regions (fig. 11-4). The spectral qualities of the substrate (usually glass) combine with those of the coating. The combined characteristics differ depending on the location of the film (exterior or interior).

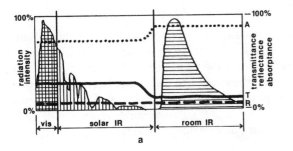

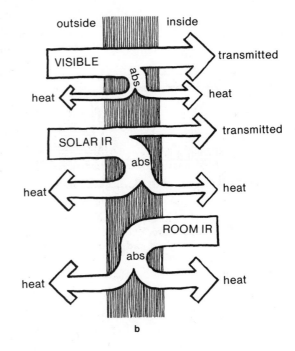

11-3. Ideal "heat-absorbing" green glass:
(a) spectral transmission, absorption, and
reflection; (b) section.

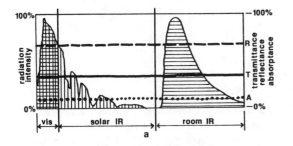

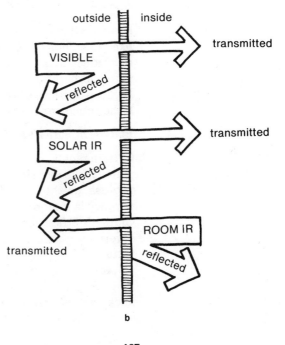

11-4. Ideal light-reflective film: (a) spectral
transmission, absorption, and reflection;
(b) section.

ROOM IR REFLECTIVE FILM

Selkowitz (1979) has described commercially available reflective films that, like clear glass, have a high visible and solar IR transmittance. Unlike glass, which absorbs room IR, these coatings reflect in this region, further reducing heat loss (fig. 11-5). Theoretically, this would be the ideal glazing for passive solar heating applications. In practice, available commercial products have significantly reduced visible and solar IR transmittance compared with clear glazing, making it less suited for passive heating than for non-south residential window applications.

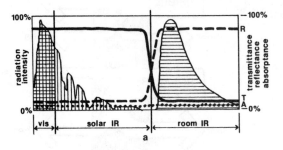

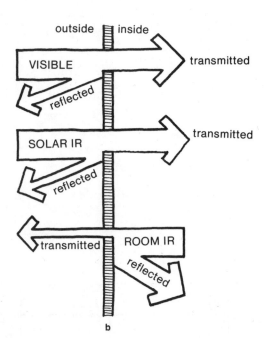

11-5. Ideal room IR reflective film ("residential heat mirror"): (a) spectral transmission, absorption, and reflection; (b) section.

SOLAR IR REFLECTIVE FILM

Rosen (1981 and 1982) has described a more recent development: a film which, like glass, has a high visible transmittance, but, unlike glass, has a high reflectance in both solar and room IR regions (fig. 11-6). This combination is particularly attractive for daylighting in internal-load-dominated buildings because of the rejection of the nonvisible solar region (which contributes only to the structure's heat gain).

ROOM IR TRANSPARENT PLASTICS

Certain plastic materials (e.g., polyethylene and nylon 6) are highly transparent in the room IR spectrum. This reduces the "greenhouse" effect common to glass, greatly increasing heat loss to the exterior (fig. 11-7). This transparency is important, however, for certain radiative cooling applications. Clark (1979) has described the use of IR transparent plastics for windscreen coverings to reduce convective warming of night-sky roof radiation cooling panels. Other plastics, more commonly used for building glazing (acrylic, polycarbonate, etc.) are also more transparent to room IR than glass, but less so than polyethylene. Since spectral qualities vary considerably with thickness as well as material, manufacturer's specifications should be consulted.

FENESTRATION

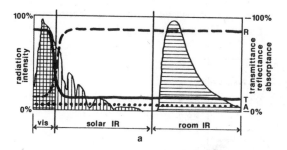

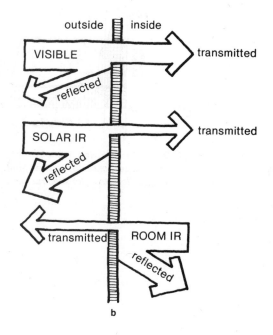

11-6. Ideal solar IR reflective film ("commercial building heat mirror"): (a) spectral transmission, absorption, and reflection; (b) section.

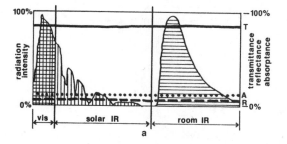

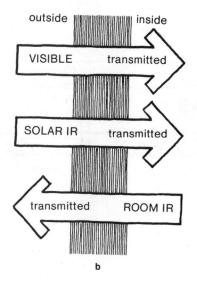

11-7. Ideal room IR transparent plastic: (a) spectral transmission, absorption, and reflection; (b) section.

MULTIPLE GLAZING

The spectral response of multiple layers of the same material differs little from that of an individual layer. However, combining two or more types into a "sandwich" may produce a totally different response. This is particularly true in the common case where one layer is glass and one layer is a reflective film. Placing the reflective layer on the outside causes the room IR to be absorbed and the heat dissipated to each side by convection and by reradiation to the interior. Conversely, placing the reflective layer on the room side reflects room IR before it can be absorbed by the glass (fig. 11-8).

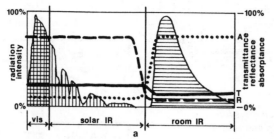

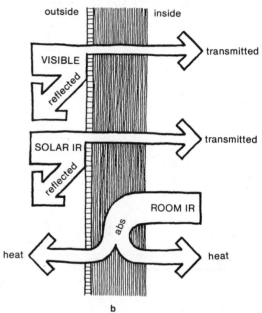

11-8. Multiple glazing, reflective out: (a) spectral response; (b) section. Multiple glazing, reflective in: (c) spectral response; (d) section.

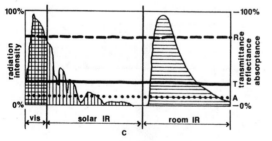

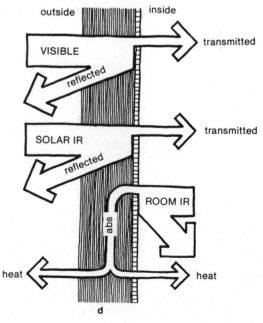

FENESTRATION

A discussion of the ideal spectral behavior of all of the possible glazing layer combinations is beyond the scope of this book. However, the reader can derive the ideal response for any combination from the individual layers discussed above. It should be noted that commercially available products (especially IR reflective types) will differ from these ideal examples. In some cases, the performance difference will be so great as to make it unsuitable for the application recommended for the ideal sample. For this reason, manufacturers' test results for spectral response in each of the three regions should be studied. Unfortunately, many manufacturers do not differentiate between transmission in visible and solar IR regions in standard literature.

SHADING COEFFICIENT

The *shading coefficient* is a widely used index of the effective solar rejection performance of fenestration. *ASHRAE* (1981) has defined it as "the ratio of the solar heat gain through a glazing system under a specific set of conditions to the solar gain through a single light of double-strength sheet glass under the same conditions." Most glazing manufacturers publish shading coefficient data in their technical literature.

GLAZING DIFFUSION

In general, the transmittance and reflectance discussed above is primarily a function of the material used to form the glazing. If the glazing surfaces are flat and polished, then transmission and reflection are specular (i.e., transmitted light continues in the same direction and reflections are mirrorlike). If one or both surfaces are rough, then reflection and transmission are diffused. In most cases this diffusion depends only on surface texture; in some materials (such as translucent white glass or plastic) white pigment suspended in the material diffuses the light internally. Transmission can be characterized as clear, diffuse (where diffusion is complete and uniform in all directions), or spread (where diffusion is complete but not uniform, with the largest component in the incident direction).

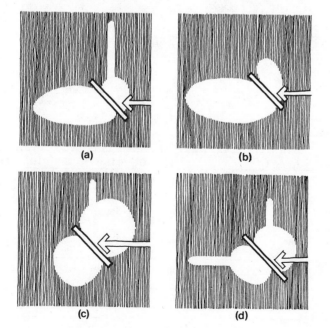

(a) (b) (c) (d)

11-9. Transmitted light diffusion: (a) spread transmission on smooth side of figured, etched, ground, or hammered glass; (b) spread transmission on rough side of the same types; (c) diffuse transmission through solid opalescent and flashed opalescent glass, white plastic, and thin marble; (d) mixed transmission through opalescent glass. (After I.E.S., 1981)

While the exact amount of transmission, reflection, and spread of diffusion can only be determined by laboratory measurement, useful design information can be gained by visual inspection of glazing samples. As a general rule, for commercially available glazing materials, increased diffusion results in decreased transmission. Light transmission, diffusion, and the shading coefficients of window draperies are influenced by yarn color and weave, as shown in figures 11-10 and 11-11.

11-10. Lecture room, Art Museum, Miami University (Skidmore, Owings and Merrill, Architects). With white drapes 60 percent closed and black-out drapes 30 percent closed. Window draperies can be used to block or diffusely transmit light (becoming a secondary-source luminous wall).

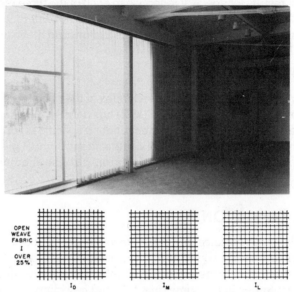

11-11. Effect of drapery fabrics on various window functions. (Reprinted, by permission, from ASHRAE 1981 Handbook of Fundamentals)

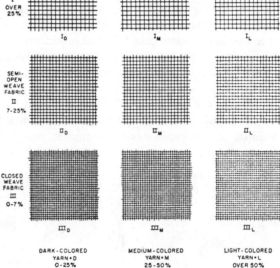

	Designator (Figs. 17, 18)								
Item	I_D	I_M	I_L	II_D	II_M	II_L	III_D	III_M	III_L
1. Protection from Direct Solar Radiation and Longwave Radiation to or from Window Areas	Fair	Fair	Fair	Fair	Good	Good	Fair	Good	Good
2. Effectiveness in Allowing Outward Vision through Fenestration	Good	Good	Fair	Fair	Fair	Some	None	None	None
3. Effectiveness in Attaining Privacy (Limiting in Inward Vision from Outside)	None	None	Poor[b] Good[b]	Poor	Fair	Fair[b] Good[b]	Good[c]	Good[c]	Good[c]
4. Protection against Excessive Brightness and Glare from Sunshine and External Objects	Mild	Mild	Mild[d] Poor[d]	Good	Good	Good[d] Poor[d]	Good	Good	Good[d] Poor[d]
5. Effectiveness in Modifying Unattractive or Distracting View out of the Window	Little	Little	Some	Some	Good	Good	Blocks	Blocks	Blocks

[b] Good when bright illumination is on the viewing side.
[c] To obscure view completely, material must be completely opaque.
[d] *Poor* rating applies to white fabric in direct sunlight. Use off-white color to avoid excessive transmitted light.

OPAQUE REFLECTORS

For all commonly available building materials (including paints and metal surfaces) reflectance in the solar IR region is similar to reflectance in the visible region and can be evaluated on the basis of lightness or darkness of color. Therefore, sunlight maintains the same proportion of visible and solar IR radiation after being reflected by a white surface. Thus there is little thermal advantage in reflecting sunlight from a white roof surface before it enters a room compared with transmitting a comparable amount of direct sunlight. (This is not literally true because the outside white surface does absorb some radiation in both regions, and this is dissipated by convection outside of the building envelope. However, this advantage is not due to any selective reflectance.)

In the room IR region, high reflectance is primarily associated with metallic surfaces; virtually all other nonmetallic opaque materials are highly absorptive in the room IR region.

REFLECTED DIFFUSION

Flat, polished, metallic surfaces reflect specularly. Conversely, ideal matte surfaces reflect diffusely, with an even distribution in all directions. In practice, most building materials exhibit some combination of specular and diffuse reflection (fig. 11-12).

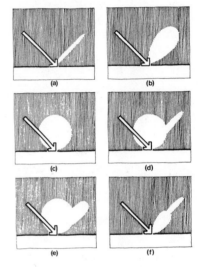

11-12. Reflected light diffusion: (a) specular (polished mirror surface); (b) spread (pebbled mirror surface); (c) diffuse (ideal matte surface); (d) diffuse/specular (polished white surface); (e) diffuse/spread (pebbled, glass white surface); (f) specular/spread (rippled mirror surface). (After I.E.S., 1981)

REFERENCES

American Society of Heating, Refrigerating and Air Conditioning Engineers. *ASHRAE Handbook 1981 Fundamentals.* New York: American Society of Heating, Refrigerating, and Air Conditioning Engineers, 1981.

Clark, G. and Blanpied, M. "The Effect of IR Transparent Windscreens on Net Nocturnal Cooling From Horizontal Surfaces." In *Proceedings, 4th National Passive Solar Conference,* edited by Franta, G., pp. 509–513. Boulder, CO: American Solar Energy Society, 1979.

Kaufman, J., ed. *IES Lighting Handbook 1981 Reference Volume.* New York: Illuminating Engineering Society of North America, 1981.

Rosen, J.E. "Daylighting and Energy Conservation: Innovative Solutions for Office Buildings." Master of Architecture thesis, M.I.T., 1982.

Rosen, J.E. "Heat Mirror Coatings for Internal-Load-Dominated Buildings." In *Proceedings, 6th National Passive Solar Conference,* edited by Hayes, J., and Kolar, W., pp. 626–630. Boulder, CO: American Solar Energy Society, 1981.

Selkowitz, S.E. "Transparent Heat Mirrors for Passive Solar Heating Applications." Report LBL-7829. Berkeley, CA: Lawrence Berkeley Laboratory, 1979.

Chapter 12
Integration with Electric Lighting

A daylighted building, no matter how well designed, saves energy only if the daylighting can effectively and reliably displace electric lighting usage. Most daylighting designers agree that, in nonresidential buildings, no amount of provision for convenient manual switching (even for 50 percent reduction of fixtures in use) will result in useful energy savings. For significant savings to be achieved (in lighting and cooling energy and in peak-demand utility costs), electric lighting control must be automatic. Automatic controls are made up of a combination of a sensing device (to measure daylight) and a controller that either switches or dims the electric lighting.

The recent increase in daylight utilization in commercial buildings has been facilitated by the increased availability of electronic lighting controls. These controls can be either switching or dimming and may be further categorized by lamp type (incandescent or fluorescent) as shown in figure 12-1. The graphs in this figure show the total interior lighting levels (top curve) that are the sum of daylight and electric light used throughout the day. Optimum performance (minimum electricity usage) occurs when the shaded area is minimized and when the top curve is lowest (while still maintaining the desired light level). Each system has certain characteristics that may be desirable or undesirable depending on the application. Most of the following discussion of control systems is derived from Sain (1983).

SWITCHING CONTROLS

Switching controls simply turn off artificial lights when there is ample daylight. The most common switching control is the photocell, similar to those used on exterior lights. Referred to as a *task-switching device,* it controls one or two fixtures by sensing the light level at the task location. Photocells that are used to control interior lights must be adjustable and capable of sensing at least two levels of light. An adjustment control makes the same device appropriate for various spaces with different lighting requirements. This two-level sensing is illustrated in figure 12-1a. The device should sense when there is twice as much daylight as required (to compensate for electric light) and turn off the lights and also sense when the quantity of light drops below the required level and turn the lights back on. Either a time-delay feature or a "dead band" (cut-on setting is less than cut-off setting) will prevent annoying on/off switching during partly cloudy days. The other type of switching control is a *source-switching device.* This device senses the quantity of daylight only by installing a sensor on the exterior of the building at the "source" of the daylight. This has the advantage of requiring only one sensing level. However, the operating mechanism must be adjustable for high levels of light (100 to 2,000 footcandles) so that the required inside light level (50 footcandles, for example) can be matched with the appropriate source level (as much as 1000 footcandles). A properly-sized air-conditioning system is required to prevent overheating due to excess solar gain.

Both switching devices can be connected directly to one fixture, to an entire circuit, or relays can be added to switch several circuits (depending on the relative location of those fixtures to the sensor).

114

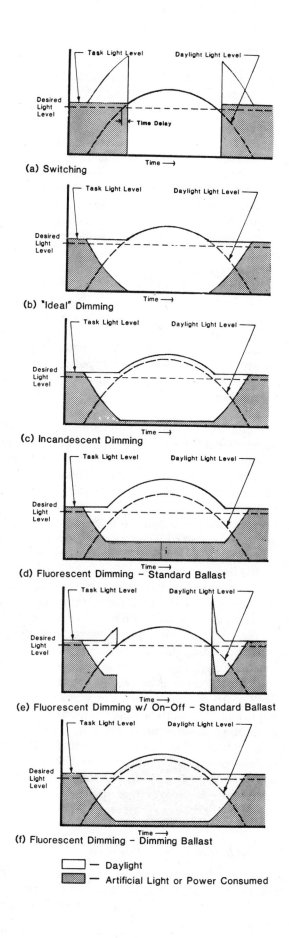

12-1. *Schematics of various control devices.* (*Reprinted, by permission, from Sain, 1983*)

DIMMING CONTROLS

Dimming controls reduce electric light proportionally as the daylight increases. An ideal dimming control sequence would provide only as much electric light as required to meet desired levels (with a small "dead band" allowance) and consume no power when sufficient daylight was present. Such a control sequence is shown graphically in figure 12-1b. Unfortunately, ideal dimming devices are not available at this time because some power is required to operate the controls (although some approach this ideal).

Dimming controls for incandescent lamps are the closest to the ideal. These dimmers reduce power consumption proportionally to light output; however, the dimming control does consume a small amount of power itself. Figure 12-1c shows the control schematic for an incandescent dimmer, with a slight increase in power consumption over an ideal dimmer. Incandescent dimming systems for daylighting purposes are not commercially available as an integrated unit but can be readily assembled from available components (sensors and dimmers).

FLUORESCENT WITH STANDARD LAMPS/BALLASTS

Dimming controls for fluorescent lights with standard lamps and ballasts are available in a variety of forms and with many special features. They can be divided into two generic types: multiple- and single-fixture dimmers. The power consumption patterns are the same for each, as illustrated in figure 12-1d.

Multiple-fixture dimmers are useful when simultaneous dimming is required for a large number of fixtures. One sensor is used to read the daylight level; this is converted to an electronic signal to operate a controller and dim the lights. In this type of system, one sensor and one controller dim several hundred watts of lighting. Overall costs are decreased when the maximum number of watts possible is dimmed by each controller. However, care should be taken to ensure that all areas dimmed are receiving equal daylight.

Single-fixture dimmers normally control one or two ballasts only. Typically, this type of system uses a fiber-optics tube to sense the light level on the workplane below the fixture, transferring this light signal to the control box on top of (or inside) the ballast housing. The control box contains all electrical and/or mechanical devices, thus reducing the cost of the sensing device. Each fixture in a daylit area is equipped with a sensor and controller to make maximum use of the daylight available. However, a controller that is adjustable from below the ceiling should be selected for ease of maintenance.

One manufacturer of daylighting controls has added an on/off switch to their dimming system for standard lamps. The control dims the lights to the minimum level of 25 percent light output, then waits until daylight can provide all of the required light before turning the electric lights off. When the daylight decreases, the lights are turned back on. Designers should recognize, however, that standard fluorescent lamps and ballasts must first be turned to 100 percent power and then dimmed. This control sequence is shown in figure 12-1e. Note that not all lamps can be dimmed by the fluorescent controls. Some energy-saving lamps cannot be dimmed; manufacturer's literature should be consulted before combining dimmers and energy-saving lamps.

FLUORESCENT WITH DIMMING BALLASTS

Dimming controls for fluorescent lights with dimming ballasts are very similar to dimmers for standard lamps except that they can dim the full 100 percent range (fig. 12-1f). At present, this type of system is only available in the multiple-fixture form described above.

HIGH INTENSITY DISCHARGE (H.I.D.)

Dimming controls for H.I.D. lights are not commercially available at present, although several companies have successfully dimmed these lamps in the laboratory. The power-consumption characteristics are similar to those of fluorescent controls. However, dimming H.I.D. lamps has a severe effect on the color rendition of the lamps and may reduce the life of both lamps and ballasts. Manufacturer's literature should be consulted for recent developments in these products.

SELECTION OF ELECTRIC LIGHTING CONTROLS

Proper selection of electric lighting controls is an important step in the design of a daylighted building. Sain (1983) has suggested the following considerations:

QUALITY OF SPACE

Daylighting controls can affect the quality of the interior space. They can cause annoying changes in the light level, poor color rendition, the appearance of burned-out lamps, and other items that may reduce the quality and/or rentability of building space. The control schematics in figure 12-1 show the task light level as the combination of daylight and electric light. If this curve has a sharp vertical section where lamps are turned on or off, occupants may be annoyed. This is critical in task areas such as office spaces, where light switching may reduce productivity, resulting in economic losses that far exceed the energy savings. Some recent installations have utilized various occupant sensors that prevent lowering electric lighting when anyone is present in the room. Color rendition and perceived burn-out must also be addressed for each application and control system.

LAMP/BALLAST TYPE

The type of lamps and ballasts used in the space will affect the selection of electric light controls. Several controls are made specifically for certain types of lamps, but some controls, such as switching devices, can be used on any lamp type. The designer should be aware of this compatibility of controls and lamp types. For example, switching H.I.D. or fluorescent lamps can reduce their life, but if they are switched off during half of the normal working hours and their life is reduced by 25 percent, they will still last 25 percent longer than standard lamps with no controls.

FIXTURE LAYOUT AND ROOM SIZE

The selection of controls can be affected by the fixture layout or room size. Multifixture dimming and switching systems rely on layouts in which many fixtures are receiving similar quantities of daylight. In large buildings where this occurs, the multifixture systems are typically cheaper and easier to maintain than numerous single-fixture controls. However, in small buildings or individual rooms, single-fixture controls are more appropriate.

QUANTITY OF LIGHT

The daylighting strategy and its resulting daylight level in the space can affect the control device selection. Since most dimming devices have a minimum power consumption of approximately 30 percent, they may not be appropriate for areas where large amounts of daylight are available, or where low illuminance levels are required. On the other hand, in areas where the required light level is high and the daylight source is small, a switching device may never operate. The effects of daylight level on control selection are shown graphically in figure 12-2.

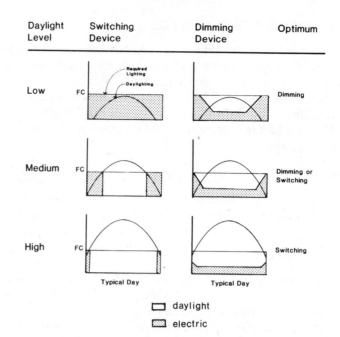

12-2. Control strategies appropriate for various daylighting levels. (Reprinted, by permission, from Sain, 1983)

COST

The cost of daylighting controls will have a major effect on final system selection. When a designer bases a decision on economic feasibility, he is attempting to save the most energy for the lowest initial cost. Prices for each control system will vary slightly between manufacturers, but the actual cost of the total system will vary much more depending on the application. (This is especially true for retrofit projects.) For instance, using a multifixture device on a few fixtures will cost more than two single-fixture units.

One system that is very high in initial cost is a fluorescent dimming system with dimming ballasts. Such a system would be extremely hard to justify on the basis of energy savings alone.

OTHER CONSIDERATIONS

Several miscellaneous items can also affect the control selection. Control systems will require some maintenance, and some devices are easier to maintain than others. They may also cause radio interference with other equipment in the space. Another concern with dimming or switching fluorescent lights is the adverse effect this may have on the power factor. If the space contains a large inductive motor load, fluorescent lights will help alleviate the problem. However, if the fluorescent lights are not there, a capacitor bank may be required to control the power factor.

PHOTOCELL PERFORMANCE

The control system performance illustrated in figure 12-1 is schematic and seldom achieved under actual operating conditions. Rubinstein (1983) has analyzed the ability of various photocell sensor types to provide constant illumination levels using a dimming system. In the simplest case, the photosensor is located on the workplane, and the system operates by maintaining a constant light level on the sensor itself. However, this location is impractical since the sensor is then sensitive to the effects of body shadows, loose papers, and other light-obstructing objects. Figures 12-4 through 12-6 illustrate comparisons between three types of illuminance sensors based on computer simulations (validated using results from two test rooms) and show relative effectiveness at maintaining designed workplane illuminance using a dimming control system.

118   FENESTRATION

12-3. *Operational characteristics of electric lighting controls. (After Sain, 1983)*

CONTROL TYPE	LIGHT QUALITY	SYSTEM MAINTENANCE	APPLICABILITY TO NEW PROJECTS	APPLICABILITY TO RETROFIT PROJECTS	SPACES BEST SUITED FOR USE
Task-switching	1, 2	4	8, 9, 10, 11	19, 20, 21, 22	30, 31, 32, 33
Source-switching	1, 2	4, 5	8, 9, 10, 11, 12, 13	19, 20, 21, 22, 23	30, 31, 32, 33
Incandescent Dimming	2		10, 14	21, 24, 25, 26	34
H.I.D dimming	3	4	8, 9, 10, 15	19, 21, 22, 27	30, 31, 35
Fluorescent dimming : multi-fixture, std. ballast		6	10, 14, 16, 17	21, 24, 28	36
Fluorescent dimming: single fixture, std. ballast		7	14, 16, 17, 18	24, 28, 29	
Fluorescent dimming: Multi-fixture, dimming ballast		6	14, 16, 17	26, 28	36

LEGEND

1 - May be annoying in task areas.
2 - Perceived burnouts.
3 - Poor color rendition.
4 - May reduce life of some lamps and ballasts.
5 - Outdoor sensor must be cleaned.
6 - Few additional components.
7 - Non-task areas.
8 - Non-task areas.
9 - Large ratio of daylight to artificial light.
10 - Hybrid systems.
11 - All lamp types.
12 - Where screening devices will be installed.
13 - Vandal areas.
14 - Any task or non-task area.
15 - H.I.D. lamps only.
16 - Fluorescent lamps only.
17 - High required light level.
18 - Small daylight room with fluorescent lights.

19 - Non-task areas.
20 - All lamp types.
21 - Many fixtures on one power panel.
22 - Large ratio of daylight to artificial light.
23 - When screening divices are not being used properly.
24 - Any area.
25 - Incandescent lamps only.
26 - Add sensor to existing dimmer system.
27 - H.I.D. lamps only.
28 - Fluorescent lamps only.
29 - Small daylit rooms with fluorescent lights.
30 - Corridors / stairs.
31 - Gymnasium.
32 - Cafeteria.
33 - Entry / Lobby.
34 - Any daylit space with incandescent lighting.
35 - Warehouses.
36 - Anydaylit space with a large number of Flu. lights.

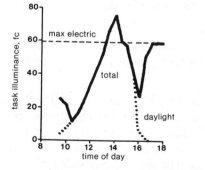

12-4. *Simulated performance of ceiling-mounted illuminance sensor. (Solid line = total task illumination; dotted line = daylight illumination; after Rubinstein, 1983.)*

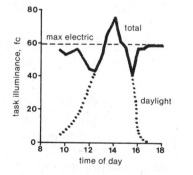

12-5. *Simulated performance of ceiling-mounted illuminance sensor (shielded from the window). (Solid line = total task illumination; dotted line = daylight illumination; after Rubinstein, 1983.)*

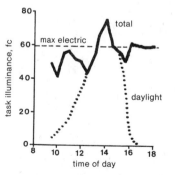

12-6. *Simulated performance of ceiling-mounted, wide-angle illuminance sensor (aimed at the floor). (Solid line = total task illumination; dotted line = daylight illumination; after Rubinstein, 1983.)*

The ceiling-mounted sensor performs poorly with large variations in the total light levels at the task (solid line). Between 10:30 A.M. and 1:00 P.M. and between 2:30 P.M. and 3:30 P.M., this sensor control strategy supplied no electric illumination even though the daylight component was less than the designed light level.

The shielded sensor whose performance is shown in figure 12-5 does not provide sufficient electric illumination to maintain the target light level, but its performance is clearly an improvement over the unshielded photosensor system, as evidenced by the lower level of variability and the generally higher maintained illuminance levels.

The performance of the wide-angle illuminance sensor (figure 12-6) system is comparable to the previous system, but electric illuminance is still insufficient to maintain designed levels.

Rubenstein concludes that more sophisticated sensor systems are required in order to maintain designed illuminance levels.

EXPERIENCE IN CONTROL SELECTION

Sain (1983) has summarized some of the experiences of the firm of Burt Hill Kosar and Rittelman Associates, Architects (Butler, Pennsylvania) in applying these control system design considerations to a variety of new and retrofit projects.

NEW PROJECTS

The addition of daylighting controls was selected as an energy conservation measure in the following new projects:

- The Firstside Parking Garage in Pittsburgh, Pennsylvania will be equipped with a multifixture source-switching control system. Conditions include a similar daylighting configuration on each side of all ten floors, a H.I.D. lighting system, and the need for preventing vandalism of the sensors.

- A multifixture fluorescent dimming system was considered for the atrium of the L.K. Comstock Office Building in Pittsburgh. The ten-story-high atrium with a skylight top and a west-facing, eight-story vertical glazing system would provide equal daylighting on all floors. However, the low level of daylight prevented dimming for economic reasons.

- Single-fixture fluorescent dimmers were selected for the American Hardware Office in Charleston, Illinois. West-facing private offices were equipped with a light shelf and a small vertical window for view glazing. Each room required individual control for its wall-mounted fluorescent up/down fixture.

- An underground field office for Fox Oil and Gas also required individual control for each room's fluorescent fixtures; single-fixture dimmers were used for control.

- A gymnasium at Fort Story (near Norfolk, Virginia) was analyzed for the economic feasibility of adding skylights and a control system to reduce electric lighting power consumption. Because of the use of H.I.D. fixtures and a uniform layout of skylights, a multifixture source-switching system was selected for analysis, which indicated a fifteen year payback period.

RETROFIT PROJECTS

The following projects are examples of studies performed to find economical ways to reduce energy consumption in existing buildings. Although the daylighting conditions would seem to suggest the installation of controls, the actual analyses revealed that not all such installations were economical.

The classrooms at Bethel Park and Gateway Senior High Schools in Pittsburgh are typical of those built in the 1950s. The exterior walls are comprised of continuous eight-foot-high windows (single clear glazing). The desks along the window receive 100 footcandles of daylight on rainy days. Since wiring was concealed in a plaster ceiling, and the wall switches were not conducive to the installation of automatic dimming controls, single-fixture fluorescent dimmers were selected as the appropriate control system.

When the school administration was asked about having a fragile fiber-optic sensor mounted on the side of each row of fixtures, they expressed concern that the sensors would last a week . . . maybe. All electric controls were eliminated on the basis of economic or maintenance considerations. However, Gateway Gymnasium has been successfully equipped with a multifixture source-switching system for its new H.I.D. system. Since the old incandescent system was being replaced, it was simple to wire all new fixtures to a single panel and control them with one controller and one sensor. The daylight source is a sixteen-foot-wide skylight that runs the length of the gym. This system has been in operation since September 1981.

An office building for Rodale Press in Emmaus, Pennsylvania was analyzed for possible daylighting because the one-story building was equipped with skylights. Since a task-ambient lighting system was used, and the general lighting was provided by indirect H.I.D. fixtures, a switching control system was analyzed. However, an analysis of daylight availability revealed that the H.I.D. fixtures would seldom, if ever, be turned off, and therefore not be economical.

REFERENCES

Rubinstein, F. "Photo-Electric Control of Equi-Illumination Lighting Systems." In *Proceedings of the International Daylighting Conference*, edited by Vonier, T., pp. 373–376. Washington, DC: American Institute of Architects Service Corporation, 1983.

Sain, A.M. "Daylighting and Artificial Lighting Control." In *Proceedings of the International Daylighting Conference*, edited by Vonier, T., pp. 363–367. Washington, DC: American Institute of Architects Service Corporation, 1983.

PART IV: ANALYSIS

Chapter 13
Preliminary Design Nomographs

A nomograph is a graphic representation of the relationships that exist between the several variables of a mathematical equation. It allows the user to determine quickly the numerical values in formulae having three or more variables. Nomographs have the advantage (compared with mathematical formulae) of representing relationships in a graphic format and thus visually revealing the relative importance of various parameters to the overall solution.

Nomographs are effective in assessing the potential of daylighting for saving energy early in the schematic design phase. As such, they provide an indication of the importance that should be assigned to further investigations of daylighting strategies. A design scheme that performs poorly on the nomographs indicates that daylighting probably will not be a significant energy conservation strategy: if large potential savings are indicated, additional effort should be expended to better define the impact of daylighting on all building systems.

Nomographs provide the designer with an all-important "feel" for energy considerations because the relative importance of the various parameters is visible graphically. Thus, for the schematic design phase (when the most important decisions affecting building energy usage are made), they are superior to other methods that require more detailed information. However, the very simplicity and generality that make the nomographs so valuable during the schematic design phase make them less suitable during the design development phase, where more detailed design tools are required.

L.B.L. DAYLIGHTING NOMOGRAPHS

The Lawrence Berkeley Laboratory has developed a set of nomographs designed specifically for daylighting applications (Selkowitz and Gabel, 1983). The nomographs provide data that suggest general design directions for cost-effective, daylighted buildings. They do *not* provide detailed design solutions. They offer a quick estimate of the magnitude of potential savings but do not provide the level of detail required to guarantee a workable solution.

The L.B.L. nomographs address electric lighting energy savings and peak electric impacts. They do not address the thermal effects of fenestration systems. These estimates of savings due to daylighting were derived from analysis using DOE-2.1B, a mainframe computer program with an hour-by-hour daylighting simulation model (see description in chapter 18). The method accommodates both top- and sidelighting. The nomographs assume the use of on/off or continuous dimming electric lighting control and the use of a simple interior shade or blind system when window glare exceeds specified values or when solar gain creates thermal discomfort for the occupant.

The user should read through this entire chapter first and test the nomographs step by step. The small diagram on each nomograph indicates the direction of movement through that nomograph. With a little practice, the reader should find the nomographs simple and easy to use. Note, however, that these nomographs and charts are based on certain assumptions (see *Assumptions* at the end of this chapter) that must be noted before this method can be applied properly; carefully review these before using the method.

DESIGN VARIABLES

The nomographs and charts provide flexibility in accounting for numerous aspects of a building's design, including:

- Latitude of building location
- Annual hours of occupancy
- Daily occupancy schedule
- Total building floor area (square feet)
- Daylit floor area (percent of total floor area)
- Visible light transmittance of glazing, including a "well factor" for toplighting
- Glazing area
- Choice of dimming or one-step (on/off) lighting controls
- Maximum light dimming factor (percent)
- Interior illumination level (footcandles)
- Installed lighting load (watts/sf)
- Nonlighting electrical load (watts/sf)
- Electricity cost ($/kWh)
- Peak demand rate ($/kW-month)

These variables are reflected in the values entered in worksheet I. The answers that come out of the nomographs are entered on worksheet II.

Other design features (such as glare control shades, interior reflectances, skylight spacing, window shape, etc.) are accounted for in the nomographs through the use of average values for fixed assumptions (explained at the end of this chapter).

Any one of the following economic variables or requirements may be tested while all of the others are held constant:

- Justifiable investment ($/sf-yr)
- First year savings ($/sf)
- Rate of return on investment or discount rate
- Energy escalation rate
- Payback period, years

USE OF THE L.B.L. NOMOGRAPH METHOD

Once the user becomes familiar with the input requirements and organization of each nomograph, several alternative designs can be compared in only a few minutes. Each nomograph is constructed so that the design choices that are most likely to be varied are located near the end of the nomograph calculation sequence.

WORKSHEETS AND CHARTS

The worksheets serve to keep track of assumptions that affect the daylighting performance of new or retrofit building designs under study. Values used in the base-case design and in several design variations are recorded on the worksheet and then used as the basis for nomograph studies. The worksheet documents the process by which specific design variations and assumptions are compared. Supplementary charts S-1 through S-7 (figs. 13-3 to 13-11) provide reference material from which appropriate worksheet input values can be selected.

WORKSHEET I, ITEMS 1–11 (REQUIRED PRELIMINARY DESIGN DATA):

These items must be completed in order to use the supplementary charts and nomographs. The small boxes to the left of each item of required information on the worksheet indicate the nomograph for which that item is either an input (i) or output (o) value. Those items that are not self-explanatory are explained below:

Item 2: *Daily occupancy schedule* refers to the normal hours of operation of the building.

Item 4: *Typical floor shape* may be expressed as a length-to-width ratio, or may be a graphic symbol that represents a particular building configuration. It is used in conjunction with charts S-5, S-6, and S-7 in determining item 13, *daylit area (%)*. For buildings not shaped like rectangular boxes, *daylit area (%)* is calculated directly from floor plans after the depth of the daylight zone is established. For sidelighting, a nominal fifteen-foot-deep perimeter zone is suggested, assuming a floor-to-ceiling height of 8′6″. (The daylight zone increases proportionally as the floor-to-ceiling height is increased above 8′6″.)

Items 5a–5d: These items include, respectively, the type of lighting control, the specification of design illuminance level, the fractional glazing area above the workplane, and the visible light transmittance of the glazing (*TVIS* = 0.0–1.0). For sidelighting, *glass area fraction* is the square feet of glazing above the workplane divided by the total (gross) wall area between floor and ceiling. For toplighting, *glass area fraction* is the square feet of glazed aperture divided by the flat ceiling area (or floor area) that it daylights. Skylights are assumed to be horizontal. The *well factor* is a correction factor (0.0–1.0) used to account for losses due to skylight well geometry and well reflectance. It typically ranges from 0.0 for a shallow, high-reflectance well to 0.5 for a well with moderate depth and reflectance.

Prepared By _____   Date _____

Project Title _____

Description of Study / Remarks _____

Input (i) or output (o) value for the specified nomograph or chart.

Worksheet Item No.	Description of Worksheet Item	\[Nomographs\] I	II	III	IV	\[Charts S.1 – S.7\] 1	2	3	4	5	6	7	Base Case	Case 1.	Case 2.	Case 3.	Case 4.
1	Latitude of Building Location					i	i										
2	Daily Occupancy Schedule					i	i										
3	Gross Area Per Floor (ft^2)								i	i	i	i					
4	Typical Floor Shape: Length-to-Width Ratio								i	i	i	i					
5a	Lighting Control Type						i	i									
5b	Illumination Level (fc)						i	i	i								
5c	Side Lighting Glass Area Fraction						i	i	i								
	Top Lighting; Glass Area Fraction																
5d	Side Lighting; Glass Visible Transmittance (TVIS)						i	i									
	Top Lighting; Glass Visible Transmittance (TVIS) X Well Factor																
6	Annual Hours of Occupancy		i														
7	Installed Lighting Load (watts/ft^2)		i														
8	Electricity Cost ($/kWh)		i														
9	Gross Total Building Area (ft^2)		i														
10	Non-Lighting Electric Loads (watts/ft^2)		i														
11	Peak Demand Rate ($/kW-month)	i	i				o	o									
12	Daylit Hours (%)	i	i				o	o									
13	Total Daylit Area (%)	i	i						o	o	o						
14	Control Effectiveness (%)	i	i						o	o							
15	Dimming Factor (%)	i	i														

Project Title _____   Date _____   Prepared By _____

Description of Study / Remarks

Nomographs I	II	III	IV	Charts S.1 - S.7 1	2	3	4	5	6	7	Worksheet Item No.	Description of Worksheet Item	Base Case	Case 1.	Case 2.	Case 3.	Case 4.
o											16	Annual Energy Savings Due to Daylight (%)					
o											17	Daylight Peak Load Savings (%)					
	o										18	Non-Daylit Lighting Energy Consumption (kWh/ft^2-year)					
	o										19	Non-Daylit Lighting Cost ($\$/ft^2$-yr)					
	o										20	Daylighting Energy Consumption Saving (kWh/ft^2-year)					
	o										21	Daylighting Saving ($\$/ft^2$-year)					
	o										22	Annual Daylighting Savings ($\$/building$)					
		o									23	Non-Daylit Peak Demand (kW)					
		o									24	Non-Daylit Monthly Demand Charge ($\$/ft^2$-month)					
		o									25	Non-Daylit Annual Demand Charge ($\$/ft^2$-year)					
		o									26	Daylit Peak Demand Saving (kW)					
		o									27	Daylit Monthly Demand Saving ($\$/ft^2$-month)					
		o									28	Daylit Annual Demand Saving ($\$/ft^2$-year)					
	o	o	i								29	Total Annual Savings ($\$/ft^2$-year)					
		o	i								30	Justifiable Investment ($\$/ft^2$ or $\$/building$), j					
		o	i								31	First Year Saving ($\$/ft^2$ or $\$/building$), s					
		o	i								32	Payback Period (years), n					
		o	i								33	Rate of Return on Investment or Discount Rate, i					
			i								34	Energy Escalation Rate, e					

Input (i) or output (o) value for the specified nomograph or chart.

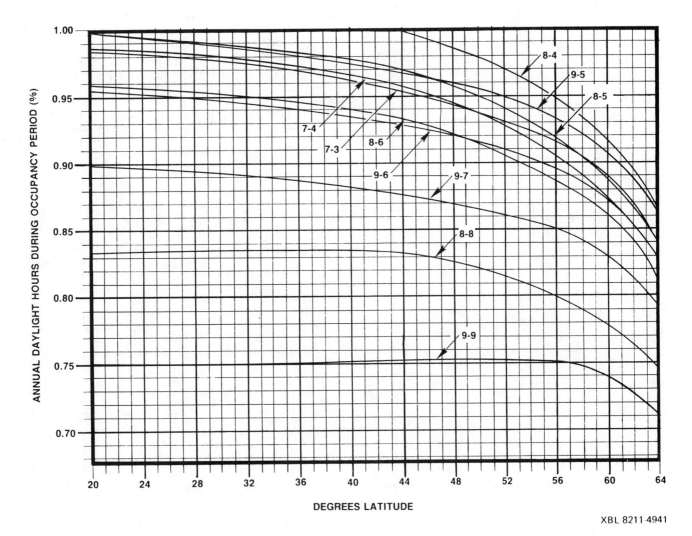

XBL 8211-4941

13-3. *Chart S-1: annual daylight hours during occupancy period.*

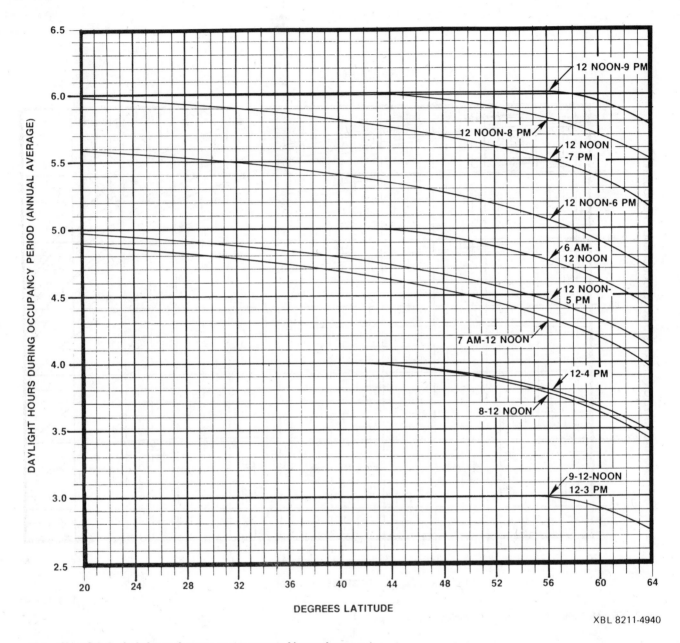

XBL 8211-4940

13-4. Chart S-2: daylight hours during occupancy period (annual average).

ANALYSIS

SIDE LIGHTING

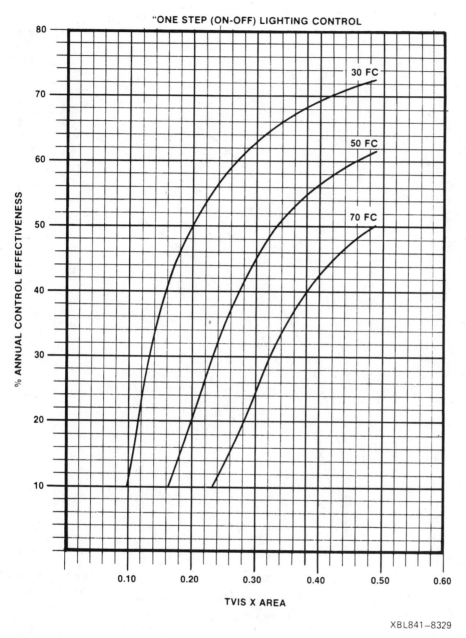

"ONE STEP (ON-OFF) LIGHTING CONTROL

XBL841—8329

13-5. Chart S-3: annual control effectiveness (on/off control—sidelighting).

TOP LIGHTING

"ONE STEP (ON-OFF) LIGHTING CONTROL"

XBL841—8331

13-6. Chart S-3A: annual control effectiveness (on/off control — toplighting).

ANALYSIS

SIDE LIGHTING

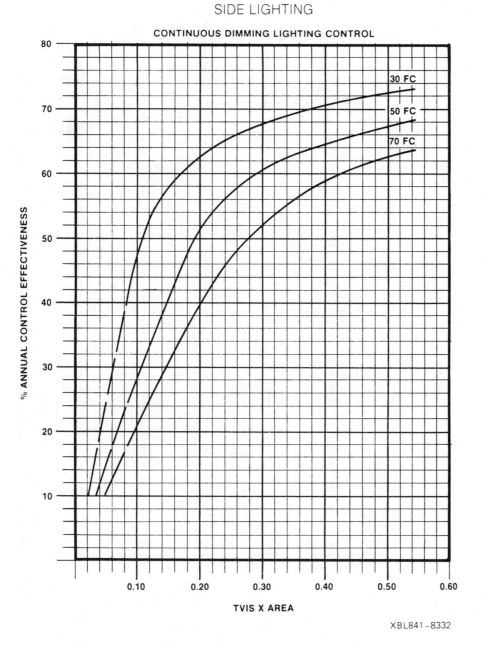

CONTINUOUS DIMMING LIGHTING CONTROL

30 FC
50 FC
70 FC

% ANNUAL CONTROL EFFECTIVENESS

TVIS X AREA

XBL841–8332

13-7. Chart S-4: annual control effectiveness (continuous dimming—sidelighting).

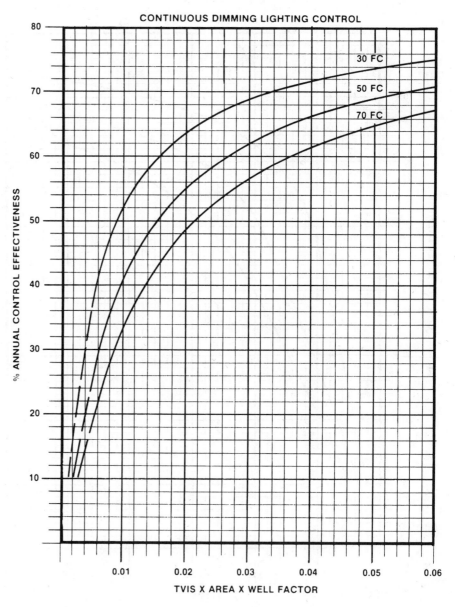

CONTINUOUS DIMMING LIGHTING CONTROL

13-8. Chart S-4: annual control effectiveness (continuous dimming—toplighting).

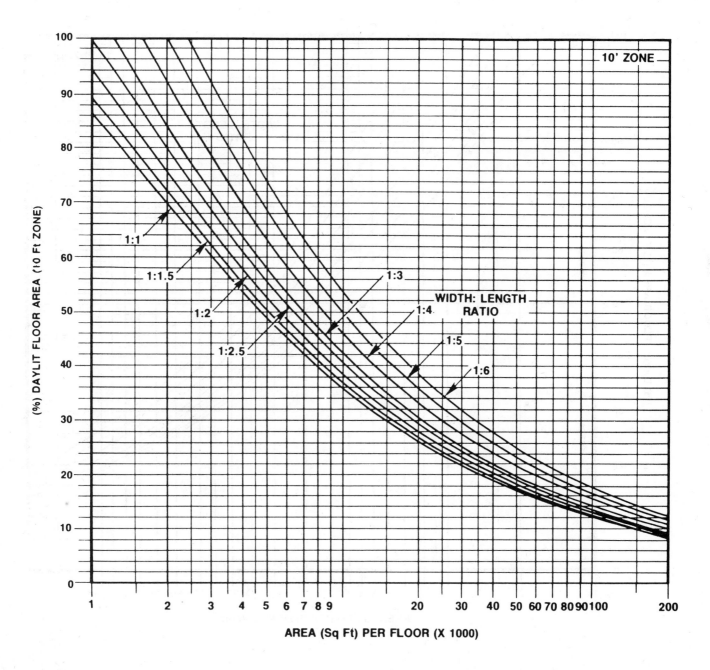

13-9.   Chart S-5: % daylit floor area (10 ft. zone).

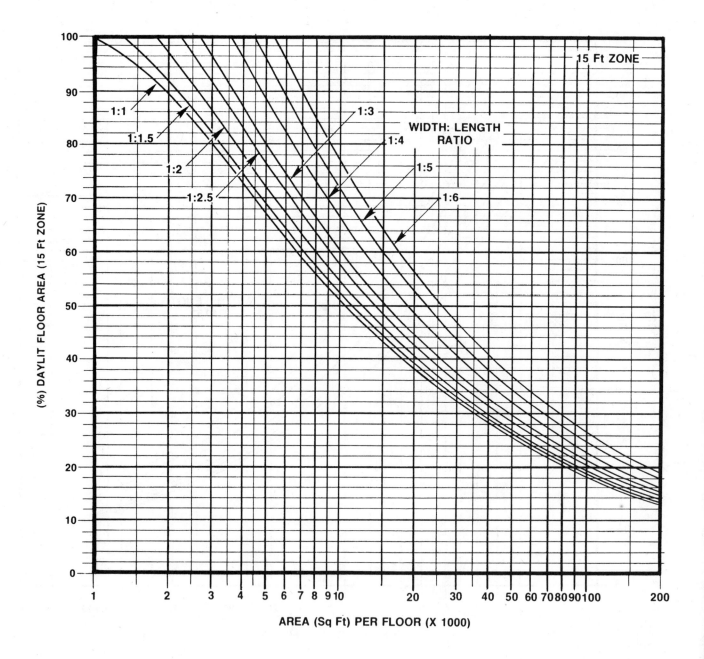

13-10. Chart S-6: % daylit floor area (15 ft. zone).

ANALYSIS

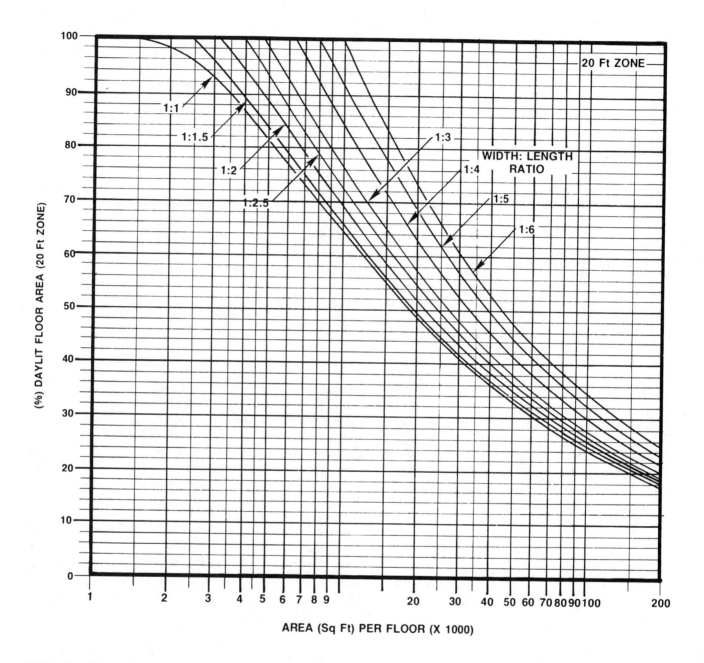

13-11. Chart S-7: % daylit floor area (20 ft. zone).

Item 12: For *daylight hours (%)*, refer to chart S-1 (fig. 13-3). Find the appropriate latitude on the horizontal axis, proceed vertically to intersect with the appropriate occupancy period, then horizontally left to read the annual daylight hours during the occupancy period (%). If the occupancy schedule of the building being studied is not found in S-1, use chart S-2 (fig. 13-4) as follows: choose the curve corresponding to the A.M. portion of the desired occupancy, find the point where the latitude line crosses the curve, and read off the value on the left vertical axis labeled *daylit hours during occupancy.* Do the same with the P.M. portion of the occupancy and add the A.M. and P.M. hours together. Divide the sum by the total number of daily occupancy hours and multiply by 100. The result is the same as *daylight hours (%)* found directly in chart S-1. Note that charts S-1 and S-2 account for daylight savings time.

Item 13: *Total daylit area (%)* is read from charts S-5, S-6, and S-7 (figs. 13-5, 6, and 7) assuming a ten-, fifteen-, or twenty-foot-deep perimeter daylighted zone, respectively, for a specified length-to-width ratio and total area per floor. For irregularly shaped buildings without a consistent length-to-width ratio, or with different floor plans on each level, the daylighted area can be calculated by dividing the floor area of the daylighted perimeter zone by total building floor area. For a skylighted building with uniform skylight distribution, *total daylit area* would be the entire floor area (100 percent). Sidelighted and toplighted areas may be treated as one using a weighted average, or may be handled separately.

Item 14: *Control effectiveness* is found from charts S-3 or S-3A (fig. 13-5 or 13-6) (one step, on/off) and charts S-4 or S-4A (fig. 13-7 or 13-8) (for continuous dimming) from the specification of item 5a. Overall control effectiveness, expressed as percent saving, is defined as a function of: (a) design illuminance level (in footcandles), (b) TVIS, and (c) area. TVIS is the total visible light transmittance of the glazing assembly (does not include the effect of operable shading). It should include the effect of any fixed shading solutions (e.g., reflective coatings, sunscreens, etc.) and any allowance for a maintenance factor to account for dirt accumulation on the glazing. Area is the net glazed window area above the workplane divided by the total (gross) wall area between the floor and ceiling. TVIS × area is the product of those two values.

To determine control effectiveness for toplighting (in charts S-3A and S-4A), a *well factor* is included in the TVIS × area product. A well factor of 1.0 is used when the skylight is virtually flush with the finished ceiling, (e.g., when each light well has a depth of 0 feet and/or a net reflectance of 100 percent). As the depth of the light well increases, and the reflectance of the light well surfaces decreases, the well factor is reduced.

If a building has more than one type of glazing assembly, calculate a weighted average as follows:

Overall Control Effectiveness =

$$\frac{(\text{type 1 glazing control effectiveness}) \times (\text{area daylit by type 1 glazing})}{\text{total daylit area}} +$$

$$\frac{(\text{type 2 glazing control effectiveness}) \times (\text{area daylit by type 2 glazing})}{\text{total daylit area}} +$$

. . . etc.

ANALYSIS

Alternatively, one could use the nomographs on a zone-by-zone basis, treating each distinct building zone as a separate "building" for analysis. If a building has daylighted areas with several different occupancy schedules, calculate each type separately and add the results at the end.

Item 15: *Dimming factor* is the maximum reduction of electric lighting power in the daylighted zone. Expressed as a percent, this value is a function of the lighting control hardware and the type of load management strategy being employed.

The dimming factor is calculated as follows:

$$\frac{LP_{min}}{LP_{max}} \times 100$$

where:

LP_{min} = minimum lighting power required to operate dimmers, and

LP_{max} = maximum lighting power required to operate dimmers.

WORKSHEET II, ITEMS 16–34 (OUTPUT DATA FROM NOMOGRAPHS)

Nomograph I:

Item 16: Annual energy savings due to daylight (%)

Item 17: Peak load savings due to daylight (%)

Nomograph II:

Item 18: Nondaylighted lighting energy consumption (kWh/sf-yr)

Item 19: Nondaylighted lighting cost ($/sf)

Item 20: Daylighting energy savings (kWh/sf-yr)

Item 21: Daylighting savings ($/sf)

Item 22: Annual daylighting savings ($/building)

Nomograph III:

Item 23: Nondaylighted peak demand (kW)

Item 24: Nondaylighted monthly demand charge ($/kW-month)

Item 25: Nondaylighted annual demand charge ($/kW-yr)

Item 26: Daylighted peak demand savings (kW)

Item 27: Daylighted monthly demand savings ($/sf-month)

Item 28: Daylighted annual demand charge ($/sf-yr)

Item 29: Total annual savings ($/sf-yr)

Nomograph IV:

Item 30: Justifiable investment ($/sf-yr), j

Item 31: First-year savings ($/sf)

Item 33: Rate of return on investment or discount rate, i

Item 34: Energy escalation rate, e

Nomograph IV can be used in several ways depending upon the approach one chooses to take. For example, the *payback period* can be found according to the values selected for the discount rate (*i*), the energy cost escalation (*e*), the incremental installation cost or justifiable investment (*j*), and the first year savings (*s*). In order to find the *rate of return on investment*, work back through the nomograph to the appropriate discount rate. Parameters can be alternately fixed or varied to examine the sensitivity to various economic assumptions.

NOMOGRAPH I: RELATIVE IMPORTANCE OF DAYLIGHTING
REQUIRED PRELIMINARY DATA: WORKSHEET I, ITEMS 1–5, 12–15.

This nomograph is used to determine the magnitude of potential energy and load savings from daylighting relative to a base-case electrical lighting system in which no daylighting is used. Note that peak load reduction assumes that the peak load occurs at the peak daylighting time. However, this may not always be true for buildings with unusual loads and/or occupancy schedules.

POTENTIAL FRACTIONAL ENERGY SAVINGS

1. Enter the nomograph at the upper right-hand scale. Find the place along that vertical scale (*daylight hours*) corresponding to the value designated in item 12. This value represents the average daylit hours of occupancy as a percent, given the latitude of the building site and the occupancy pattern.

2. Move horizontally to the left, stopping at or near the appropriate diagonal line labeled *daylit areas (%)*, item 13. This number is the percent of the floor area that is daylit, as a function of the total area and configuration of each floor.

3. Move down vertically from that point toward the diagonal line labeled *control effectiveness* in the segment of the nomograph marked *I-B*. Stop at the value of control effectiveness taken from item 14.

4. Finally, move horizontally to the right to intersect the vertical scale at the lower right entitled *energy saving due to daylight (%)*. Note the point of intersection, and record that value as item 16.

5. Repeat steps 1–4 using different building massing, floor layouts, lighting control systems, etc. Making systematic changes in each of the design variables will illustrate which factors have the greatest influence on total daylighting savings.

POTENTIAL FRACTIONAL POWER (ELECTRICAL LOAD) SAVINGS

1. Retrace steps 1 and 2 described above. Then move down vertically to the diagonal lines designated *dimming factor (%)*. Stop at or near the line corresponding to the value of item 15, which depends upon the lighting control hardware and load management strategy. It generally will be greater than the similar value selected in item 14, which is an annual reduction factor. A reasonable value for the dimming factor is 80 percent of the maximum lighting power reduction. Be sure to use the percent reduction in power, not light output, since these may have different values.

2. Move horizontally to the right to intersect the vertical scale labeled *daylight peak load savings (%)*. Record the value at that point as item 17, the percent of total electrical lighting peak load that the daylighting system would save. It generally will be higher than item 16, which is the

savings in annual energy consumption.

3. Repeating steps 1–4 with design variations will quickly indicate which
   design choices have the greatest overall impact. Note that these results
   are percent savings relative to the electric load only.

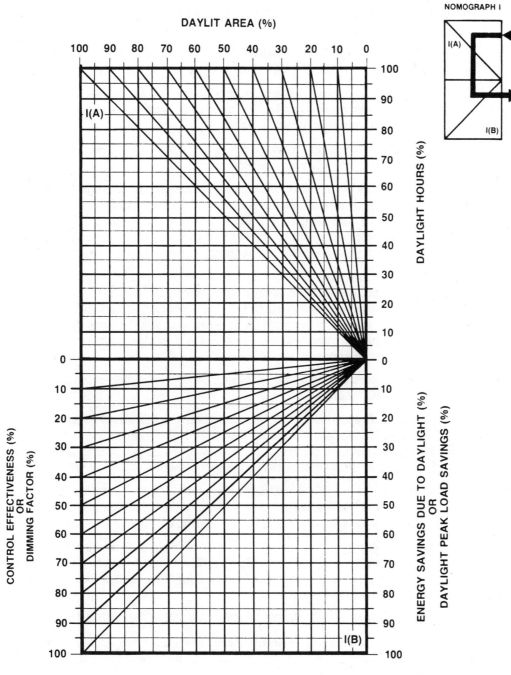

XBL 8211-4948

*13-12. Nomograph I: relative importance of daylighting. (Reproduced courtesy of Lawrence
Berkeley Laboratory, University of California)*

NOMOGRAPH II: ANNUAL ENERGY USE AND COST FOR DAYLIGHTED VERSUS NONDAYLIGHTED BUILDINGS REQUIRED PRELIMINARY DATA: WORKSHEET I, ITEMS 1–8, 12–15

This nomograph is used to determine (1) annual energy consumption and associated costs for an electrically lighted (i.e., nondaylighted) building, and (2) the potential energy and cost savings that would accrue if daylighting strategies were utilized.

LIGHTING ENERGY CONSUMPTION AND COST IN A NONDAYLIGHTED BUILDING

1. Enter the nomograph at the upper left-hand horizontal scale entitled *hours/year occupancy*. Use the appropriate number of hours per year that the building is occupied, item 6.

2. Move upward vertically, stopping at the intersection with the diagonal line labeled *100% daytime occupancy.*

3. From that point, move horizontally to the right into nomograph section II-B, stopping at or near the correct diagonal labeled *installed lighting load,* item 7. If the installed lighting load varies within the building, use an area-weighted average of installed watts per square foot (W/sf) for each building zone. Include all task lighting as well as general lighting loads.

4. Move down vertically to section II-C, stopping at the intersection with the diagonal line labeled *100% control effectiveness.* Note: if some building zones (e.g., conference room, cafeteria) have scheduled occupancies that are less than the occupied hours selected in step 1 above, do not include them in this analysis; treat them instead in a separate analysis using these same procedures.

5. Move horizontally to the left to segment II-D, stopping at the line labeled *100% daylit area.*

6. Move down vertically from that point to the horizontal scale of the segment II-E marked *kWh/sf-yr.* The value at this intersection is the average lighting energy consumption in kilowatt-hours per year for each square foot of building. Record this number as item 18.

7. Continue moving down vertically, stopping at or near the appropriate diagonal line marked *electricity cost, $/kWh,* item 8. For initial estimates, use the average cost per kWh for buildings of similar size and type.

8. From this point, move horizontally to the right until intersecting the vertical scale marked *light cost/savings.* This value, in $/sf/building-yr, is the annual lighting cost to electrically light each square foot of building. Record it as item 19.

ENERGY AND COST SAVINGS IN A DAYLIGHTED BUILDING

1. Enter the nomograph at the upper left-hand horizontal scale entitled *hours/year occupancy.* Use the number of hours per year the building is occupied (item 6).

2. Move upward vertically, stopping at or near the appropriate *daytime occupancy, %,* item 12.

3. Move horizontally to the right to segment II-B, stopping at or near the appropriate diagonal line *installed lighting load,* item 7.

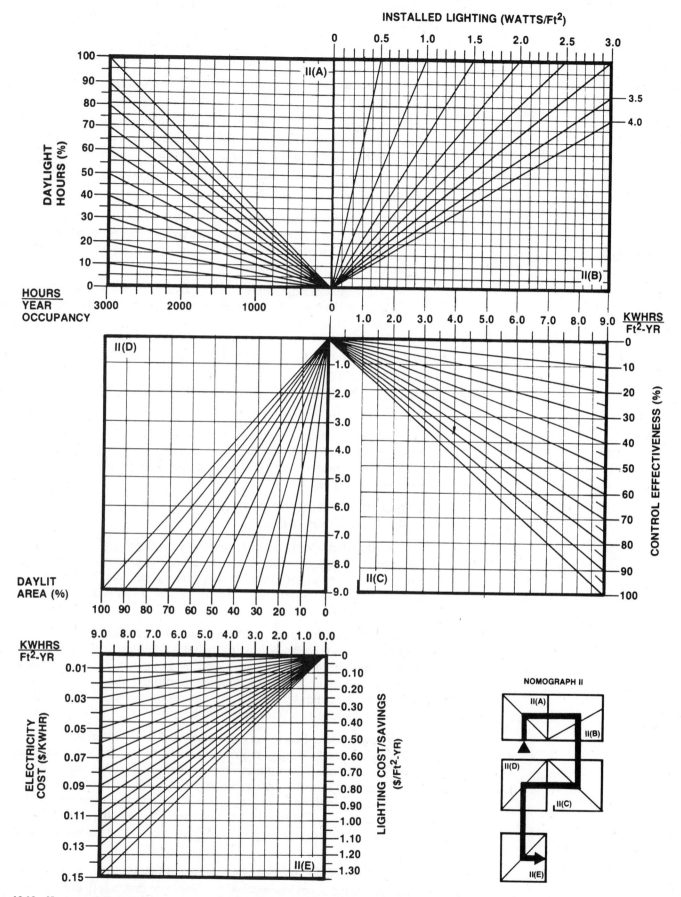

INSTALLED LIGHTING (WATTS/Ft²)

DAYLIGHT HOURS (%)

II(A)

II(B)

HOURS YEAR OCCUPANCY

KWHRS Ft²-YR

II(D)

CONTROL EFFECTIVENESS (%)

II(C)

DAYLIT AREA (%)

KWHRS Ft²-YR

ELECTRICITY COST ($/KWHR)

LIGHTING COST/SAVINGS ($/Ft²-YR)

II(E)

NOMOGRAPH II

II(A)

II(B)

II(D)

II(C)

II(E)

13-13. Nomograph II: annual energy use and cost for daylighted vs. nondaylighted buildings. (Reproduced courtesy of Lawrence Berkeley Laboratory, University of California)

PRELIMINARY DESIGN NOMOGRAPHS

4. Move down vertically to segment II-C, stopping at or near the correct line entitled *control effectiveness*, item 14.

5. Move horizontally to the left to segment II-D, stopping at or near the appropriate diagonal line marked *daylit area, %*, item 13.

6. Move down vertically to the horizontal scale in segment II-E labeled *kWh/sf-yr*. The value at this intersection is the energy *saved* in kilowatt-hours per year for each square foot of the building. Record this value as item 20.

7. Continue moving down vertically and stop at or near the correct diagonal line labeled *electricity cost, $/kWh*, item 8.

8. Finally, move horizontally to the right, intersecting the vertical scale labeled *light cost/savings ($/sf-yr)*. This value represents the *annual savings* in dollars per square foot of building that a reasonably good daylighting design can provide.

9. To find the potential daylighting energy savings for the entire building, multiply the value above by the building area, item 9. Record the result as item 22.

NOMOGRAPH III: LOAD MANAGEMENT WITH DAYLIGHTING
REQUIRED PRELIMINARY DATA: WORKSHEET I, ITEMS 3–5, 7, 9–11, 13, 15.

This nomograph is used to determine: (1) the contribution a building's lighting system makes to peak electrical load and its associated cost, and (2) the potential load management and cost savings possible from effective use of daylighting strategies.

LIGHTING ELECTRICAL DEMAND AND COST IN A NONDAYLIGHTED BUILDING

In this case, the peak electrical load is estimated without daylighting credits, and the resultant demand charge is calculated. The procedure involves estimating all electrical loads in the building (or zone) and can be repeated for a typical summer and winter month in order to account for seasonal demand charges.

1. Because this is the nondaylighted case, enter the nomograph at the middle left-hand, horizontal scale labeled *lighting load (W/sf)*, just below nomograph segment III-B; use the value from item 7. Include power consumption for both task and ambient lighting. If the levels differ significantly throughout the building, use an area-weighted average or calculate the results separately for each zone.

2. Move down diagonally to the right, following the W/sf value parallel to the broken lines leading to the vertical scale labeled *building electrical load (W/sf)*. Move down the scale in order to add to this value the net electrical load in watts per square foot that results from all nonlighting electrical use in the building: air conditioning and heating, fans, office equipment, and other miscellaneous loads. The specific load selection should be based upon the type of HVAC envisioned and the season being considered.

3. Move horizontally to the right into segment III-C, stopping at or near the appropriate diagonal line marked *total building area (sf)*, item 9. Move up vertically to the intersection with the horizontal scale labeled *KW peak demand* and record the value as item 23. Note: if the total building area is

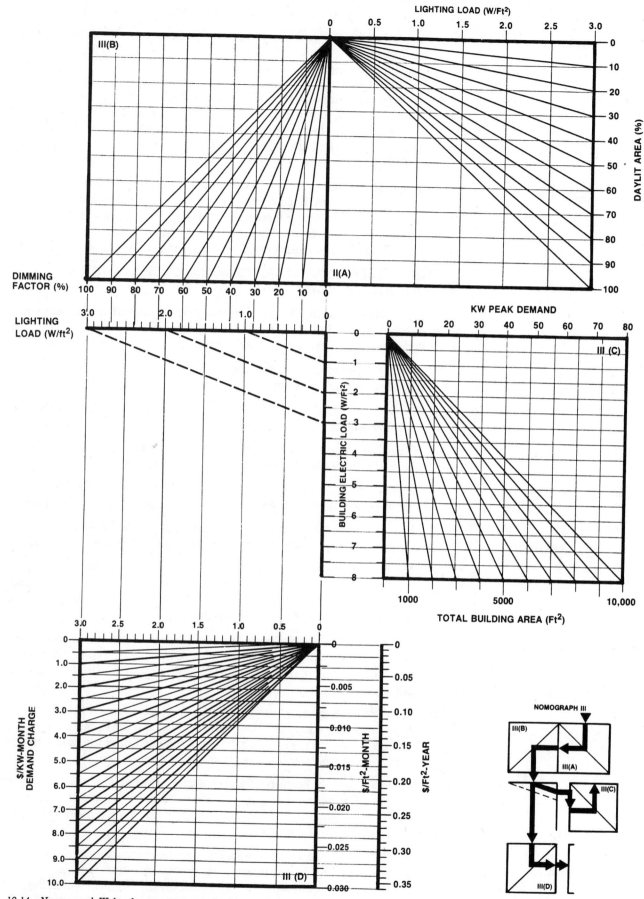

13-14. Nomograph III: load management in buildings. (Reproduced courtesy of Lawrence
Berkeley Laboratory, University of California)

PRELIMINARY DESIGN NOMOGRAPHS

more than 10,000 square feet, use a multiplier (e.g., 5, 10, 50) to obtain the correct result. For a 70,000 sf building, for example, use the *7000 sf* line and multiply the final value by 10.

4. Now return to the point on the *lighting load* described in step 1. Move down vertically to segment III-D, stopping at or near the appropriate diagonal line labeled *$/KW-month demand charge*, item 11. The appropriate demand charge should be obtained from local utility rates based on the building peak demand determined in the previous step.

5. Move horizontally to the right until intersecting the first vertical scale marked *$/sf-month*. Record this value as item 24. Continue moving to the right until intersecting the second vertical scale marked *$/sf-year*, recording the value as item 25. These figures are the demand charges for electric lighting per month and per year in the nondaylighted building.

LIGHTING ELECTRIC REDUCTIONS AND COST SAVINGS IN A DAYLIGHTED BUILDING

The procedure is now repeated while incorporating several additional factors to reflect the use of lighting controls in daylighted buildings. Reductions in peak demand and resultant cost savings are calculated.

1. Enter the nomograph at the upper right-hand horizontal scale labeled *lighting load (W/sf)*, item 7.

2. Move down vertically, stopping at or near the appropriate diagonal line marked *daylight area (%)*, item 13.

3. Move horizontally to the left to segment III-B, stopping at or near the diagonal line labeled *dimming factor (%)*, item 15.

4. Move down vertically to the line intersecting the horizontal scale labeled *lighting load*, item 7. Mark this point in order to return to it in step 7 below.

5. Move diagonally down to the right, parallel to the broken lines, until intersecting the vertical scale labeled *building electrical load (W/sf)*.

6. Move horizontally to the right, stopping at or near the correct diagonal line corresponding to the *total building area*, item 9. If the building area is larger than 10,000 square feet, use a multiplier as explained in step 3 in the nondaylighted case described above.

7. Move up vertically to the scale marked *KW peak demand*, and record it as item 26. This is the peak demand reduction from the daylighting system. Now return to the horizontal scale labeled *lighting load* and move to the point marked in step 4 above.

8. Move all the way down vertically to nomograph segment III-D, stopping at or near the diagonal line representing the *$/KW-month demand charge*, item 11. This is obtained using the peak demand calculated in step 7 and the local utility rate structure.

9. Move to the right horizontally, intersecting the two vertical scales that indicate *$/sf-month* and *$/sf-year*, the savings in demand charges per month and per year as a result of daylighting. Record these values as items 27 and 28, respectively.

   Note: The $/sf-year scale is simply twelve times the value on the monthly scale. Depending on location and utility rate structures, the monthly peak load savings should only be credited for those months in which the rate applies.

NOMOGRAPH IV: JUSTIFIABLE INVESTMENT IN DAYLIGHTING STRATEGIES
REQUIRED PRELIMINARY DATA: WORKSHEET I, ITEMS 9, 22, 28, 29

Building designs that maximize the use of daylighting will generally require additional investment in lighting and fenestration controls. The purpose of this nomograph is to estimate the justifiable investment in daylighting strategies based upon: (1) estimates of costs/savings for electrical energy and peak load as determined from nomographs II and III, and (2) the investment criteria of the building owner or operator. This nomograph can be used in a number of ways as explained below. Note that nonenergy issues may influence the decision: aesthetics, lighting quality, additional rental value on floor space having windows, reduced dependence on mechanical systems and nonrenewable energy sources, and so on. If an economic value ($/sf-yr) can be assigned to these factors, they can be accounted for in the nomograph. These can also be considered as modifiers to the results derived from the nomograph. Note also that this analysis does not account for reductions or increases in heating/cooling loads. The total annual savings (item 29) is the sum of daylighting energy savings (item 21) and daylighting demand savings (item 28).

SIMPLE PAYBACK CALCULATION

The simplest decision-making criterion frequently will be the desire for a relatively fast payback of investment (typically two to five years). Determining the justifiable investment in daylighting design then follows quickly from a four-step calculation. (Nomograph IV is not used in this case.):

1. Determine s, total annual savings ($/sf) in energy and demand (item 19), and any other factors to be considered.

2. Determine n, the maximum acceptable payback period, in years.

3. Calculate sn.

4. Multiply sn by the total building area to determine the total justifiable dollar investment. Note that this sum probably will not be spent on the entire building but only in the daylighted zones.

OTHER INVESTMENT CRITERIA

A variety of other decision-making criteria and economic factors may be utilized. Electric energy prices will generally escalate with time, increasing the magnitude of future savings. The return on alternative investments, or discount rate, will reduce the present value of apparent future savings. Depending upon the investment criteria, one might calculate (1) savings over the life cycle of a particular investment, (2) the time required to pay back an investment, or (3) the rate of return on investments in energy conservation. Common to all of these calculations is the requirement that future costs or savings be converted to an equivalent present worth. The calculation technique used in this nomograph is based upon a modified uniform present worth factor (*MUPW* or *m*).

Case 1: Maximum Justifiable Investment Given Desired Payback Period

This calculation determines the maximum investment, or first cost, that is justifiable based upon projected savings and a given payback period. It includes the discounted value of future savings and the effects of escalating energy costs.

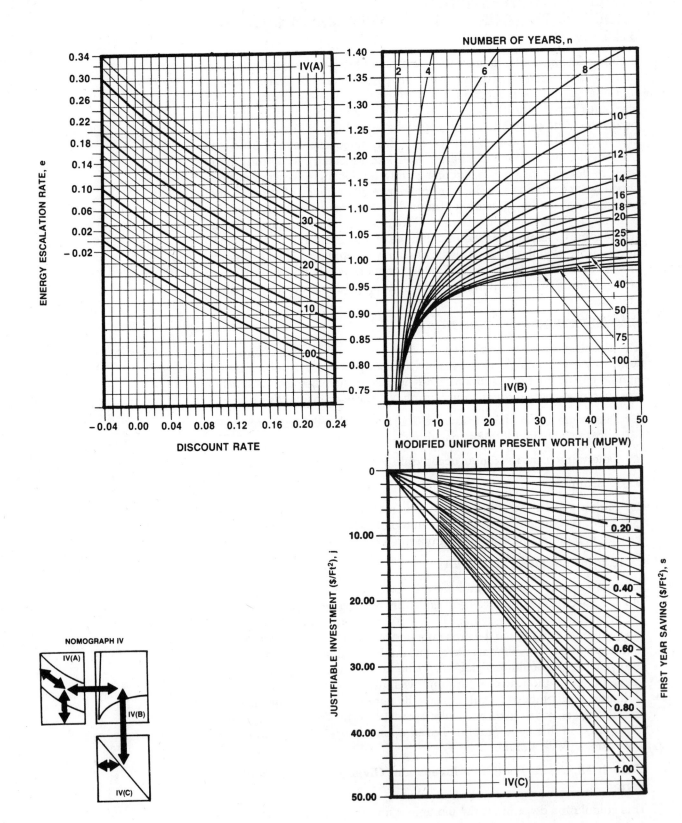

13-15. *Nomograph IV: justifiable investment in daylighting strategies. (Reproduced courtesy of Lawrence Berkeley Laboratory, University of California)*

ANALYSIS

1. Enter the nomograph at the horizontal scale labeled *discount rate*, segment IV-A. From the point corresponding to the discount rate *i* (item 33), move up vertically, stopping at or near the appropriate curve representing *e*, energy cost escalation rate, item 34.

2. From that point of intersection move horizontally to the right into segment IV-B, stopping at or near the curve having a value *n*—the desired payback period in years—item 32.

3. Move down vertically until crossing the horizontal scale labeled *modified uniform present worth*. The value of this factor, when multiplied by the first-year savings, becomes the maximum justifiable investment.

4. Continue to move down vertically from the present worth into segment IV-C, stopping at or near the diagonal line that represents the *first-year savings ($/sf)*, item 31.

5. Move horizontally to the left to intersect the vertical scale *justifiable investment ($/sf)*. Multiply this value by the area of the building, item 9, to calculate the total justifiable dollar investment, item 30. Note that this sum generally will not be spent throughout the building but will probably be spent on lighting controls in the perimeter zone and on glare and sun controls for glazed areas.

Case 2: Minimum Savings Required to Justify a Given Investment

This case is the inverse of case 1. Here, the size of the initial investment in energy conservation is given, and we want to determine the first-year savings necessary to justify that investment.

1. Given a discount rate, energy cost escalation rate, and payback period, follow steps 1–3 described in case 1 above. Mark that value along the *modified uniform present worth* scale.

2. Find the value (in $/sf) of the initial investment on the left-hand vertical scale of segment IV-C (labeled *justifiable investment*).

3. Move horizontally to the right from that point and down vertically from the *MUPW* value until the two lines intersect. The point of intersection gives the required value of first-year energy savings by interpolation between the values of the two nearest diagonal lines. Record the value as item 31.

Case 3: Required Payback Period Given First-year Savings and Conservation Investment

In this case the user is given the annual savings and available investment figures and must find the number of years required to pay back that investment.

1. Enter the nomograph at the upper left-hand scale labeled *discount rate*, item 33. Move up vertically to intersect the curve corresponding to the energy escalation rate.

2. From that point, move horizontally to the right to intersect the vertical scale (with the range of 0.75 to 1.40). Mark that value, which will be used in step 5 below.

3. Find the value of the initial investment on the vertical *justifiable investment* scale, item 30, segment IV-C. Move horizontally to the right, stopping at or near the appropriate diagonal line representing *first-year savings*, item 31.

4. Move up vertically to the horizontal scale of segment IV-B, *modified uniform present worth*.

5. Continue to move up vertically from the *MUPW* scale. Find the value from step 2 along the vertical scale, and move horizontally from that point to the right until the two lines intersect in segment IV-B. The required payback period is found by interpolating between the two curved lines nearest the intersection point, item 32. If the intersection point lies below the lowest curve marked *100*, the payback period is greater than 100 years.

Case 4: Rate of Return on Investment

The rate of return on initial investment is equivalent to the discount rate, which was a given in case 3. This calculation is similar to case 1, except that the user reverses the movement through the nomograph.

1. Follow steps 3 and 4 described in case 3 above, arriving at a point along the horizontal *modified uniform present worth* scale.

2. Move vertically, stopping at the appropriate curve in segment IV-B representing the given payback period, item 32.

3. Move horizontally to the left into segment IV-A to intersect the curve corresponding to the given energy escalation rate, item 34.

4. Finally, move down vertically to intersect the horizontal scale labeled *discount rate*. This value is the *rate of return on investment*, item 33.

EXAMPLE BUILDING

The following example building will be used to illustrate the four nomographs. It has the following specifications. Note that this is the level of design detail the user needs to make use of the nomographs:

Building type: 45,000 sf office building

Annual hours of occupancy: 2500

Daily occupancy schedule: 8 A.M.–6 P.M.

Location: Berkeley, California; 37.5° N. latitude

Building shape and dimensions: 5 stories, rectangular; 60' by 150'

Typical floor-to-ceiling height: 8'6"

Windows: Double-glazed; a horizontal "glass strip" from 3'0" to 7'0" above the floor on each level. Glass visible light transmittance is 80 percent. All four sides of the building have the same type of fenestration

Lighting controls: Continuous dimming is contemplated in the perimeter zone; the maximum dimming factor is 85 percent reduction in power

Illumination level: 50 footcandles of general and task lighting

Installed lighting load: 2.5 watts per square foot

Nonlighting electrical load: 3.0 watts per square foot

Electricity cost: average unit cost is $0.10/kWh

Peak demand rate: $1.70/kW-month

The following pages illustrate the analysis of the example building using the worksheets, the supplementary charts (S-1–S-7), and the nomographs. Under the column marked *base case*, worksheet items 1–11 and 15 are taken directly from the building specifications above or are obtained through simple calculations. For example, item 5c, *sidelighting: glass area fraction* is calculated as follows:

$$\frac{\text{(height of glass)}}{\text{(floor ceiling height)}} = \frac{4.0 \text{ ft.}}{8.5 \text{ ft.}} = 0.471$$

To find item 12, use chart S-1 as indicated. Item 13, *total daylit area (%)*, can be obtained as shown with chart S-6 for a fifteen-foot daylight zone depth, or by direct calculation. The value selected for *control effectiveness*, item 14, is taken from chart S-4 for *sidelighting, continuous dimming*.

A few case studies (cases 1–4) are worked out to show how the user can vary design and other parameters and record the results.

Case 1: Variation in the economic analysis used in nomograph IV, where the maximum justifiable investment is fixed and the minimum first year savings is determined.

Case 2: Change in the lighting control type from continuous dimming to one-step (on/off) switching.

Case 3: A change back to continuous dimming, and glass changes from clear to reflective. *TVIS* = 0.14.

Case 4: Same as base case, with the addition of uniformly spaced, diffusing dome skylights over the interior zone (previously nondaylighted portion) of the top floor.

These are the kind of variations that the user might test and compare. Example worksheet II illustrates each case worked out to the end.

Notice that *justifiable investment*, item 30, and *first-year savings*, item 31, may be expressed in $/sf or $/building. On the example worksheet, a slash is used so that these items can be listed both ways. An alternative way of quantifying these items with sidelighting is in $/linear foot of perimeter wall. Much of the investment attributable to daylight would be for solar controls and lighting controls, the cost of which may lend itself to $/linear foot of window wall.

Project Title __EXAMPLE BUILDING__   Date __1/19/84__   Prepared By __M. GABEL__

Description of Study / Remarks 'BASE CASE' (ILLUSTRATED IN EXAMPLE CHARTS & NOMOGRAPHS) AND OTHER CASE STUDIES

Nomographs I II III IV	Charts S.1 – S.7 1 2 3 4 5 6 7	Worksheet Item No.	Description of Worksheet Item	Base Case	Case 1.	Case 2.	Case 3.	Case 4.
	i i	1	Latitude of Building Location	77.5	MINIMUM 1st YR SAVING	→	REFLECTIVE, 5' GLASS	→
	i i	2	Daily Occupancy Schedule	8AM–6PM	→	→	→	→
	i i	3	Gross Area Per Floor (ft²)	9000	→	→	→	→
	i i	4	Typical Floor Shape: Length-to-Width Ratio	2.5:1		→	→	→
	i i	5a	Lighting Control Type	DIMMING		ON/OFF	DIMMING	→
	i i	5b	Illumination Level (fc)	50		→	→	→
	i i	5c	Side Lighting Glass Area Fraction	.471		→	.588	→
		5c	Top Lighting; Glass Area Fraction	(NONE)		→	→	.05 (OF TOP FLOOR)
	i i	5d	Side Lighting; Glass Visible Transmittance (TVIS)	.80		→	.14	.80 (MIRROR ZONE)
		5d	Top Lighting; Glass Visible Transmittance (TVIS) X Well Factor	(NONE)		→	→	.56
i		6	Annual Hours of Occupancy	2500		→	→	→
i	i	7	Installed Lighting Load (watts/ft²)	2.50		→	→	→
i	i	8	Electricity Cost ($/kWh)	0.100		→	→	→
i	i	9	Gross Total Building Area (ft²)	45000		→	→	→
i		10	Non-Lighting Electric Loads (watts/ft²)	3.00		→	→	→
i	o	11	Peak Demand Rate ($/kW-month)	1.70		→	→	→
i	i o	12	Daylit Hours (%)	94.4		→	→	→
i	i o	13	Total Daylit Area (%)	60.0		→	68.0	→
i	i o	14	Control Effectiveness (%)	64.0		61.0	28.0	65.9 *
i	i	15	Dimming Factor (%)	85		→	→	→

SEE NEXT PAGE, NOMOGRAPH IV

* WEIGHTED AVERAGE CALCULATION = (.882)(66.5) + (.118)(61.0) = 65.9

(SIDE LIGHTED # / TOTAL DAYLIGHTED #) = .882

(CONTROL EFFECTIVENESS FOR TVIS = .80, AREA = .588) = 66.5

(TOP LIGHTED # / TOTAL DAYLIGHTED #) = .118

(CONTROL TOP EFFECTIVENESS FOR TVIS X WELL FACTOR = .56, AREA = .05) = 61.0

13-16. *Example worksheet I (inputs).*

ANALYSIS

Project Title __EXAMPLE BUILDING__ Date __1/19/84__ Prepared By __M. GABEL__

Description of Study / Remarks __"BASE CASE" ... AND OTHER CASE STUDIES.__

Work-sheet Item No.	Description of Worksheet Item	Base Case (BASE)	Case 1. (MINIMUM 1ST YR. SAVINGS)	Case 2. (ON/OFF)	Case 3. (REFLECTIVE SL. GLASS)	Case 4. (SKYLIGHTS)
16	Annual Energy Savings Due to Daylight (%)	36.2	→	34.6	21.5	42.3
17	Daylight Peak Load Savings (%)	48.1	→	→	→	54.6
18	Non-Daylit Lighting Energy Consumption (kWh/ft²-year)	6.25	→	→	→	→
19	Non-Daylit Lighting Cost ($/ft²-yr)	.625	→	→	→	→
20	Daylighting Energy Consumption Saving (kWh/ft²-year)	2.27	→	2.16	1.74	2.64
21	Daylighting Saving ($/ft²-year)	.227	→	.216	.134	.264
22	Annual Daylighting Savings ($/building)	10 200	→	9 700	6 000	11 900
23	Non-Daylit Peak Demand (kW)	247.5	→	→	→	→
24	Non-Daylit Monthly Demand Charge ($/ft²-month)	.00425	→	→	→	→
25	Non-Daylit Annual Demand Charge ($/ft²-year)	.051	→	→	→	→
26	Daylit Peak Demand Saving (kW)	57.4	→	→	65.0	→
27	Daylit Monthly Demand Saving ($/ft²-month)	.00217	→	→	→	.00246
28	Daylit Annual Demand Saving ($/ft²-year)	.0260	→	→	→	.0295
29	Total Annual Savings ($/ft²-year)	.253	→	.242	.160	.294
30	Justifiable Investment ($/ft² or $/building), J	117 000 / 2.60	180 000 / 4.00	112 000 / 2.48	74 000 / 1.64	136 000 / 3.02
31	First Year Saving ($/ft² or $/building), s	11 400 / .253	17 500 / .390	10 900 / .242	7 200 / .160	13 200 / .264
32	Payback Period (years), n	10				
33	Rate of Return on Investment or Discount Rate, i	.080				
34	Energy Escalation Rate, e	.085				

Input (i) or output (o) value for the specified nomograph or chart — Nomographs I III IV, Charts S.1–S.7 (1 2 3 4 5 6 7).

13-17. *Example worksheet II (outputs).*

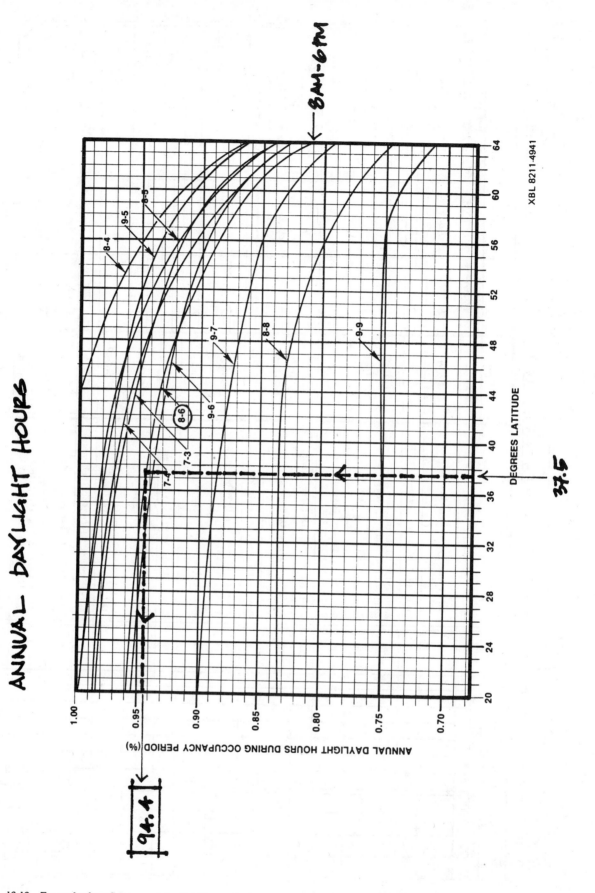

ANNUAL DAYLIGHT HOURS

8AM-6PM

37.5

94.4

XBL 8211-4941

13-18.   *Example chart S-1: annual daylight hours during occupancy period.*

154

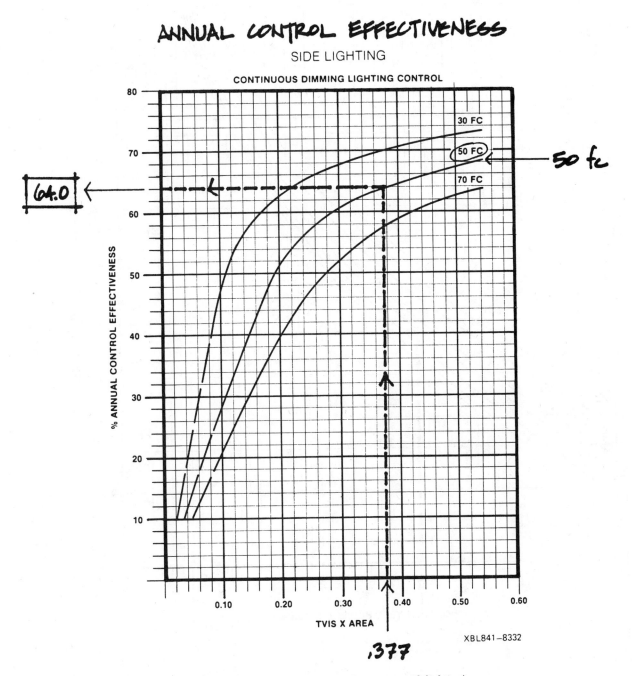

ANNUAL CONTROL EFFECTIVENESS

SIDE LIGHTING

CONTINUOUS DIMMING LIGHTING CONTROL

% ANNUAL CONTROL EFFECTIVENESS

30 FC
50 FC
70 FC

64.0

50 fc

TVIS X AREA

.377

XBL841-8332

13-19. Example chart S-4: annual control effectiveness (continuous dimming— sidelighting).

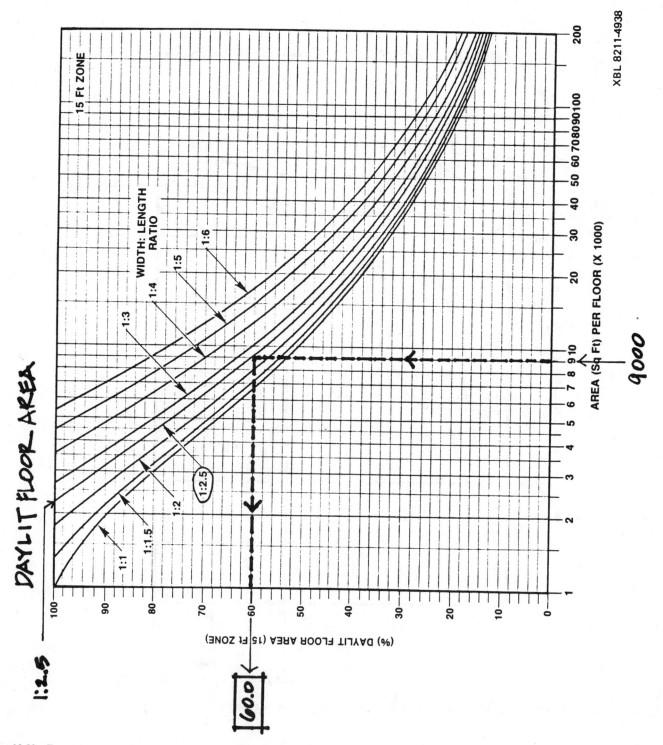

13-20. Example chart S-6: % daylit floor area (15 ft. zone).

ANALYSIS

POTENTIAL FRACTIONAL ENERGY SAVINGS

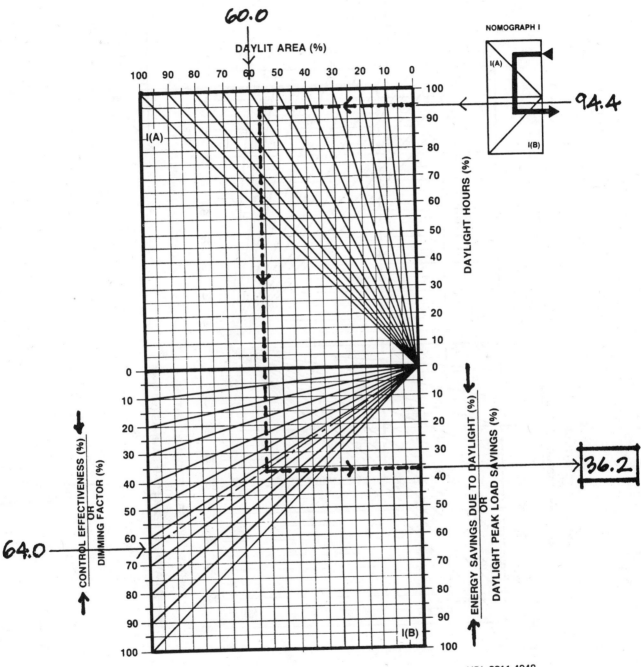

13-21. *Example nomograph I: relative importance of daylighting.*

XBL 8211-4948

POTENTIAL FRACTIONAL POWER SAVINGS

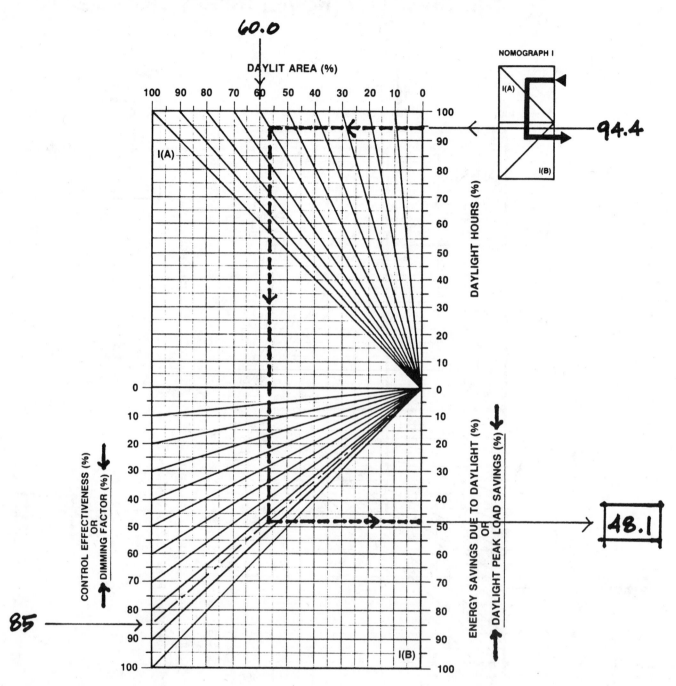

13-22. *Example nomograph I: relative importance of daylighting.*

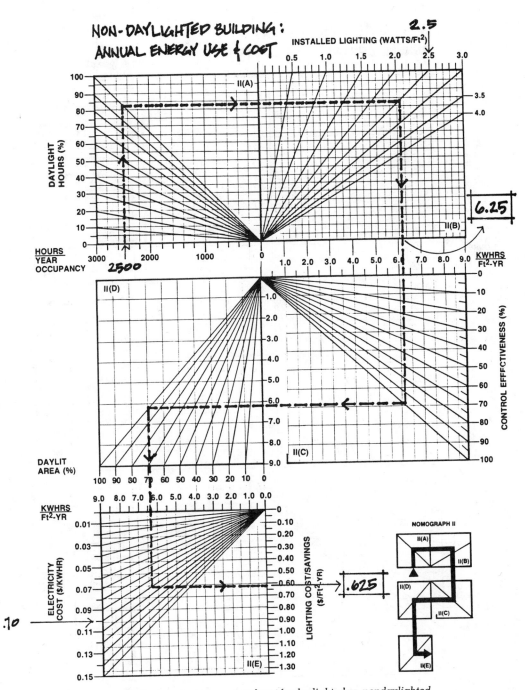

NON-DAYLIGHTED BUILDING:
ANNUAL ENERGY USE & COST

2.5

INSTALLED LIGHTING (WATTS/Ft²)

13-23. Example nomograph II: annual energy use and cost for daylighted vs. nondaylighted buildings.

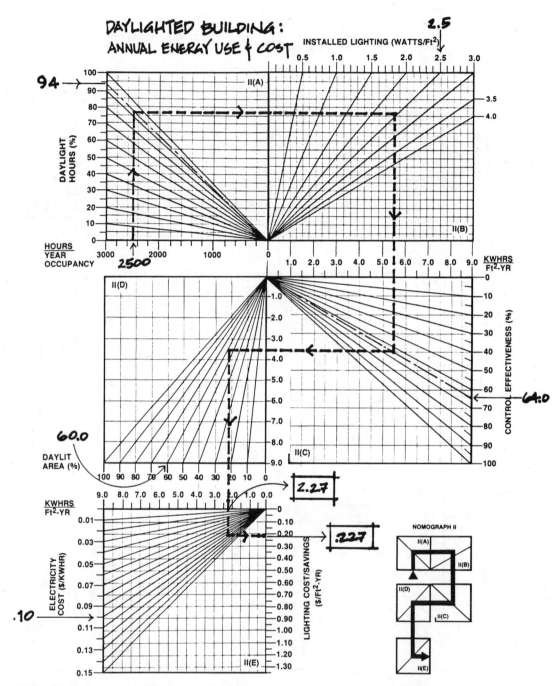

13-24. Example nomograph II: annual energy use and cost for daylighted vs. nondaylighted buildings.

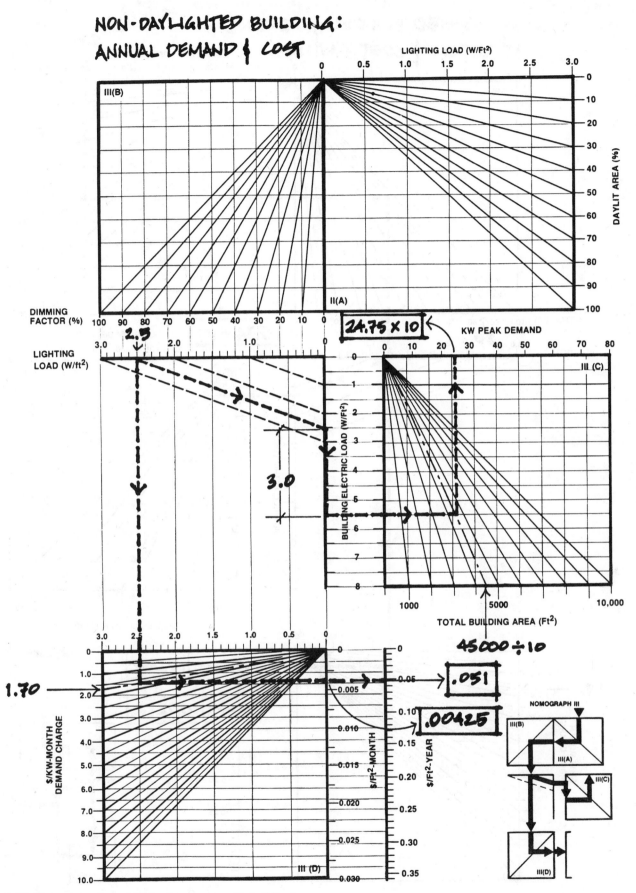

NON-DAYLIGHTED BUILDING:
ANNUAL DEMAND & COST

LIGHTING LOAD (W/Ft²)

III(B)

DAYLIT AREA (%)

II(A)

24.75 × 10

KW PEAK DEMAND

DIMMING FACTOR (%)

LIGHTING LOAD (W/ft²)

BUILDING ELECTRIC LOAD (W/Ft²)

III (C)

3.0

TOTAL BUILDING AREA (Ft²)

45000 ÷ 10

1.70

.051

.00425

NOMOGRAPH III

III(B)

III(A)

III(C)

III(D)

$/KW-MONTH DEMAND CHARGE

$/Ft²-MONTH

$/Ft²-YEAR

III (D)

13-25. *Example nomograph III: load management in buildings.*

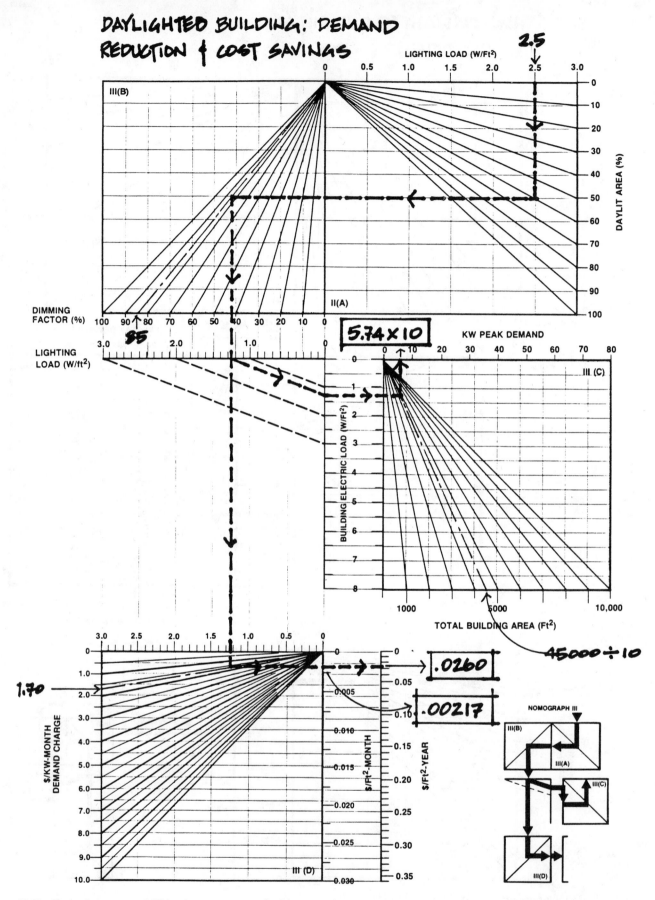

DAYLIGHTED BUILDING: DEMAND REDUCTION & COST SAVINGS

2.5

LIGHTING LOAD (W/Ft²)
0   0.5   1.0   1.5   2.0   2.5   3.0

III(B)

DAYLIT AREA (%)

II(A)

DIMMING FACTOR (%)
100 90 80 70 60 50 40 30 20 10 0

85

LIGHTING LOAD (W/ft²)
3.0   2.0   1.0   0

5.74 X 10

KW PEAK DEMAND
0   10   20   30   40   50   60   70   80

III (C)

BUILDING ELECTRIC LOAD (W/Ft²)

TOTAL BUILDING AREA (Ft²)
1000   5000   10,000

45000 ÷ 10

$/KW-MONTH DEMAND CHARGE
3.0 2.5 2.0 1.5 1.0 0.5 0

1.70

$/Ft²-MONTH

$/Ft²-YEAR

III (D)

.0260

.00217

NOMOGRAPH III

III(B)

III(A)

III(C)

III(D)

13-26. Example nomograph III: load management in buildings.

MAXIMUM JUSTIFIABLE INVESTMENT

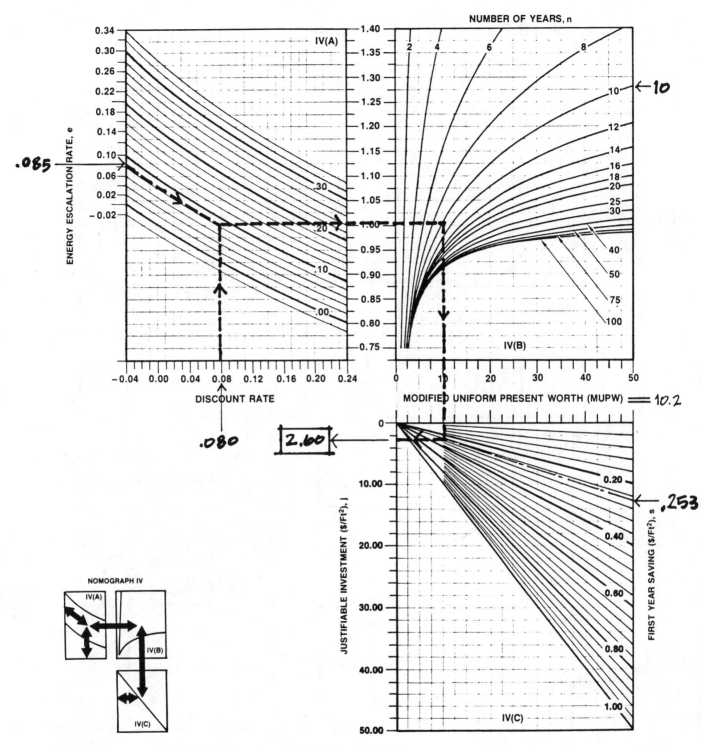

13-27. Example nomograph IV: justifiable investment in daylighting strategies.

MINIMUM FIRST YEAR SAVING

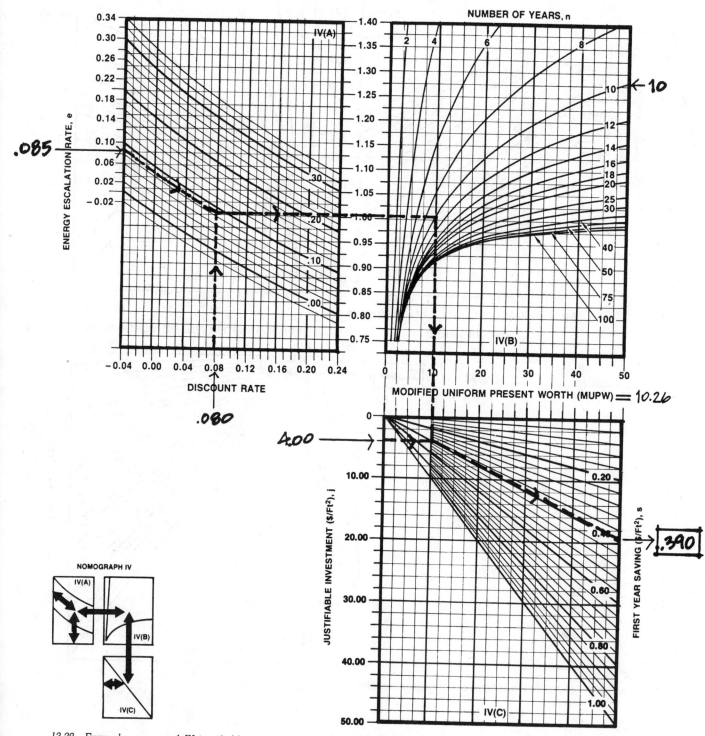

13-28. *Example nomograph IV: justifiable investment in daylighting strategies.*

NOMOGRAPH ASSUMPTIONS

The following assumptions are "built in" to the nomographs and charts. They are reasonable for an analysis of this type in which the main focus of the daylighting performance is annual energy use. Analysis of a building design whose parameters vary slightly from the values assumed here is not likely to introduce major sources of error. Altering fixed parameters might produce significant differences in illumination levels for a daylighting calculation method that predicts performance at a particular instant. However, daylighting performance calculated hourly throughout the entire year (assuming a specific electric lighting control and illumination level) reduces the magnitude of distinctions obtained in instantaneous calculations.

■ The curves predicting annual control effectiveness (charts S-3, S-3A, S-4, and S-4A) are derived from analysis using DOE-2.1B, a computer program that contains an hour-by-hour daylighting simulation model (see chapter 18). The data for sidelighting in S-3 and S-4 were calculated for each orientation but are shown in the charts as averages of all orientations. The toplighting results in S-3A and S-4A assume the use of diffusing domed skylights. The assumption of "average orientation" of glazing may appear to be simplistic. However, study of the data indicates the assumption is quite reasonable. At 70 footcandles, with one-step (on/off) switching, the annual performances of south and north glazing diverge no more than 2–4 percent from the average annual performance of all four orientations.

■ The results assume that a simple interior shade or blind system is utilized when window glare exceeds specified values or when solar gain creates thermal discomfort for the occupant.

■ The analysis is based on the use of a standard 8 A.M.–6 P.M. office occupancy schedule and was generated for a high latitude, predominantly overcast city (Seattle). For most other U.S. locations these values will be conservative.

■ The daylighting model assumes the use of a one-step (on/off) lighting control (charts S-3, S-3A) or a continuous dimming system (charts S-4, S-4A). The dimming system operates linearly between 100 percent light/100 percent power and 0 percent light/10 percent power.

■ The standard office used in the DOE-2.1B analysis of sidelighting was eight feet, six inches high, ten feet wide, and fifteen feet deep; the lighting control (reference) point was located at a depth of ten feet from the window wall and workplane height was two feet, six inches. Reflectances of internal surfaces were: ceiling, 70 percent; walls, 50 percent; and floor, 30 percent.

■ For toplighting, uniformly-spaced, square, diffusing dome skylights were assumed. The reference point was located at the crossing (X) of imaginary diagonal lines intersecting the centers between the skylights. The uniform light distribution spacing of skylights should not be wider than 1.5 times floor-to-ceiling height.

■ Charts S-5, S-6, and S-7 provide fractional daylighted areas for zone depths of ten, fifteen, and twenty feet. Savings in the shallower zone would be greater than those indicated in charts S-3 and S-4, while the deeper zone will have lower savings. Data for the fifteen-foot-deep zone can be used for the twenty-foot-deep zone if the ceiling height is increased proportionally to eleven feet, four inches. With additional supporting calculations and experience, the nomographs can be used for variable zone depths and for more architecturally sophisticated fenestration solutions.

■ For sidelighting, daylight illuminance was calculated assuming that the glazing area was a single horizontal strip above the workplane (two feet, six inches), with a horizontal centerline five feet, six inches above the floor. Maximum size glazing extended from the workplane (two feet, six inches) to the ceiling (eight feet, six inches).

REFERENCES

Sain, A., Rockwell, P., and Davy, J. "Energy Nomographs as a Design Tool for Daylighting." In *Proceedings of the International Daylighting Conference*, edited by Vonier, T., pp. 125–128. Washington, DC: American Institute of Architects Service Corporation, 1983. (Complete set available from Burt Hill Kosar and Rittelmann, Architects, Butler, PA.)

Selkowitz, S., and Gabel, M. "LBL Daylighting Nomographs." LBL report 13534. Berkeley, CA: Energy Efficient Buildings Program, Lawrence Berkeley Laboratory, University of California, 1984.

ANALYSIS

Chapter 14
Physical Models

Physical models of a building provide a means of accurately predicting interior daylight illumination. Unlike most other physical models where the behavior of the phenomenon does not scale down properly (for example, thermal conduction, structural bending, acoustics, and airflow), light model studies require no scaling correction. A daylighting model that exactly duplicates a full-scale building space, if tested under identical sky conditions, will yield identical results. Although it is not always practical to duplicate a full-scale space exactly, the advantages of using physical scale models can significantly outweigh the disadvantages. These advantages include:

■ Accurate, quantitative results, even when crude models are used;

■ Ease of making comparisons by changing a single design component;

■ Familiarity of most designers with constructing and using scale models; and

■ Opportunity for qualitative evaluation (such as identification of potential glare problems) through visual observation or photography.

It is essential that sky exposure and obstruction geometry be accurate if models are to be used for daylighting analysis. The sectional models (where one wall or the ceiling is removed) that are often used for other architectural studies obviously admit extraneous light and are thus useless for illumination analysis (fig. 14-1). Similarly, by observing a model interior through window openings, the observer's head (or camera) becomes a significant obstruction. It is thus essential that observation intrusion be considered and minimized throughout the design, construction, and use of daylight models.

MODEL CONSTRUCTION

SCALE

Theoretically, illumination effects in a model are scaleless; thus, any scale can be used. Practically, the scale should depend on the use intended.

For interior illumination studies, the relative size of the photometric sensor required for measurement may cause a disturbance when inserted into a small scale model. In addition, since illumination measurements are usually taken at a thirty-inch (desk) height, the sensor's height should be considered.

Until recently, rectifier-type photometric sensors were used for model studies. Their sensitivity was proportional to surface area and a one-inch diameter was the minimum size recommended for daylighting measurements. This large sensor size necessitated large models to ensure that measurements approximated the actual illumination at the center of the sensor area. (No sensor actually measures illumination at a point; instead they measure an *average* illumination over the sensor area.) The silicon photovoltaic sensors now available and preferred are less than half an inch in diameter, effectively eliminating sensor size as a source of concern on any but the smallest-scaled models.

14-1. (a) Sectional study model used by Alvar Aalto for the design of the Riola Church admitted extraneous light and thus could not have been used in this configuration for illumination study without considerable error; (b) interior of completed church.

Other factors such as available construction materials and portability affect model scale. The following scales are recommended for quantitative measurements:

- 1 inch = 100 feet to 1 inch = 20 feet for large urban site studies (larger for street level illuminance measurements).

- 1/8 inch = 1 foot for schematic design and massing studies.

- 1/2 inch = 1 foot for medium to large interiors (one inch = one foot for small spaces with ceilings up to 10 feet high).

- 3 inches = 1 foot to full scale mock-up for detailed design development of repetitive spaces, permitting integration with other building systems.

For qualitative studies, these scales should be doubled to permit greater construction detail and allow for the minimum focusing distances desirable for the eye and camera.

CONSTRUCTION

Because most models will be used for design purposes to compare various alternatives, the construction should be modular to accommodate inserts representing competing configurations. For example, for comparisons of sidewall configurations, the entire sidewall should be replaceable. To vary room heights, either the floor or ceiling should be adjustable.

Special care should be taken to detail all fenestration accurately. The three-dimensional aspects of openings and mullions should be reproduced. For example, a white window sill reflects substantial light onto the ceiling; the effect of this would be lost if the window were modeled simply by an opening cut in a thin sheet of cardboard.

Similarly, mullions create an important louver effect. Deep skylight wells shield direct sunlight. It is important that such geometries be accurately preserved.

Less care need be taken with interior details and furnishings, especially if the model is for quantitative study only. Block shapes are typically used to represent major furnishings (such as desks, filing cabinets, and library stacks) and may be reused for future studies.

Care should be taken to eliminate extraneous light from entering (or leaving) the interior. Where appropriate, make sure that construction materials are opaque. Foam-board, a favorite model material of many designers, is translucent and should be used only with an opaque covering. Joints should be covered on the exterior with aluminum foil or black tape (such as electrical or photographic tape).

Symmetrical spaces can be accurately represented using half- or quarter-models in conjunction with mirrors to reflect the remaining spaces (fig. 14-2). Note, however, that this technique is applicable only for overcast sky conditions and can create substantial error when direct sunlight enters the space.

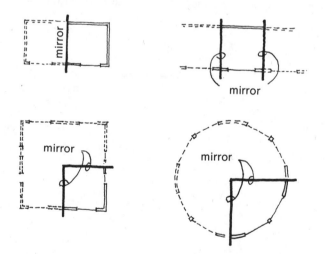

14-2. Mirrors may be used to reflect remaining model space.

Model surface reflectances should match those of the building. For quantitative studies, shades of gray can be used; for qualitative studies, colors should be used. It is useful to prepare a set of gray samples covering reflectances from 10 percent to 80 percent as measured using a footcandle meter with a surface of known reflectance (such as a standard 18 percent-reflectance gray card, available from most camera stores). These samples can then be used to visually estimate reflectances of various model materials before purchasing (fig. 14-3).

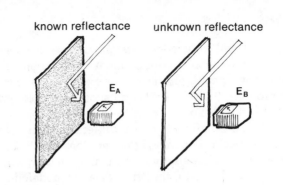

known reflectance   unknown reflectance

E_A E_B

14-3. Method for determining surface reflectances using a sample of known reflectance: $R_b = R_a \times E_b/E_a$
where:

R_b = *reflectance of sample b,*

R_a = *reflectance of sample a,*

E_a = *illuminance reflected from sample a, and*

E_b = *illuminance reflected from sample b.*

The specularity of interior finishes is important in daylighting. Gloss and semigloss finishes can cause reflected glare and substantially affect interior illuminances. Most illustration boards have a relatively matte finish. Gloss can be increased by the application of transparent contact paper or various tapes. For quantitative models, it may be convenient to use the actual room finish material (for example, floor tile or carpet); this approach is not recommended for qualitative models because the textures will be out of scale.

GLAZING

Clear glazing materials can be omitted from the model, and a correction factor (typically .9 for single glazing transmittance multiplied by .9 for dirt factor; $0.9 \times 0.9 = 0.81$) applied to the interior illuminance measurements at a later time to allow for glazing transmission losses. Alternatively, glazing can be represented by the actual material (full thickness) or by an acrylic plastic of similar transmittance. If the proposed glazing is diffusing, it is recommended that a sample of the actual material be used if possible. If a substitute material is used, it must match both the actual transmittance and the directional transmittance (diffusion spread) of the actual material (fig. 14-4). This match is especially critical if the glazing is designed to diffuse direct sunlight.

14-4. Method of measuring diffusion properties of glazing materials: (a) average transmittance (measured with illuminance meter); (b) directional transmittance (measured with luminance meter).

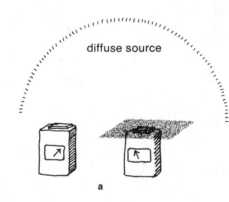

diffuse source

a

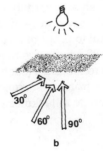

30°   60°   90°

b

170   ANALYSIS

MODEL TESTING

Daylight model testing can be conducted under a real or artificial sky. Testing under a real sky is the cheapest and easiest method. However, unpredictable weather and sky conditions change absolute interior illuminances considerably. Even on two "identical" days, sky luminance measurements will typically vary by more than 15 percent. For that reason, it is recommended that relative illuminance measurements be used as a basis for comparing alternative designs.

REAL SKY: OVERCAST CONDITIONS

The relative illuminance of an overcast sky at any given time varies from darkest near the horizon (0 degrees altitude) in all directions, to three times as bright at the zenith (overhead, 90 degrees altitude). The absolute luminance varies with the altitude of the hidden sun (that is, an overcast sky is brightest at midday), but the 1-to-3 horizon to zenith luminance ratio remains constant. Because of this, the daylight factor for a particular building design will remain constant. That is, the ratio of interior horizontal illuminance (at a given location) to exterior horizontal illuminance will not change under an overcast sky, even though the absolute illuminances may change substantially throughout the day.

This allows outdoor testing to be conducted with a high expectation of accuracy under a completely overcast sky. Even when sky conditions are not completely overcast, useful design comparisons can be obtained provided that sky brightness distribution is relatively constant and measurements can be completed within a brief time span.

REAL SKY: CLEAR CONDITIONS

If the design of a building is intended to utilize direct or reflected sunlight as a major daylight component, outdoor testing can be effective under clear sky conditions. Sun angles throughout the year can be simulated by tilting the model relative to the sun to achieve the desired solar altitude and azimuth angle (fig. 14-5).

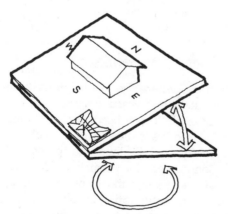

14-5. *Simple model tilt table. Adjust so that sundial shadow points to desired day and time (see chapter 6).*

It is obvious that such tilting exposes the model to a different "view" of the sky and ground (fig. 14-6). However, if the design is intended to utilize diffused sunlight (e.g., via a translucent skylight or south window with white louvers) the illumination component due to sunlight is typically so great that variations in ground and sky contributions are insignificant (O'Laughlin and Porter, 1983). In practice, even daylight through fenestrations that do not receive direct sunlight is affected by moderate model tilt less than might be expected because of the similar luminances of sunlit ground surfaces and clear skies.

Comparisons of design alternatives tested under clear sky conditions should be based on a "window factor" ratio of interior illuminance to exterior illuminance in the plane of the primary fenestration, and the relative solar altitudes and azimuths should be identical.

14-6. *Errors introduced by tilted model studies. These are insignificant for designs where direct and reflected sunlight is the major daylight component. (1) sky seen by real building; (2) sky seen by model; (3) sky error associated with model: (a) summer simulation; (b) winter simulation.*

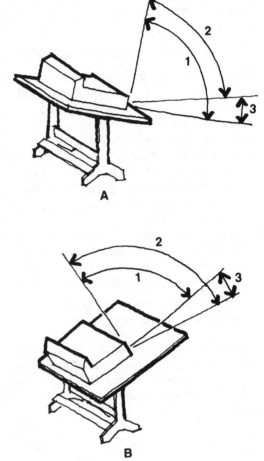

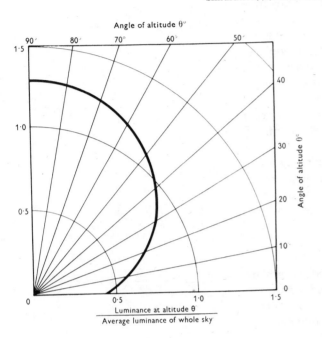

14-7. *Luminance distribution of C.I.E. standard overcast sky, expressed as a relationship between the average sky luminance and the angle of altitude. (Reprinted, by permission, from Hopkinson, et al., 1963)*

REAL SKY: PARTLY CLOUDY CONDITIONS

Partly cloudy conditions, where the sky brightness distribution changes considerably throughout the test period, are unsuitable for model testing and should be avoided if possible. This is because cloud luminance varies greatly depending on location relative to the sun (front-lit clouds are much brighter than surrounding blue sky; back-lit clouds may or may not be darker than the surrounding sky depending on cloud density). If testing under these conditions is unavoidable, it is suggested that a control configuration be employed: testing of each alternative configuration should be followed immediately by a control test so that variations due to changing sky conditions can be estimated and compensated with a correction factor.

ARTIFICIAL SKIES

To control the problems associated with varying and unpredictable sky conditions, many daylight researchers prefer to work with an artificial sky that approximates the luminance distribution of an "ideal" overcast sky (i.e., the 1 to 3 C. I. E. standard overcast sky luminance distribution as shown in figure 14-7).

HEMISPHERICAL DOME ARTIFICIAL SKY

One type of artificial sky in general use is the dome. Skydomes are usually opaque white and illuminated by interior perimeter lights. The model is located in the center and receives reflected light from the surrounding dome in a manner similar to that by which a building receives light from an overcast sky. The luminance distribution of such a sky can be fine-tuned by adjustment of perimeter lights. (Extreme variations in luminance distribution are not possible because of multiple reflections within the dome.)

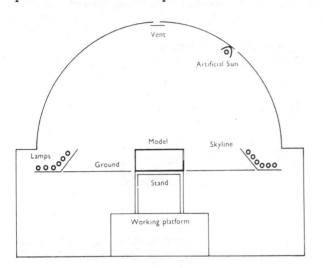

14-8. A typical dome artificial sky section. (Reprinted, by permission, from Hopkinson, et al., 1963)

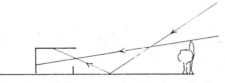

Light from the real sky never reaches a horizontal ceiling direct, but only by reflection from the ground. Direct light to back wall is often obstructed.

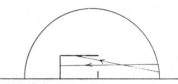

Horizon error in hemisphere sky. Direct light on ceiling and too much light on back wall.

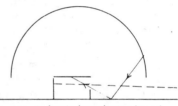

14-9. Horizon error inherent in dome skies. (Reprinted, by permission, from Hopkinson, et al., 1963)

Horizon error in hemisphere sky can be reduced by lowering model to eliminate ceiling error. Back wall now receives insufficient light, but this may not be serious.

Because the dome is of finite size, it presents a horizon that does not accurately represent a true, infinitely distant horizon (fig. 14-9). To minimize this horizon error, domes must be relatively large compared to the model. Most research domes are twenty feet in diameter or larger, making them expensive to construct and maintain. Selkowitz (1982) and Hopkinson (1966) have described and referenced such domes. Most of these have been calibrated for C. I. E. standard overcast sky conditions; some have the additional capability of simulating clear sky luminance distribution, with and without direct sunlight capability.

MIRROR BOX ARTIFICIAL SKY

A less expensive alternative to the artificial skydome is a mirror box. This combines a luminous ceiling and mirrored walls to create a sky with an "infinite" horizon as a result of multiple interreflections. Because some light is absorbed with each mirror reflection, this configuration tends to approximate naturally the luminance distribution of an overcast sky (brighter at the zenith than at the horizon). The height-to-width ratio of the box controls the actual luminance distribution.

While a large (room-sized) box can be used, allowing the insertion of a free-standing model, most are smaller, with the model window exposed to the box interior through an opening in one mirrored wall. Such boxes can be modified to allow a portion of the model to penetrate into the box (thus allowing skylights to be tested).

One error inherent in mirror-box skies is the multiple reflected image of the model itself (appearing as several adjacent models, with spacing equal to the box dimension). This error can be reduced by covering the exterior model walls with a mirror or white surface.

Mirror boxes have been modified to provide a clear sky luminance distribution without direct sun (White, 1983); however, most have been used only to simulate overcast skies. Because of the suitability of these boxes for use by designers, a detailed description (Airy, 1981) is presented in Appendix F.

14-10. *Section perspective, mirror-box artificial sky: (a) model; (b) gray ground plane; (c) mirrored walls; (d) translucent diffuser; (e) fluorescent lamps.*

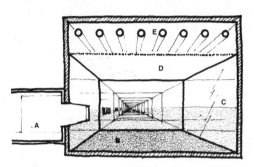

MEASUREMENT

An important (and expensive) aspect of physical modeling is the need for accurate and convenient measurement of interior and exterior model illuminances. These measurements are taken with a cosine-corrected, color-corrected photometer. Cosine correction is necessary to measure illuminance in a plane. (Incident-reading photographic meters incorporate a hemispherical diffuser, are intentionally not cosine corrected, and are not suitable for lighting measurements.) Color correction requires that the sensitivity of the photometer match that of the human eye. (Ordinary photocells and solar pyranometers are sensitive to ultraviolet and infrared as well as visible radiation and are thus unsuited for lighting measurements.)

For daylighting measurements, the photometer should have a range from 1 to 10,000 footcandles (approximately full sun at sea level). To cover this wide range, some photometers require a perforated cap that allows a fixed percentage of light to penetrate to the sensor, thus requiring the application of a standard multiplication factor (usually 10) to be applied to the reading.

Photometers that incorporate the sensor and the display in the same enclosure are poorly suited for model studies because of their large size and because of the difficulty in observing the readings without obstructing the windows. If such a meter must be used, it should be locked in the "on" position, inserted into the model at the test location, and observed through a small viewing opening. Taking horizontal readings at thirty-inches (scale) desk height is usually difficult because of the meter size. Alternatively, the sensor can be inserted through an opening in the floor of the model, allowing the display to project below for observation. The user should ensure that extraneous light through the opening is minimized by the use of a shielding "skirt" fitted around the neck of the meter.

Sensors that are remote (on a wire) from the display are a desirable alternative to the self-contained meter (fig. 14-11). Multisensor photometers allow near-simultaneous measurements to be made at several locations inside and outside the model, saving time and minimizing the effect of changing sky conditions (fig. 14-12). Multisensor photometers can be combined with a data-acquisition microcomputer to facilitate calibration in the field, storing data on cassette or paper tape, and simultaneous data analysis to compute and

174   ANALYSIS

plot daylight and other factors. (Dwyer, 1983; see fig. 14-13). See Appendix F for a survey of daylighting instrumentation.

Luminance measurements made within the model provide a basis for the qualitative assessment of glare. Luminance meters measure the brightness of a very small (usually less than 2 degrees) portion of a surface or sky within the field of view. Many use a sighting lens separate from the sensor opening, resulting in a parallax error. Meters of this type usually provide an adjustment to create a convergence at the estimated viewing distance. This is satisfactory for building surveys, but not for models where the parallax effect is exaggerated. For model measurements, a reflex-type luminance meter permits direct observation of the measured areas and is thus preferable.

14-11. Remote photometer mounted on a stick to facilitate placement at model reference locations. (Care should be taken to exclude extraneous light through these wall openings.)

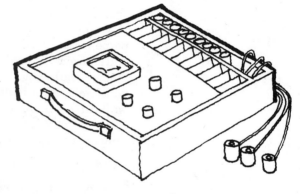

14-12. "Megatron" multisensor photometer for model measurements (see Appendix G).

14-13. Ensar Group multisensor model photometer system, with Hewlett-Packard HP-85 microcomputer and Licor photometric sensors (see Appendix G).

PHYSICAL MODELS

INTERIOR MODEL PHOTOGRAPHY

TYPE OF CAMERA

Single-lens reflex 35mm cameras are preferred for documenting model studies because:

- they are compact and relatively inexpensive;

- the view through the viewfinder matches the view recorded on film;

- they accept wide-angle, interchangeable lenses;

- most incorporate a through-the-lens meter; and

- a wide selection of films is available.

A tripod should be used with a cable release to allow the long time exposures (typically longer than one second) required by slow-speed film (fine-grained with wide exposure latitude) and small lens apertures (to maximize the depth of focus).

CAMERA POSITION

To prevent convergence of vertical edges in the photograph, the film plane should be vertical relative to the model (this may not be obvious through the viewfinder). Usually, photographs made through a viewport in the wall perpendicular to the window produce the best results, simulating a section and showing the daylighting effects throughout the room. Interior objects are thus sidelighted for better definition (as opposed to front- or backlighted, which minimizes texture and form). Horizontal convergence of the opposite wall can be eliminated by orienting the film plane parallel to that wall. A shielding "skirt" fitted around the lens is recommended to exclude extraneous light through the viewport.

FILM

If a tripod is available, then a relatively slow-speed film (which typically has lower contrast and greater exposure latitude) is preferred. Note, however, that if extremely low light levels necessitate exposures longer than five seconds with color film, a slight color shift may result from "reciprocity failure." (Some color films produce a color shift and require disproportionately greater exposure for exposure times longer than one second.) This may be avoided where color balance is critical by using a faster film speed or opening the lens aperture.

If color slide film is used, select a type that is color-balanced for the primary light source (or compensated for with an appropriate conversion filter). In general, color prints can be made from slides by most photo labs, but these are of poorer quality (higher contrast and grainier) and more expensive than prints from original color negatives. Similarly, black-and-white prints made from color slides (usually via an internegative) are poorer than those made from either black-and-white or color negatives. Custom labs can prepare high-quality slides from color negatives; these are typically better than slide duplicates. Kodak 5293/5247 and Fuji 8518 motion picture films are available spooled for use in 35mm cameras from mail-order photo labs (see photography magazine advertisements); when returned for processing, these films yield both high-quality color negatives and color slides at modest cost.

EXPOSURE

Determining exposure for photographing daylighted model interiors, like building interiors, is difficult because of the extreme brightness range between the fenestration and shadow areas. The exposure latitude of any film is much shorter than that of the human eye. Extremely bright areas, such as the sky and surrounding exterior, tend to completely dominate the camera meter. Invariably, if these areas are visible within the sensitivity zone of the camera meter, the interior will be underexposed. When taking the exposure reading, aim the camera so that the fenestration is just out of the field of view. Set the exposure, and then return to the desired view to take the photograph. (Automatic exposure modes are typically unsuccessful; use the "manual" mode on automatic cameras.) If the interior model surfaces are very light in color, exposure should be about one f-stop greater to avoid underexposure (the camera meter is programmed to "expect" an average 18 percent reflectance).

If an incident light meter (or an incident attachment to cover the lens) is available, insert the meter through a viewport on the opposite wall, aiming it toward the camera. For this application, incident readings are usually more reliable than the reflected-light readings made by camera meters. No correction needs to be made for the model interior color with incident readings.

Exposure for interior photographs is, at best, an art. Even technically correct exposures frequently fail to represent the view as perceived by the eye. Because of this, it is recommended that exposures be "bracketed" one f-stop over and one f-stop under. (For shots toward the window, use one, two, and three f-stops over.)

LENSES

Wide- to ultrawide-angle lenses (15 to 28 mm) are recommended to provide maximum coverage and because of their inherently great depth of focus. Some daylight researchers also prefer these focal lengths because they most closely approximate the field of view of the eye and thus better simulate the perceived depth of the room. It should be noted that this only occurs when the angular field of view observing the final photograph matches the angular field of view of the lens; an 8" × 10" print taken with a 20 mm lens would have to be viewed at the uncomfortably close distance of 5 inches to accurately recreate the correct room perspective (Moore, 1976).

Relatively inexpensive 28 mm lenses produce excellent results, although the field of view is somewhat narrow for interior model photography. Less expensive ultrawide lenses tend to lose sharpness at the corners and exhibit noticeable "barrel" distortion (slight "fisheye" effect—straight lines near the edge bow out). All ultrawide lenses tend to suffer from "edge fall-off", resulting in less exposure (darkening) at the edges. This is most obvious at the large apertures. If fall-off is significant, reduce the shooting aperture; this will also increase the depth of field. Other remedies to fall-off include very expensive graded filters (darker at the center than at the edge), and custom "dodging" during printing.

Fisheye lenses (lenses with a 180 degree field of view) can be used to assess the relative contribution of various distributed light sources (sky, reflective walls, ceiling, and so on) to the illumination of a given reference point (fig. 14-14). The camera is positioned so that the lens replaces the photometer at the reference location (usually aimed at the ceiling). The size, brightness, and location of the area source in the photograph indicate its relative contribution of light to the reference point. Accurate measurements from such photographs are difficult and are possible only if the lens is cosine corrected (for example, the Nikkor 10 mm OP lens).

A Modelscope is a thin periscope with a wide field of view that is useful for observing the interior of otherwise inaccessible architectural models. Its optical quality is inferior to comparable camera lenses, and while it can be adapted to a camera, it is not recommended for daylighting model photography.

14-14. Reading room, Rovaniemi Library, Finland (Alvar Aalto, Architect). This photograph was taken with a fisheye lens at the reference plane. Luminances and luminance areas are approximately proportional to their illuminance contribution on a horizontal plane at the camera position.

DOCUMENTATION

Careful documentation of each model test is essential. As much of the relevant information as possible should be displayed within the model photograph. A convenient method is to locate a small display board on the wall opposite the camera, with a matrix of different testing variables (time and date, experiment number, sky condition, photographic exposure, and so on) with movable push-pins to identify the configuration being tested. The panel can be used to cover a wall opening, allowing changes to be made from the outside.

REFERENCES

Airy, A. "An Artificial Sky Chamber for Daylighting Studies." In *Daylighting Design Tools Workshop Workbook*, pp. 35–45. Washington, DC: American Institute of Architects Service Corporation, 1983.

Dwyer, L., and Franta, G. "An Interactive Tool for Daylighting Analysis." In *Proceedings of the International Daylighting Conference*, edited by Vonier, T., pp. 131–134. Washington, DC: American Institute of Architects Service Corporation, 1983.

Hopkinson, R., et al. *Architectural Physics: Lighting.* London: Her Majesty's Stationery Office, 1963.

Moore, F. "Perceptual Distortion of Space in 2-D Architectural Media." Chapter in McGinty, T., *Architectural Graphics.* Dubuque, IA: Kendall-Hunt, 1976.

O'Laughlin, P., and Porter, R. "Relative Contributions of Beam, Sky, and Ground Components to Diffusely Reflected Sunlight Illuminance in Physical Models." In *Progress in Passive Solar Energy Systems*, edited by Hayes, J., and Andrejko, D., pp. 143–146. Boulder, CO: American Solar Energy Society, 1983.

Selkowitz, S., MacGowan, D., McSwain, B., and Nawab, M. "A Hemispherical Sky Simulator for Daylighting Studies." Paper #41. Toronto: Annual I.E.S. Technical Conference (also available from Windows and Daylighting Program, Lawrence Berkeley Laboratory, Berkeley, CA), 1981.

White, R. "The Conversion of a Mirrored Artificial Sky to a Clear Sky Distribution." In *Proceedings of the International Daylighting Conference*, edited by Vonier, T., pp. 283–285. Washington, DC: American Institute of Architects Service Corporation, 1983.

Chapter 15
Graphic Methods

A variety of graphic methods are available for estimating interior illuminance due to daylighting. They include protractors, nomographs, prototypical iso-lux contours ("daylight footprints"), and dot charts. (Nomographs are treated separately in chapter 13; annual energy-saving graphs are covered in chapter 17.) All of these graphic methods were derived from computational methods. They allow one to estimate daylight illuminance using the format with which designers are most familiar: graphic. In addition to their ease of use, graphic methods reveal the relative effect of various design parameters, providing the designer with additional insight that may help to improve the design.

PROTRACTORS

Chapter 6 described a conceptual model that recognizes interior illuminance as a function of three variables: (1) luminance of the light source, (2) apparent (angular) size of the light source, and (3) the position of the source relative to the reference plane (cosine effect). Virtually all protractor methods are based on this conceptual model; that is, they involve measuring the angular field of view of the primary daylight source (the sky) from a selected interior reference point, assume a sky luminance, and provide a correction for the cosine effect.

LUNE PROTRACTOR

Jones (1983) has described a very simple *lune protractor* for rapid graphic estimation of daylight illumination. (A lune is a pie-shaped section of a sphere.) The protractor considers the contribution of the sky and of the major interior reflecting surfaces. While the principle behind the protractor is simple, actual usage is laborious for any but the most simple applications. Its greatest value lies in its clear demonstration of the fundamental principles, especially the quantitative relationship between units of luminance (foot-lamberts) and illuminance (footcandles). Because these principles are less obvious in more sophisticated protractors, study of the following example (shown in figures 15-2 to 15-7) demonstrating the lune protractor is recommended before proceeding to other, more practical methods:

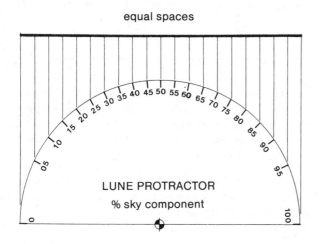

15-1. *Construction of the lune protractor. Equal divisions are projected orthographically onto a semicircle, producing a cosine-corrected protractor.*

1. Select the reference point P for which daylight illuminance is to be determined.

2. Identify the center of the major surface brightnesses (A, B, C, and O) within the field of view of P (fig. 15-2).

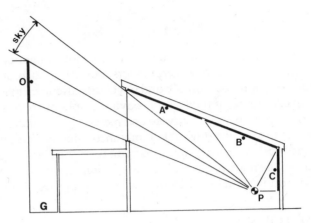

15-2. Building section showing major bright areas visible from P.

3. Determine the luminance of the sky seen from the reference point P from the table in figure 15-3.

15-3. Sky luminance and horizontal illuminance, 34° latitude. (After Jones, 1983)

Condition	Dec 21	Mar/Sep 21	Jun 21
Illuminance (Footcandles)			
Overcast sky	900	1600	2200
Clear sky: Sun only	2700	5600	7100
Sky only	800	1400	1600
Sun + Sky	3500	7000	8700
Luminance (Footlamberts)			
Overcast sky	900	1600	2200
Clear: North	550	800	1400
South	1900	2600	1600
East 10 A.M./West 2 P.M.	1400	2600	2700
West 10 A.M./East 2 P.M.	700	900	1000

4. Determine the luminance of the exterior surfaces that are major reflectors of light to A, B, and C (in this example, roof R and ground G): *luminance (footlamberts) = illumination (in footcandles from figure 15-3) × surface reflectance.* (Surface reflectance is based on specified surface color and ranges from 0.0 to 1.0.)

5. Calculate shape factors (the difference between two readings on the lune protractor) using lune protractor for sky, obstruction, and roof as seen from A, B, and C (fig. 15-4).

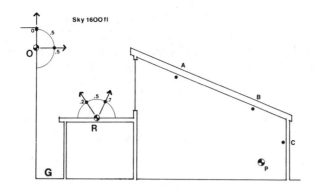

15-4. *Section showing example calculation of ground and roof luminances using shape factors (SF), read from lune protractor (overcast sky, March 21):*

Illuminance at O = 0.5SF × 1600fl
= 800 fc.

Luminance at O = 800fc × 20% ref.
= 160 fl.

Illuminance at R = 0.5SF × 1600fl
= 800fc.

Luminance at R = 800fc × 50% ref.
= 400fl.

6. Calculate the illuminances at *A, B,* and *C,* where *illuminance = (ground luminance × ground shape factor) + (roof luminance × roof shape factor) + (sky luminance × sky shape factor)*(fig. 15-5).

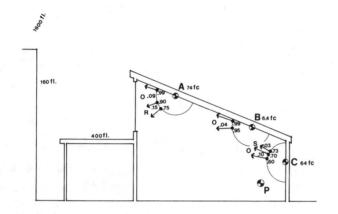

15-5. *Illuminance = SF × luminances "seen" from* A, B, *and* C:

Illuminance at A = (.09SF × 160fl)
+ (.15SF × 400fl) = 74fc.

Illuminance at B = .04SF × 160fl
= 6.4fc.

Illuminance at C = (.03SF × 1600fl)
+ (.10SF × 160fl) = 64fc.

7. Calculate the luminances of *A, B,* and *C* by multiplying their respective illuminances and reflectances.

8. Position the protractor center at *P* with the base on the reference plane (horizontal in this case), and determine the shape factors of the sky and the areas represented by *A, B,* and *C*(fig. 15-6).

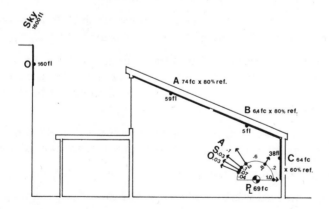

15-6. *Calculation of illuminance at* P *(for "long window"):*

Ep = (.03SF × 160fl) + (.03SF × 1600fl)
+ (.1SF × 59fl) + (.6SF × 5fl)
+ (.2SF × 38)
= 69fc.

9. Calculate the illuminance contribution (in footcandles) of the sky and areas *A, B,* and *C* by multiplying their shape factors times their luminances (footlamberts). Temporarily assuming that the window is "very long" (approaches infinite length), the total illuminance (in footcandles) is the sum of these contributions.

10. This value should be reduced by a width shape factor, determined by using the protractor in plan with the base parallel to the glazing (fig. 15-7). (The width shape factor is the difference between the protractor readings for the left and right sides of the window.)

15-7. Plan at clerestory window showing correction for "short" windows using horizontal shape factors. (Base of protractor is parallel to glazing.)

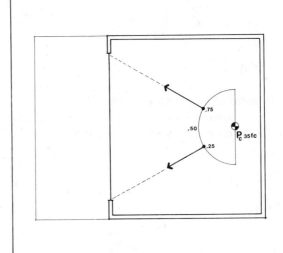

B. R. S. DAYLIGHT FACTOR PROTRACTOR (OVERCAST SKY)

The B. R. S. (British Research Station) protractors were first developed by Dufton (1946) for uniform sky conditions to simplify the calculation of daylight and to enable daylight measurements to be made directly from architectural drawings. These were revised in 1967 to include the C.I.E. standard overcast sky and more recent information on glazing transmission (Longmore, 1967). The B. R. S. protractors are based on the daylight factor method (also known as the C.I.E. method) for calculating the interior illuminance under overcast sky conditions.

The daylight factor is the sum of three components (each of which is a percentage of exterior unobstructed illuminance):

■ Sky component—the illuminance received at the interior reference point directly from the sky through the window or skylight.

■ External reflected component—the illuminance received at the interior reference point from reflecting exterior surfaces above the horizon (surfaces below the horizon cannot be "seen" directly from the horizontal reference plane).

■ Internal reflected component—the illuminance received at the interior reference point from all light reflected from interior room surfaces.

Sky Component (Overcast Sky)

Each B.R.S. protractor is actually two protractors. The *primary* protractor is overlaid on a building section for measuring the sky component for an infinitely long window. The *auxiliary* protractor is overlaid on a corresponding floor plan to determine a correction factor for the given window length (figs. 15-8, 15-9).

External Reflected Component (Overcast Sky)

The external reflected component is first calculated for the area of exterior obstruction visible from the reference point in a manner similar to the sky

ANALYSIS

component. This value is then multiplied by a factor of 0.1 (because the brightness of external obstructions averages 10 percent of sky brightness). Thus for the above example, the external reflected component (infinitely long window) = 0.3%. The width correction = 0.3 + 0.15 = 0.45. Thus the external reflected component = 0.3% × 0.45 × 0.1 = 0.0135%.

It is obvious that the external reflected component tends to be very small because of the 0.1 reflectance correction and because of the cosine effect due to its low average elevation. Generally the ERC can be ignored as insignificant if its angular size is smaller than the sky component.

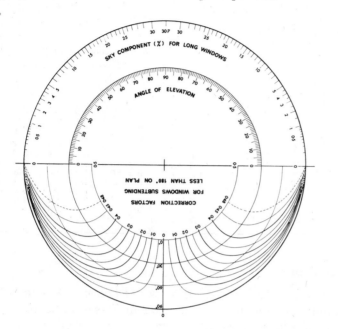

15-8. B.R.S. daylight factor protractor: (a) top half is primary protractor for use over section; (b) bottom half is auxiliary protractor for use over floor plan to determine the width correction factor. A complete set for various glazing slopes for both overcast and uniform sky conditions is available (see Longmore in References). (Reprinted from Hopkinson, 1963, courtesy of Her Majesty's Stationery Office)

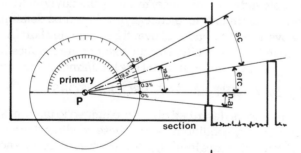

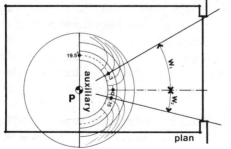

15-9. Use of the B.R.S. daylight protractor: (a) sky component (SC) (above the external obstruction) at reference point P for infinitely long window = 3.5% − 0.3% = 3.2%; (b) correction for window length (for 19.5° average sky elevation) = 0.3 + 0.15 = 0.45. The sky component at P = 3.2% × 0.45 = 1.44%.

Internal Reflected Component (Overcast Sky)

The internal reflected component (IRC) is determined from the table in figure 15-10. The appropriate column is determined by the floor and wall reflection factors (reflectance × 100). The appropriate row is determined by either the actual glass area as a percentage of floor area or the ratio of glass area to floor area.

15-10. Internal reflected component of daylight factor. (Reprinted from Hopkinson, 1963, courtesy of Her Majesty's Stationery Office)

Ratio— Actual glass area to floor area	Actual glass area as % of floor area	Floor Reflection Factor (%)											
		10				20				40			
		Wall Reflection Factor (%)											
		20	40	60	80	20	40	60	80	20	40	60	80
		(%)	(%)	(%)	(%)	(%)	(%)	(%)	(%)	(%)	(%)	(%)	(%)
1 : 50	2	—	—	0·1	0·2	—	0·1	0·1	0·2	—	0·1	0·2	0·2
1 : 20	5	0·1	0·1	0·2	0·4	0·1	0·2	0·3	0·5	0·1	0·2	0·4	0·6
1 : 14	7	0·1	0·2	0·3	0·5	0·1	0·2	0·4	0·6	0·2	0·3	0·6	0·8
1 : 10	10	0·1	0·2	0·4	0·7	0·2	0·3	0·6	0·9	0·3	0·5	0·8	1·2
1 : 6·7	15	0·2	0·4	0·6	1·0	0·2	0·5	0·8	1·3	0·4	0·7	1·1	1·7
1 : 5	20	0·2	0·5	0·8	1·4	0·3	0·6	1·1	1·7	0·5	0·9	1·5	2·3
1 : 4	25	0·3	0·6	1·0	1·7	0·4	0·8	1·3	2·0	0·6	1·1	1·8	2·8
1 : 3·3	30	0·3	0·7	1·2	2·0	0·5	0·9	1·5	2·4	0·8	1·3	2·1	3·3
1 : 2·9	35	0·4	0·8	1·4	2·3	0·5	1·0	1·8	2·8	0·9	1·5	2·4	3·8
1 : 2·5	40	0·5	0·9	1·6	2·6	0·6	1·2	2·0	3·1	1·0	1·7	2·7	4·2
1 : 2·2	45	0·5	1·0	1·8	2·9	0·7	1·3	2·2	3·4	1·2	1·9	3·0	4·6
1 : 2	50	0·6	1·1	1·9	3·1	0·8	1·4	2·3	3·7	1·3	2·1	3·2	4·9

Daylight Factor

The uncorrected daylight factor = sky component + external reflected component + internal reflected component. This is further reduced by multiplying factors for mullions, glazing transmittance (if other than single clear glass), and dirt. The final product is the corrected daylight factor (%). To determine the footcandle illuminance, multiply the daylight factor by the horizontal exterior illuminance (overcast sky). This can be determined from the illuminance overlays (Appendix C) over the sun angle chart (Appendix B), or from the table in figure 15-11. (Horizontal exterior illuminance in footcandles is numerically equal to the equivalent sky luminance in footlamberts.)

CLEAR SKY DAYLIGHT FACTOR PROTRACTORS

The B. R. S. protractors described above are limited to uniform sky and C.I.E. standard overcast sky conditions. While these conditions are representative of northern Europe, they are less suited for the greater occurrence of clear sky conditions characteristic of many parts of North America. As discussed previously, under clear sky conditions, sky brightness is greatest near the sun and least perpendicular to the sun (approximately 10 to 1 ratio). Thus, not only does the average sky luminance change throughout the day (as with an overcast sky), but the location of greatest luminance changes with the sun's location. The luminance range throughout the clear sky is much greater than it is for the overcast sky.

Bryan and Carlsberg (1982) have developed a set of daylight factor protractors that is based on the C.I.E. clear sky function and is similar in format to the B.R.S. protractors (fig. 15-12). These have been constructed for solar altitudes of every 10 degrees. For every 10 degrees, there are five protractors: one for every 45 degrees of solar azimuth relative to the window (i.e., 0°, 45°, 90°, 135°, and 180°), the positive direction being clockwise from the sun. Since the protractors are transparent, the positive orientations are derived by reversing the protractors (because the clear sky is symmetrical about the axis

ANALYSIS

Latitude	8 AM 4 PM		9 AM 3 PM		10 AM 2 PM		11 AM 1 PM		Noon	
	cd/m²	fL	cd/m²	fL	cd/m²	fL	cd/m²	fL	cd/m²	fL
December 21										
30° N	1440	420	2540	740	3490	1020	4150	1210	4350	1270
32	1200	350	2400	700	3290	960	3940	1150	4110	1200
34	1100	320	2230	650	3120	910	3770	1100	3910	1140
36	890	260	2060	600	2880	840	3490	1020	3670	1070
38	790	230	1880	550	2710	790	3220	940	3430	1000
40	650	190	1710	500	2540	740	3080	900	3190	930
42	510	150	1540	450	2260	660	2810	820	2950	860
44	340	100	1300	380	2060	600	2600	760	2710	790
46	210	60	1160	340	1880	550	2330	680	2500	730
48	140	40	990	290	1610	470	2160	630	2230	650
50	0	0	820	240	1440	420	1920	560	1990	580
March 21 or September 21										
30° N	3120	910	4520	1320	5860	1710	6890	2010	7330	2140
32	3010	880	4420	1290	5650	1650	6650	1940	7096	2070
34	2950	860	4280	1250	5480	1600	6410	1870	6780	1980
36	2880	840	4180	1220	5340	1560	6170	1800	6510	1900
38	2740	800	4110	1200	5140	1500	5960	1740	6300	1840
40	2710	790	3910	1140	5000	1460	5720	1670	6030	1760
42	2600	760	3840	1120	4830	1410	5480	1600	5790	1690
44	2540	740	3700	1080	4590	1340	5280	1540	5550	1620
46	2430	710	3530	1030	4420	1229	5040	1470	5310	1550
48	2360	690	3390	990	4250	1240	4830	1410	5070	1480
50	2230	650	3220	940	4040	1180	4560	1330	4800	1400
June 21										
30° N	4350	1270	5930	1730	7710	2250				
32	4390	1280	5930	1730	7670	2240				
34	4420	1290	5930	1730	7610	2220				
36	4420	1290	5930	1730	7540	2200	10140	2960		
38	4420	1290	5890	1720	7400	2160	9730	2840		
40	4420	1290	5820	1700	7260	2120	9080	2650	10480	3060
42	4450	1300	5790	1690	7130	2080	8700	2540	9800	2860
44	4420	1290	5720	1670	7020	2050	8330	2430	9110	2660
46	4420	1290	5620	1640	6890	2010	7980	2330	8630	2520
48	4420	1290	5550	1620	6710	1960	7710	2250	8220	2400
50	4320	1260	5450	1590	6510	1900	7400	2160	7810	2280

15-11. *Equivalent overcast sky luminance in candelas per square meter and footlamberts. Unobstructed horizontal illuminance in lux (footcandles) is numerically equal to equivalent sky luminance in candelas per square meter (footlamberts). (Reprinted, by permission, from I.E.S., 1981)*

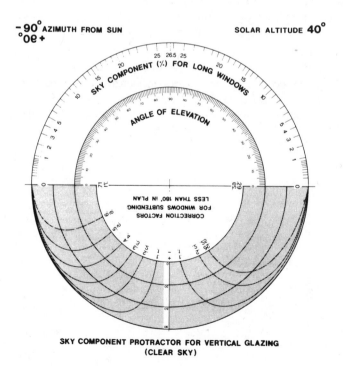

SKY COMPONENT PROTRACTOR FOR VERTICAL GLAZING (CLEAR SKY)

15-12. *Clear sky protractor for vertical glazing. (Reprinted, by permission, from Bryan and Carlsberg, 1982)*

that bisects the hemisphere through the sun). This is facilitated by placing protractor values on both sides. A recently developed version combines these five protractors into a single unit.

Sky Component (Clear Sky)

The sky component is determined using the appropriate protractor for solar altitude and relative solar azimuth, using the procedure outlined above for the B.R.S. protractor.

External Reflected Component (Clear Sky)

Bryan and Carlsberg (1982) have not developed an external reflected component for this procedure. They note that the contribution of the underside of an overhang is small and can usually be ignored, and that the procedure can be used with no loss in accuracy when no external obstructions are visible from the reference location.

However, daylight reflected from an exterior sunlit surface (such as an adjacent building) may be significant and even exceed the sky component. This contribution can be calculated as follows:

1. Determine the illuminance on the exterior reflecting surface using the illuminance overlay for vertical surface (Appendix C) over the appropriate sun angle chart.

2. Calculate the luminance of this surface by multiplying its illuminance times its average reflectance.

3. Using the lune protractor, determine the vertical (section) and horizontal (plan) shape factors. The illuminance at the reference point is the product of the exterior surface luminance times these two shape factors.

4. Convert this to an external reflected component by dividing the external reflected illuminance by the clear sky horizontal exterior illuminance (excluding direct sunlight, from Appendix C or fig. 15-13), and convert to a percentage by multiplying by 100 percent.

Internal Reflected Component (Clear Sky)

Bryan and Carlsberg (1982) recommend that the *split flux method* be used to calculate the internal reflected component. This method divides the light entering the room into two parts: light received directly from the sky and light received directly from the ground. The light from the sky, on entering the room, is considered to be modified by the average reflectance of the floor and those parts of the walls below the midheight of the window. The light from the ground is considered to be modified by the average reflectance of the ceiling and those parts of the walls above the midheight of the window.

Latitude	December 21					March and September 21					June 21				
	8 AM	10 AM	Noon	2 PM	4 PM	8 AM	10 AM	Noon	2 PM	4 PM	8 AM	10 AM	Noon	2 PM	4 PM
North															
30° N	1540 (450)	2060 (600)	2060 (600)	2060 (600)	1540 (450)	2400 (700)	3430 (1000)	3600 (1050)	3430 (1000)	2400 (700)	5310 (1550)	4800 (1400)	3430 (1000)	4800 (1400)	5310 (1550)
34° N	1200 (350)	1880 (550)	1880 (550)	1880 (550)	1200 (350)	2740 (800)	2740 (800)	3080 (900)	2740 (800)	2740 (800)	4630 (1350)	4800 (1400)	3250 (950)	4800 (1400)	4630 (1350)
38° N	1030 (300)	1880 (550)	1880 (550)	1880 (550)	1030 (300)	2570 (750)	2740 (800)	3080 (900)	2740 (800)	2570 (750)	4630 (1350)	4450 (1300)	3250 (950)	4450 (1300)	4630 (1350)
42° N	860 (250)	1710 (500)	1710 (500)	1710 (500)	860 (250)	2400 (700)	2570 (750)	2740 (800)	2570 (750)	2400 (700)	4450 (1300)	4450 (1300)	3250 (950)	4450 (1300)	4450 (1300)
46° N	510 (150)	1540 (450)	1710 (500)	1540 (450)	510 (150)	2400 (700)	2570 (750)	2570 (750)	2570 (750)	2400 (700)	4450 (1300)	4280 (1250)	3250 (950)	4280 (1250)	4450 (1300)
South															
30° N	3770 (1100)	6680 (1950)	7710 (2250)	6680 (1950)	3770 (1100)	5820 (1700)	7880 (2300)	9590 (2800)	7880 (2300)	5820 (1700)	4110 (1200)	5480 (1600)	8220 (2400)	5480 (1600)	4110 (1200)
34° N	3770 (1100)	6510 (1900)	7540 (2200)	6510 (1900)	3770 (1100)	5820 (1700)	9080 (2650)	9940 (2900)	9080 (2650)	5820 (1700)	4630 (1350)	5650 (1650)	7880 (2300)	5650 (1650)	4630 (1350)
38° N	3080 (900)	7880 (2300)	7540 (2200)	7880 (2300)	3080 (900)	5820 (1700)	9250 (2700)	10100 (2950)	9250 (2700)	5820 (1700)	4630 (1350)	5650 (1650)	7880 (2300)	5650 (1650)	4630 (1350)
42° N	2060 (600)	7190 (2100)	7370 (2150)	7190 (2100)	2060 (600)	5820 (1700)	9250 (2700)	8390 (2450)	9250 (2700)	5820 (1700)	4630 (1350)	6850 (2000)	8570 (2500)	6850 (2000)	4630 (1350)
46° N	1370 (400)	6510 (1900)	7190 (2100)	6510 (1900)	1370 (400)	5820 (1700)	9250 (2700)	9940 (2900)	9280 (2710)	5820 (1700)	4630 (1350)	7190 (2100)	9250 (2700)	7190 (2100)	4630 (1350)
East															
30° N	5310 (1550)	5140 (1500)	3430 (1000)	2400 (700)	1370 (400)	6850 (2000)	8570 (2500)	5140 (1500)	3080 (900)	2400 (700)	9590 (2800)	9080 (2650)	4800 (1400)	3430 (1000)	2400 (700)
34° N	4630 (1350)	4800 (1400)	3250 (950)	2400 (700)	1370 (400)	8220 (2400)	8910 (2600)	5480 (1600)	3250 (950)	2230 (650)	9590 (2800)	9250 (2700)	4970 (1450)	3430 (1000)	2400 (700)
38° N	4110 (1200)	4450 (1300)	3080 (900)	2230 (650)	1200 (350)	8570 (2500)	8910 (2600)	5140 (1500)	3080 (900)	2060 (600)	9590 (2800)	9250 (2700)	4800 (1400)	3600 (1050)	2400 (700)
42° N	2570 (750)	4110 (1200)	2910 (850)	2060 (600)	860 (250)	8220 (2400)	8220 (2400)	4970 (1450)	2740 (800)	2060 (600)	9940 (2900)	8910 (2600)	4800 (1400)	3430 (1000)	2400 (700)
46° N	1710 (500)	3770 (1100)	2740 (800)	1710 (500)	510 (150)	7880 (2300)	7190 (2100)	4800 (1400)	2400 (700)	2060 (600)	9760 (2850)	8910 (2600)	4800 (1400)	3430 (1000)	2400 (700)
West															
30° N	1370 (400)	2400 (700)	3430 (1000)	5140 (1500)	5310 (1550)	2400 (700)	3080 (900)	5140 (1500)	8570 (2500)	6850 (2000)	2400 (700)	3430 (1000)	4930 (1440)	9080 (2650)	9590 (2800)
34° N	1370 (400)	2400 (700)	3250 (950)	4800 (1400)	4630 (1350)	2230 (650)	3080 (900)	5480 (1600)	8910 (2600)	8220 (2400)	2400 (700)	3430 (1000)	4800 (1400)	9250 (2700)	9590 (2800)
38° N	1200 (350)	2230 (650)	3080 (900)	4450 (1300)	4110 (1200)	2060 (600)	3080 (900)	5140 (1500)	8910 (2600)	8570 (2500)	2400 (700)	3600 (1050)	4800 (1400)	9250 (2700)	9590 (2800)
42° N	860 (250)	2060 (600)	2910 (850)	4110 (1200)	2570 (750)	2060 (600)	2740 (800)	4970 (1450)	8220 (2400)	8220 (2400)	2400 (700)	3430 (1000)	4800 (1400)	8910 (2600)	9940 (2900)
46° N	510 (150)	1710 (500)	2740 (800)	3770 (1100)	1710 (500)	2060 (600)	2400 (700)	4800 (1400)	7190 (2100)	7880 (2300)	2400 (700)	3430 (1000)	4800 (1400)	8910 (2600)	9760 (2850)

* Average values, direct sunlight excluded.

15-13. *Equivalent sky luminance in candelas per square meter (footlamberts) on clear days (direct sunlight excluded). Illuminance of a horizontal unobstructed surface (in footcandles) is numerically equal to these footlambert values. (Reprinted, by permission, from I.E.S., 1981)*

The formula for the average IRC is:

$$IRC = \frac{T \times W \times (F_s \times R_{fw} + F_g \times R_{cw})}{A(1 - R)} \times 100\% \qquad (15.1)$$

where:

T = Transmittance of glass,

W = Area of window,

A = Total area of ceiling, floor, and walls, including window,

R = Average reflectance of ceiling, floor, and walls, including window,

R_{fw} = Average reflectance of the floor and those parts of the walls below the plane of the mid-height of the window (excluding the window-wall),

R_{cw} = Average reflectance of the ceiling and those parts of the walls above the plane of the midheight of the window (excluding the window-wall),

F_s = Window factor due to the light incident on the window from the sky, and

F_g = Window factor due to the light incident on the window from the ground.

The window factor for F_s (light incident on window from sky) has been pre-calculated and included in the documentation of the protractors. The window factor due to light incident on windows from the ground (F_g) is defined as follows:

$$F_g = \frac{(E_{sun} + E_{sky}) \times R_g \times G_{cf}}{E_{sky}} \qquad (15.2)$$

where:

E_{sun} = Illumination from the sun,

E_{sky} = Illumination from the sky,

R_g = Reflectance of ground surface, and

G_{cf} = Ground configuration factor (for a horizontal surface, G_{cf} = 0.5).

Daylight Factor (Clear Sky)

As with the B.R.S. protractor, the clear sky daylight factor is the sum of the sky component, external reflected component (if any), and internal reflected component.

Interior Illuminance (Clear Sky)

The interior illuminance is the product of the daylight factor times the exterior horizontal illuminance under an unobstructed sky (excluding direct sunlight) for the appropriate solar altitude and azimuth. The values for the exterior horizontal illuminance may be determined using the illuminance overlays (Appendix C) over the sun angle charts (Appendix B), or by using the equivalent sky luminance tables (clear sky) in figure 15-13. (The exterior horizontal illuminance in footcandles is numerically equal to the equivalent sky illuminance in footlamberts.)

The protractor methods above determine daylight illuminance for a single interior reference point but provide no information as to the distribution of illumination within the space. This can be determined only by calculating illuminance for many reference point locations within the space. These values can be plotted over a floor plan as contour lines of equal daylight factor or equal footcandles. Such contours are known as isolux lines or contours. Every window or skylight opening generates a characteristic pattern of isolux contours. The proportions and scale of these contour patterns vary with opening size and location.

GRAPHIC DAYLIGHTING DESIGN METHOD (GDDM)

Millet, et al. (1979) have developed a graphic method for predicting interior illumination for C.I.E. standard overcast sky conditions based on a collection of "daylighting footprints" (isolux contours). Brown, et al. (1982) have included a basic set of these for overcast sky conditions; others are under development. The method has the advantage of showing illuminance distribution as well as illuminance at any one point. Because illuminance from multiple sources is additive, "footprints" from multiple openings can be superimposed and combined numerically to generate new contours for the particular daylighting design.

Like the B.R.S. protractor method, the contours of the GDDM method represent a daylight factor that is the sum of the sky component, external reflected component, and internal reflected component. The GDDM method, shown in figures 15-15 to 15-22, is as follows:

1. Begin by constructing a plan with a projected outline of all window openings (see figure 15-14; skylights, though not shown in this example, would be projected straight down as a reflected ceiling plan).

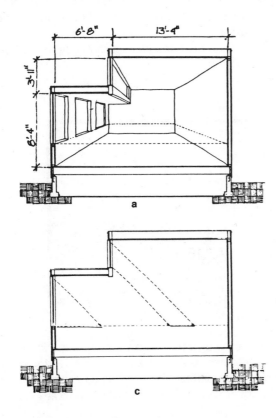

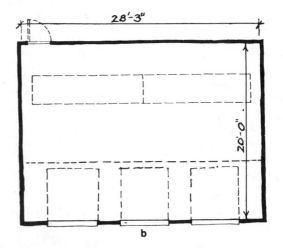

15-14. Construction of example plan with projected window openings: (a) section perspective; (b) section showing workplane and method of projecting window openings; (c) window openings projected onto workplane.

2. For each window and skylight, determine: (a) the ratio of height to width (*H/W*) and (b) the ratio of sill height above the work plane to height of window (*S/H*). For this example, for the lower windows, *H/W* = 1 and *S/H* = 0; for the clerestory windows, *H/W* = .25 and *S/H* = 2.

3. Select the appropriate daylight footprint for the computed values of H/W and S/H (figs. 15-15, 15-16).

15-15. Daylight footprint for window where H/W = 1 and S/H = 0. (Reprinted, by permission, from Millet, et al., 1979)

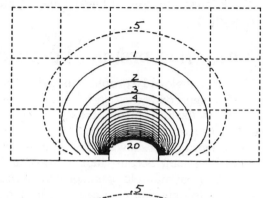

15-16. Daylight footprint for window where H/W = .25 and S/H = 2. (Reprinted, by permission, from Millet, et al., 1979)

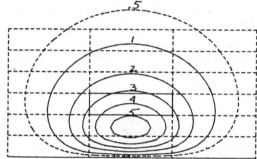

4. Transfer the daylight footprints by sketching them to scale on the plan (fig. 15-17). The solid rectangle near the center of the footprint represents the relative location of the projected window in plan. To avoid confusion, plot only three footprints on the plan; if necessary, use several plans that will be combined later.

15-17. Daylight footprints for lower three windows sketched on the plan. (Reprinted, by permission, from Millet, et al., 1979)

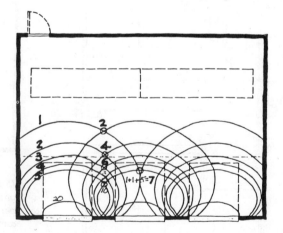

5. On a tracing overlay, draw a circle around each intersection of contours, and write the sum of the two contours next to the circle (fig. 15-18). Interpolate a new set of contours (figs. 15-19, 15-20). If necessary, repeat this process to combine several sets of footprints (fig. 15-21).

ANALYSIS

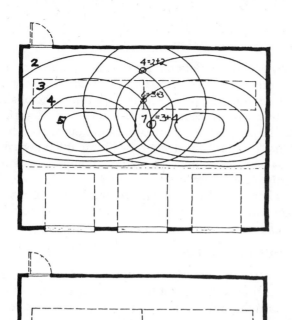

15-18. Daylight footprints for clerestory windows sketched on the plan. (Reprinted, by permission, from Millet, et al., 1979)

15-19. Daylight footprints for lower windows combined. (Reprinted, by permission, from Millet, et al., 1979)

15-20. Daylight footprints for clerestory windows combined. (Reprinted, by permission, from Millet, et al., 1979)

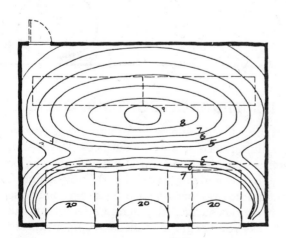

15-21. Final sky component after combining daylight footprints in figures 15-20 and 15-21. (Reprinted, by permission, from Millet, et al., 1979)

External Reflected Component

Millet, et al. (1979) proposed determining the effect of external obstructions by separating the affected window into two sections: one receiving only direct sky light and one receiving only reflected light from the obstruction. Each section is then treated as a separate window, and the daylight factor contours resulting from the obstructed part are reduced. This approach does not take into account the "occulus" effect whereby illumination near the window is affected less by an external obstruction than illumination deep in the room (from which point the sky may be totally obstructed). Thus the daylight footprint method is best suited for sites with minimal external obstructions.

In the accompanying example, the external reflected component is considered insignificant and thus excluded.

Internal Reflected Component

The internal reflected component may be presumed to be uniform throughout the room and calculated from a table (such as figure 15-10). Since this component is uniform throughout the room, the values of the contours are increased by this amount and the contours themselves need not be redrawn. In a similar manner, reductions in the daylight factor due to mullions, nonstandard glazing transmittance, and dirt accumulation can be deducted from the contour values.

Clear Sky GDDM

Millet, Adams, and Bedrick (1980) have described recent efforts to extend the daylight footprint method to clear sky conditions. The resulting patterns vary considerably with solar altitude and relative azimuth (fig. 15-22). The number of standard footprints required for clear sky conditions increases by a factor of 50 (compared with overcast sky conditions) to cover the significantly different combinations of solar azimuth and altitude conditions.

15-22. Comparison of clear sky daylight footprints for a square window for 60° solar altitude and: (a) 0° relative solar azimuth; (b) 180° relative solar azimuth. (After Millet, Adams, and Bedrick, 1980)

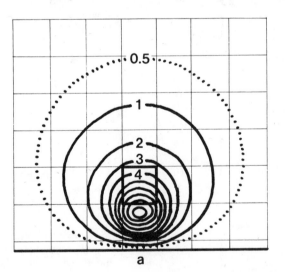
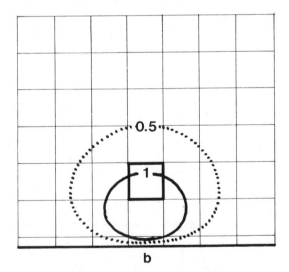

a · b

EXTERIOR ILLUMINANCE CONTOUR OVERLAYS

Selkowitz (1981) has described a series of illuminance contour overlays for estimating the illuminance on exterior surfaces. The overlays utilize equidistant projection and are thus compatible with the sun path charts (see Appendix B and L.O.F. sun angle calculator). They include C.I.E. standard clear sky and standard overcast sky conditions and can be used to determine illuminance for various surface slopes and orientations due to the beam- (direct sun only), sky-, and/or ground-reflected components of daylight. While

ANALYSIS

they are of limited direct applicability as a design tool, these illuminance values can be usefully applied to other calculation procedures (such as the lumen method described in chapter 16). Plots for 110-degree sloped surfaces are included to permit the rapid approximation of the average illuminance incident on a vertical surface (window) with an overhang. The procedures for using these overlays are described below and illustrated in figures 15-23 and 15-24. A complete set of full-size overlays is included in Appendix C.

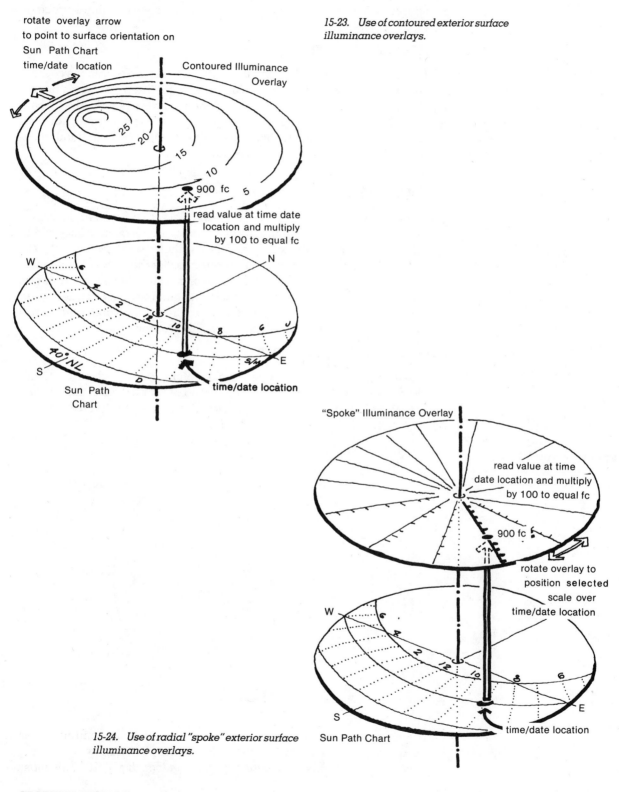

15-23. *Use of contoured exterior surface illuminance overlays.*

15-24. *Use of radial "spoke" exterior surface illuminance overlays.*

CONTOURED OVERLAYS

From Appendix C, select the overlay for the correct surface slope (horizontal, 45 degrees vertical, and 110 degrees for windows with overhangs) and daylight component (beam/sky/ground, and beam/sky). Place the overlay over the sun path chart for the correct latitude and rotate until the overlay arrow is pointing to the surface orientation. Find the sun's location for the selected time on the sun path chart and read the surface illuminance (in footcandles) from the contours on the overlay. In this example, a west-facing surface receives 900 footcandles at 9 A.M. on March 21.

RADIAL "SPOKE" OVERLAYS

Select the appropriate "spoke" on the overlay. Unlike the conditions covered by the contoured overlays, surface illuminances for these conditions are not dependent on orientation (i.e., if the illuminances were plotted, they would be concentric circles). Locate the sun's position on the sun path chart and rotate the overlay until the "spoke" intersects the sun position. Read the illuminance on the "spoke" at the sun position.

DOT CHARTS

Several authors (including Pleijel, 1954 and Turner, 1969) have described charts for graphically estimating the sky component for overcast sky conditions. The charts consist of a pattern of dots distributed as a function of the sky luminance distribution and the cosine correction for the angle of incidence. Each chart is overlayed with an obstruction mask showing the angular size and location of window/skylight openings visible from a given interior reference location. The number of dots visible in the opening area determines the sky component of the daylight factor at that location.

OVERCAST SKY DOT CHARTS

The present author has developed a sky component dot chart for C.I.E. standard overcast sky conditions using equidistant projection that is compatible with the sun path charts (Appendix B) and the L.O.F. sun angle calculator (fig. 15-25).

15-25. Sky component dot chart (C.I.E. standard overcast sky, equidistant projection). Each dot represents 0.1% daylight factor.

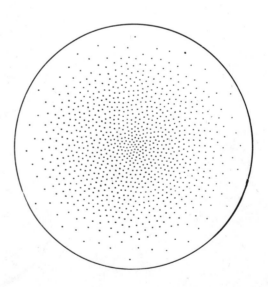

To use this overcast sky dot chart (or charts for other sky conditions), an obstruction mask for an interior reference location is plotted showing both sky and exterior obstructions visible through all openings (fig. 15-26). This mask

ANALYSIS

is overlayed on the dot chart (for overcast sky conditions orientation is not a factor, so the rotation of the chart is immaterial). The dots are counted in the visible sky area (figs. 15-27, 15-28), and divided by 10 to determine the sky component (as a percentage of exterior illuminance under an unobstructed sky). Full-size dot charts are reproduced in Appendix B.

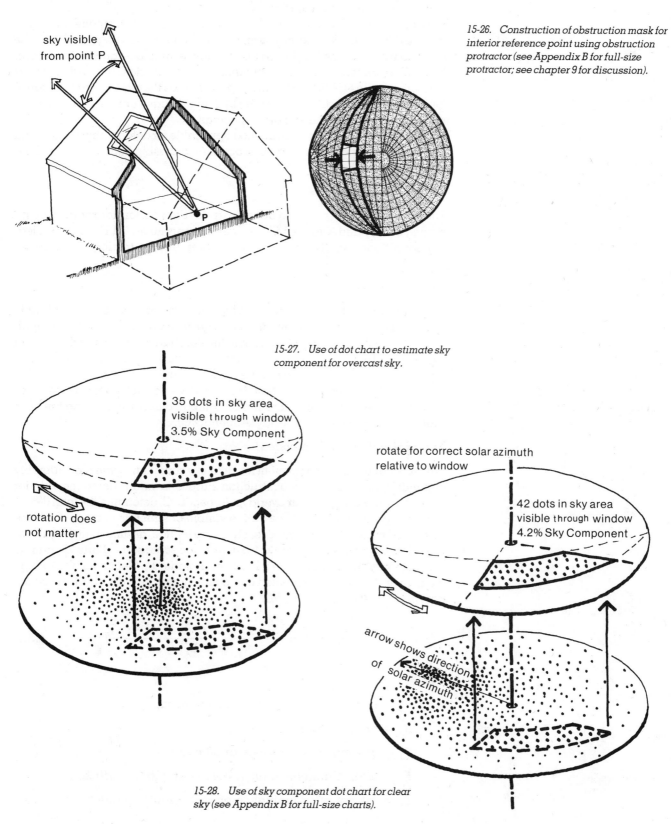

sky visible from point P

15-26. Construction of obstruction mask for interior reference point using obstruction protractor (see Appendix B for full-size protractor; see chapter 9 for discussion).

15-27. Use of dot chart to estimate sky component for overcast sky.

35 dots in sky area visible through window 3.5% Sky Component

rotation does not matter

rotate for correct solar azimuth relative to window

42 dots in sky area visible through window 4.2% Sky Component

arrow shows direction of solar azimuth

15-28. Use of sky component dot chart for clear sky (see Appendix B for full-size charts).

A different overlay (Appendix B) allows the estimation of the external reflected component for overcast skies. The dots within the area of the mask for external obstructions are counted and divided by 10 to equal the external reflected component (%). This ERC is based on an average obstruction reflectance of 0.2; if the obstruction reflectance is different than 0.2, multiply the result times the reflectance times 5.0.

Both the sky components and the external reflected components, as determined from the dot charts above, are for unglazed openings, and must be reduced using factors for glazing transmittance, mullions, and maintenance. Use 0.72% transmittance for double-glazed standard glass (this value is for a 60 degree angle of incidence, which approximates the average transmittance for distributed sources such as the sky and reflective obstructions); consult manufacturer's literature for other glazings.

There is no comparable dot method applicable for determining the internal reflected component. This may be approximated using figures 15-10 or 15-11, or by equation 15-1.

CLEAR SKY DOT CHARTS

The present author has also developed daylight factor dot charts for estimating the sky and external reflected components under C.I.E. standard clear sky conditions. An obstruction mask is prepared on tracing paper as described above.

Sky Component

From the sun path chart for the local latitude, determine the solar altitude angle. Select the sky component (clear sky) dot chart closest to this solar altitude. Place the obstruction mask over the dot chart, rotating it so that the dot chart arrow (representing the solar azimuth angle) is properly oriented relative to the mask. Divide the number of dots visible in the sky area(s) by 10 to equal the sky component (%). Note that this does not include the illuminance from direct beam sunlight; this can be computed separately using the horizontal beam illuminance overlay (Appendix C).

External Reflected Component

The external reflected component for clear sky conditions varies considerably depending on whether the obstruction surface is sunlit. Using the exterior surface illuminance contour overlays (Appendix C) determine the total (beam + sky + ground) illuminance on the visible obstruction surface, E_o. If the obstruction is randomly shaped, such as tree foliage, assume that the surface is vertical and faces the window. Next, from the same set of charts, determine the "sky-only" illuminance on a horizontal plane, E_s. Using the obstruction mask over the external reflected component (clear sky) dot chart, count the dots in the obstruction area, ND.

$$\text{ERC (\%)} = \frac{ND \times 0.1 \times R_o \times E_o \times T_g}{E_s} \qquad (15.3)$$

where:

ND = number of dots in obstruction area,

R_o = obstruction reflectance,

T_g = glazing transmittance at 60 degrees,

E_o = total illuminance on visible obstruction surface, and

E_s = "sky-only" illuminance on a horizontal plane.

REFERENCES

Brown, G., Reynolds, J., and Ubbelohde, S. *Inside Out.* New York: John Wiley and Sons, 1982.

Bryan, H., and Carlsberg, D. "Daylight Protractors: For Calculating the Effects of Clear Skies." In *Progress in Passive Solar Energy Systems,* edited by Hayes, J. and Winn, C., pp. 399–404. Boulder, CO: American Solar Energy Society, 1982.

Dufton, A. F. "Protractors for the Computation of Daylight Factors." D.S.I.R. Building Research Technical Paper No. 28. London: Her Majesty's Stationery Office (as cited by Bryan and Carlsberg, 1982), 1946.

Hopkinson, R. G., et al. *Architectural Physics: Lighting.* London: Her Majesty's Stationery Office, 1963.

Jones, B. F. "Very, Very Simple Hand Calculations for Daylighting." In *Proceedings of the International Daylighting Conference,* edited by Vonier, T., pp. 87–92. Washington, DC: American Institute of Architects Service Corporation, 1983.

Longmore, J. "BRS Daylight Protractors." Building Research Station, London: Her Majesty's Stationery Office, 1967.

Millet, M., Bedrick, J., Spencer, G., and Varey, B. "Designing for Daylight: A New Prediction Technique." In *Proceedings of the 3rd National Passive Solar Conference,* edited by Miller, H., et al. pp. 121–212. Boulder, CO: American Solar Energy Society, 1979.

Millet, M., Adams, C., and Bedrick, J. "Graphic Daylighting Design Method: Including Clear Sky Conditions." In *Proceedings of the 5th National Passive Solar Conference,* edited by Hayes, J. and Snyder, R., pp. 1183–1191. Boulder, CO: American Solar Energy Society, 1980.

Pleijel, G. "The Computation of Natural Radiation in Architecture and Town Planning." Meddelande (Bulletin) 25, Stockholm: Statens Namnd for Byggnadsforskning (as cited by Hopkinson, R. G., Petherbridge, P., and Longmore, J. *Daylighting.* London: William Heinemann Ltd., 1966).

Turner, D. P., ed. *Windows and Environment.* London: Architectural Press, 1971.

Chapter 16:
Illuminance Calculations

Two basic methods are presently available for manually calculating interior daylighting illuminance.

One, the *lumen method*, is based on calculating the illuminance on the glazing from available weather data for clear and overcast conditions, and from that determining interior illuminance at selected locations based on *utilization factors* derived from empirical testing. The lumen method has been adopted by the North American Illumination Society as part of their recommended practice of daylighting (Daylighting Committee of the I.E.S., 1979). This method is primarily used in the United States. It was derived from experimental studies and is therefore accurate only for applicable window configurations and calculation points within a room.

The other method, the *daylight factor method*, is used in Europe and recommended by the C.I.E. It is based on fundamental theoretical principles and determines the interior horizontal illuminance as a percentage of that on the exterior by adding up the contribution from sky, exterior, and interior reflections. The contribution of the sky and exterior reflections is computed as a function of source luminance, angular (apparent) size, and relative location (cosine effect). Because of this, the daylight factor method is applicable to a larger variety of window sizes, room configurations, and reference point locations than the lumen method.

THE LUMEN METHOD

Because the lumen method is based on a process of interpolating actual test data, its accuracy is limited to the general type of room, fenestration, and conditions actually tested (e.g., a room in which the top of the window is at the ceiling level, the sill is at the desk height, and so forth). With care, however, these conditions can be expanded to consider a wide variety of building designs.

Interior illumination is determined by calculating the contributions of various components (windows, skylights, sky and ground contributions, etc.) and adding them together.

LUMEN METHOD: SIDELIGHTING

The following is a summary of the I.E.S. lumen method for sidelighting. (For a more detailed explanation, especially regarding other methods for considering the effects of overhangs, see I.E.S., 1981.)

The side window calculations yield illuminances at three reference locations in the room at the thirty-inch workplane: "maximum" (five feet from the window), "middle," and "minimum" (five feet from the wall opposite the window).

A. Illuminance from an overcast sky, without window controls

C

	Room Width	6.1 M (20 FT)		9.1 M (30 FT)		12.2 M (40 FT)	
	Wall Reflectance (per cent)	70	30	70	30	70	30
	M FT						
MAX	6.1 20	.0276	.0251	.0191	.0173	.0143	.0137
	9.1 30	.0272	.0248	.0188	.0172	.0137	.0131
	12.2 40	.0269	.0246	.0182	.0171	.0133	.0130
MID	6.1 20	.0159	.0117	.0101	.0087	.0081	.0071
	9.1 30	.0058	.0050	.0054	.0040	.0034	.0033
	12.2 40	.0039	.0027	.0030	.0023	.0022	.0019
MIN	6.1 20	.0087	.0053	.0063	.0043	.0050	.0037
	9.1 30	.0032	.0019	.0029	.0017	.0020	.0014
	12.2 40	.0019	.0009	.0016	.0009	.0012	.0008

K

	Room Width	Ceiling Height 2.4 M (8 FT)		3 M (10 FT)		3.7 M (12 FT)		4.3 M (14 FT)	
	Wall Reflectance (per cent)	70	30	70	30	70	30	70	30
	M FT								
MAX	6.1 20	.125	.129	.121	.123	.111	.111	.0991	.0973
	9.1 30	.122	.131	.122	.121	.111	.111	.0945	.0973
	12.2 40	.145	.133	.131	.126	.111	.111	.0973	.0982
MID	6.1 20	.0908	.0982	.107	.115	.111	.111	.105	.122
	9.1 30	.156	.102	.0939	.113	.111	.111	.121	.134
	12.2 40	.106	.0948	.123	.107	.111	.111	.135	.127
MIN	6.1 20	.0908	.102	.0951	.114	.111	.111	.118	.134
	9.1 30	.0924	.119	.101	.114	.111	.111	.125	.126
	12.2 40	.111	.0926	.125	.109	.111	.111	.133	.130

B. Illuminance from a clear sky, without window controls

C

	Room Width	70	30	70	30	70	30
	M FT						
MAX	6.1 20	.0206	.0173	.0143	.0123	.0110	.0098
	9.1 30	.0203	.0173	.0137	.0120	.0098	.0092
	12.2 40	.0200	.0168	.0131	.0119	.0096	.0091
MID	6.1 20	.0153	.0104	.0100	.0079	.0083	.0067
	9.1 30	.0082	.0054	.0062	.0043	.0046	.0037
	12.2 40	.0052	.0032	.0040	.0028	.0029	.0023
MIN	6.1 20	.0106	.0060	.0079	.0049	.0067	.0043
	9.1 30	.0054	.0028	.0047	.0023	.0032	.0021
	12.2 40	.0031	.0014	.0027	.0013	.0021	.0012

K

	Room Width	70	30	70	30	70	30	70	30
	M FT								
MAX	6.1 20	.145	.155	.129	.132	.111	.111	.101	.0982
	9.1 30	.141	.149	.125	.130	.111	.111	.0954	.101
	12.2 40	.157	.157	.135	.134	.111	.111	.0964	.0991
MID	6.1 20	.110	.128	.116	.126	.111	.111	.103	.108
	9.1 30	.106	.125	.110	.129	.111	.111	.112	.120
	12.2 40	.117	.118	.122	.118	.111	.111	.123	.122
MIN	6.1 20	.105	.129	.112	.130	.111	.111	.111	.116
	9.1 30	.0994	.144	.107	.126	.111	.111	.107	.124
	12.2 40	.119	.116	.130	.118	.111	.111	.120	.118

C. Illuminance from a uniform ground, without window controls

C

	Room Width	70	30	70	30	70	30
	M FT						
MAX	6.1 20	.0147	.0112	.0102	.0088	.0081	.0071
	9.1 30	.0141	.0112	.0098	.0088	.0077	.0070
	12.2 40	.0137	.0112	.0093	.0086	.0072	.0069
MID	6.1 20	.0128	.0090	.0094	.0071	.0073	.0060
	9.1 30	.0083	.0057	.0062	.0048	.0050	.0041
	12.2 40	.0055	.0037	.0044	.0033	.0042	.0026
MIN	6.1 20	.0106	.0071	.0082	.0054	.0067	.0044
	9.1 30	.0051	.0026	.0041	.0023	.0033	.0021
	12.2 40	.0029	.0018	.0026	.0012	.0022	.0011

K

	Room Width	70	30	70	30	70	30	70	30
	M FT								
MAX	6.1 20	.124	.206	.140	.135	.111	.111	.0909	.0859
	9.1 30	.182	.188	.140	.143	.111	.111	.0918	.0878
	12.2 40	.124	.182	.140	.142	.111	.111	.0936	.0879
MID	6.1 20	.123	.145	.122	.129	.111	.111	.100	.0945
	9.1 30	.0966	.104	.107	.112	.111	.111	.110	.105
	12.2 40	.0790	.0786	.0999	.106	.111	.111	.118	.118
MIN	6.1 20	.0994	.108	.110	.114	.111	.111	.107	.104
	9.1 30	.0816	.0822	.0984	.105	.111	.111	.121	.116
	12.2 40	.0700	.0656	.0946	.0986	.111	.111	.125	.132

D. Illuminance from the ''uniform sky'', without diffuse window shades

C

	Room Width	70	30	70	30	70	30
	M FT						
MAX	6.1 20	.0247	.0217	.0174	.0152	.0128	.0120
	9.1 30	.0241	.0214	.0166	.0151	.0120	.0116
	12.2 40	.0237	.0212	.0161	.0150	.0118	.0113
MID	6.1 20	.0169	.0122	.0110	.0092	.0089	.0077
	9.1 30	.0078	.0060	.0067	.0048	.0044	.0041
	12.2 40	.0053	.0033	.0039	.0028	.0029	.0024
MIN	6.1 20	.0108	.0066	.0080	.0052	.0063	.0047
	9.1 30	.0047	.0026	.0042	.0023	.0029	.0020
	12.2 40	.0027	.0013	.0022	.0012	.0018	.0011

K

	Room Width	70	30	70	30	70	30	70	30
	M FT								
MAX	6.1 20	.145	.154	.123	.128	.111	.111	.0991	.0964
	9.1 30	.141	.151	.126	.128	.111	.111	.0945	.0964
	12.2 40	.159	.157	.137	.127	.111	.111	.0973	.0964
MID	6.1 20	.101	.116	.115	.125	.111	.111	.101	.110
	9.1 30	.0952	.113	.105	.122	.111	.111	.110	.122
	12.2 40	.111	.105	.124	.107	.111	.111	.130	.124
MIN	6.1 20	.0974	.111	.107	.121	.111	.111	.112	.119
	9.1 30	.0956	.125	.103	.117	.111	.111	.115	.125
	12.2 40	.111	.105	.125	.111	.111	.111	.133	.124

16-1. Coefficients of utilization. (Reprinted, by permission, from I.E.S., 1981)

1. Determine the illuminance on vertical (90-degree slope) glazing surface due to combined sun (if any) and sky (E_s), and due to ground reflectance (E_g) only for the wall orientation and latitude, using the illuminance overlays (Appendix C) over the sun angle charts (Appendix B). If a significant overhang exists, use the illuminance values for a 120 degree slope. (Note that the I.E.S., 1979, procedure for determining glazing illuminance involves the use of graphs and a different method for calculating the effect of overhangs. The above method is based on more recently developed sky models. Use of the 120-degree slope yields similar results to the more involved I.E.S. method for moderate, sunshading overhangs.)

2. Calculate the net vertical glazing area in square feet (A_g) (approximately 75 percent of gross window area).

3. From figure 16-1a–b, look up C_{max}, C_{mid}, C_{min}, K_{max}, K_{mid}, and K_{min} sky-contributed coefficients of utilization for the room conditions nearest to those being designed.

4. From figure 16-1c–e, look up C_{max}, C_{mid}, C_{min}, K_{max}, K_{mid}, and K_{min} ground-contributed coefficients of utilization for the room conditions nearest to those being designed.

5. From figure 16-2, look up the *LLF* (light loss factor).

16-2. *Light loss factors. (After Kroner, et al., 1981)*

	Office (vert.)	Factory (vert.)	Factory (30° slope)	Factory (60° slope)	Factory (horiz.)
Average over 6 months	83%	71%	65%	58%	54%
After 3 months	82%	69%	62%	54%	50%
After 6 months	73%	55%	45%	39%	34%

6. Determine the glazing transmission factor (*TG*) from manufacturer's data (0.9 for single clear, 0.81 for double clear).

7. Determine the transmission factor (*TD*) for any shades or drapes not previously accounted for when selecting the *C* and *K* coefficients of utilizations from manufacturer's literature. If none, use 1.0.

8. Calculate the sky-contributed interior illuminance for max, mid, and min:

$$E_{int, sky} = E_s \times A_g \times C \times K \times LLF \times TG \times TD. \quad (16.1)$$

9. Calculate the ground-contributed interior illuminance for max, mid, and min:

$$E_{int, gnd} = E_s \times A_g \times C \times K \times LLF \times TG \times TD. \quad (16.2)$$

10. Determine the total interior illuminance at max, mid, and min by adding the sky-contribution (step 8) and the ground-contribution (step 9) components of each.

LUMEN METHOD: TOPLIGHTING

The lumen method for toplighting determines the average illuminance on the workplane due to horizontal (or near horizontal) roof openings. The calculation procedure may be summarized as follows:

1. Calculate ratio of net to gross area of the top light (*AR*). This is typically 0.6 to 0.9.

2. From figure 16-3, determine the light well efficiency (*LE*) for the well index.

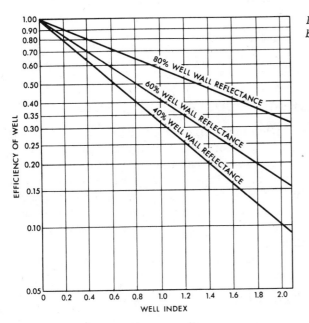

16-3. Light well efficiency factor. (Reprinted, by permission, from I.E.S., 1981)

16-4. Room coefficients of utilization for toplighting, based on 20 percent floor reflectance. (Reprinted, by permission, from I.E.S., 1981)

Room Ratio	Ceiling Reflectance			
	75 Per Cent		50 Per Cent	
	Wall Reflectance			
	50 Per Cent	30 Per Cent	50 Per Cent	30 Per Cent
0.6	.52	.49	.52	.49
0.8	.63	.60	.62	.59
1.0	.70	.67	.69	.63
1.25	.73	.71	.72	.70
1.5	.79	.77	.77	.72
2.0	.82	.80	.81	.79
2.5	.88	.83	.87	.82
3.0	.90	.88	.89	.87
4.0	.92	.89	.90	.88

3. Determine the *TG* (transmission of the glazing medium) from the manufacturer's literature.

4. Determine the transmission effectiveness of louvers or other controls (*TE*). (Prismatic lenses = 0.9, white translucent diffuser = 0.5, translucent white louvers = 0.7.)

5. Calculate the toplight transmittance (*TT*): AR × LE × TG × TE.

6. Calculate the room ratio:

$$RR = \frac{w \times l}{H_c \times (w + l)} \qquad (16.3)$$

where:

$$H_c = \text{room height} - \text{workplane height,}$$
$$w = \text{room width, and}$$
$$l = \text{room length.}$$

7. Look up the *CU* (coefficient of utilization) for this room ratio (fig. 16-4).

ILLUMINANCE CALCULATIONS

8. Select a *LLF* (light loss factor) from fig. 16-2.

9. Calculate room area (*RA*) in square feet.

10. Determine horizontal exterior illuminance (*ESS*) from sky and sun using illuminance overlays (from Appendix C) over sun path charts (from Appendix B).

11. Determine the net area of toplight (*AN*) in square feet (from manufacturer's literature).

12. Calculate the average interior illuminance due to toplighting (E_{top}) (in footcandles) as follows:

$$E_{top} = \frac{CU \times LLF \times ESS \times AN}{RA} \tag{16.4}$$

DAYLIGHT FACTOR METHOD (OVERCAST SKY)

The daylight factor (as used in this method) is defined as the ratio of horizontal interior illuminance at a selected point *P* to horizontal exterior illuminance under an unobstructed overcast sky (expressed as a percentage). It is computed by adding up the contribution of three components: the sky component (*SC* = direct light from the skydome), the external reflected component (*ERC* = direct light reflected from external obstructions above the horizon line), and the internal reflected component (*IRC* = light reflected from interior room surfaces). Tables for determining the contribution of the *SC*, *ERC*, and *IRC* for vertical windows have been developed by the Building Research Station (Hopkinson, Longmore, & Graham, 1958).

SKY COMPONENT (OVERCAST SKY)

The sky component table (fig. 16-5) gives values for the sky component for a particular relationship between the window and reference point *P* (which is always assumed to be located normal to one of the bottom corners of the window). Values for *H* (height of window head above horizontal reference plane), *D* (normal distance from window to *P*), and *H* (width of window to side of *P*) are used to determine the sky component from the table.

16-5. *Table of sky components (%) for vertical glazed windows for C.I.E. standard overcast sky. (Reprinted from Hopkinson, 1963, courtesy of Her Majesty's Stationery Office)*

WIDTH OF WINDOW TO ONE SIDE OF NORMAL : DISTANCE FROM WINDOW

RATIO H/D — HEIGHT OF WINDOW HEAD ABOVE WORKING PLANE : DISTANCE FROM WINDOW

RATIO H/D	0·1	0·2	0·3	0·4	0·5	0·6	0·7	0·8	0·9	1·0	1·1	1·2	1·3	1·4	1·5	1·6	1·7	1·8	1·9	2·0	2·2	2·4	2·6	2·8	3·0	3·5	4·0	5·0	∞
0·1	0·01	0·03	0·06	0·10	0·16	0·24	0·33	0·42	0·50	0·57	0·65	0·71	0·77	0·82	0·86	0·90	0·94	0·97	1·0	1·0	1·1	1·1	1·1	1·1	1·2	1·2	1·2	1·2	1·3
0·2	0·02	0·06	0·14	0·25	0·39	0·53	0·68	0·83	0·99	1·1	1·3	1·4	1·5	1·6	1·7	1·8	1·9	2·0	2·0	2·1	2·1	2·2	2·2	2·3	2·3	2·4	2·4	2·5	
0·3	0·02	0·09	0·18	0·34	0·52	0·74	0·97	1·2	1·5	1·7	1·9	2·1	2·3	2·4	2·6	2·7	2·8	2·9	3·0	3·1	3·2	3·3	3·4	3·4	3·5	3·6	3·6	3·7	3·7
0·4	0·03	0·11	0·26	0·45	0·70	0·98	1·3	1·6	1·9	2·2	2·5	2·7	2·9	3·2	3·3	3·5	3·6	3·8	3·9	4·0	4·1	4·3	4·4	4·5	4·5	4·6	4·7	4·8	4·9
0·5	0·03	0·12	0·30	0·54	0·82	1·2	1·5	1·9	2·2	2·6	3·0	3·3	3·6	3·8	4·0	4·2	4·4	4·6	4·7	4·8	5·0	5·2	5·3	5·4	5·5	5·7	5·8	5·9	5·9
0·6	0·04	0·14	0·34	0·62	0·97	1·3	1·7	2·2	2·6	3·0	3·4	3·8	4·1	4·4	4·6	4·9	5·1	5·3	5·4	5·6	5·8	6·0	6·2	6·3	6·4	6·6	6·7	6·8	6·9
0·7	0·04	0·16	0·38	0·70	1·0	1·5	1·9	2·4	2·8	3·3	3·8	4·2	4·5	4·8	5·1	5·4	5·6	5·8	6·0	6·2	6·4	6·6	6·8	7·0	7·1	7·3	7·4	7·6	7·7
0·8	0·05	0·20	0·42	0·75	1·1	1·6	2·1	2·6	3·1	3·6	4·3	4·8	5·2	5·6	5·9	6·2	6·5	6·7	6·9	7·1	7·4	7·7	7·9	8·1	8·2	8·5	8·7	8·8	9·0
0·9	0·05	0·21	0·44	0·82	1·2	1·7	2·2	2·7	3·3	3·8	4·6	5·0	5·5	5·9	6·2	6·5	6·8	7·1	7·3	7·5	7·9	8·1	8·4	8·6	8·7	9·0	9·2	9·4	9·6
1·0	0·05	0·21	0·47	0·89	1·3	1·8	2·3	2·9	3·4	4·0	4·6	5·0	5·5	5·9	6·2	6·5	6·8	7·1	7·3	7·5	8·7	9·1	9·3	9·6	9·8	10·1	10·3	10·5	10·7
1·2	0·06	0·22	0·49	0·92	1·4	1·9	2·5	3·1	3·7	4·3	4·9	5·4	5·9	6·4	6·8	7·2	7·5	7·8	8·1	8·3	8·7	9·1	9·3	9·6	9·8	10·1	10·3	10·5	10·7
1·4	0·06	0·22	0·50	0·95	1·4	1·9	2·5	3·2	3·8	4·5	5·1	5·7	6·2	6·7	7·1	7·5	7·8	8·2	8·5	8·7	9·1	9·5	9·8	10·0	10·2	10·6	10·9	11·1	11·6
1·6	0·06	0·22	0·50	0·95	1·4	2·0	2·6	3·3	3·9	4·6	5·3	5·9	6·4	7·0	7·4	7·8	8·2	8·5	8·8	9·1	9·6	10·0	10·2	10·5	10·7	11·1	11·4	11·7	12·2
1·8	0·06	0·22	0·51	0·96	1·5	2·0	2·6	3·3	4·0	4·7	5·4	6·0	6·6	7·2	7·6	8·1	8·5	8·8	9·2	9·5	10·0	10·4	10·8	11·1	11·3	11·8	12·0	12·3	12·6
2·0	0·07	0·23	0·51	0·96	1·5	2·0	2·6	3·3	4·0	4·7	5·4	6·1	6·7	7·3	7·8	8·2	8·6	9·0	9·4	9·7	10·2	10·7	11·1	11·4	11·7	12·2	12·4	12·7	13·0
2·5	0·07	0·23	0·52	0·97	1·5	2·1	2·6	3·3	4·0	4·8	5·5	6·2	6·8	7·4	7·9	8·4	8·8	9·2	9·6	9·9	10·5	11·0	11·4	11·7	12·0	12·6	12·9	13·3	13·7
3·0	0·07	0·23	0·52	0·97	1·5	2·1	2·7	3·4	4·1	4·8	5·6	6·3	6·9	7·5	8·0	8·5	8·9	9·3	9·7	10·0	10·7	11·2	11·7	12·0	12·4	12·9	13·3	13·7	14·2
4·0	0·07	0·23	0·52	0·97	1·5	2·1	2·7	3·4	4·1	4·9	5·6	6·3	6·9	7·5	8·0	8·6	9·0	9·4	9·8	10·1	10·8	11·3	11·8	12·2	12·5	13·2	13·5	14·0	14·6
6·0	0·08	0·24	0·53	0·98	1·5	2·1	2·8	3·4	4·2	5·0	5·7	6·3	6·9	7·6	8·1	8·6	9·1	9·5	9·9	10·2	10·9	11·4	11·9	12·3	12·6	13·2	13·6	14·1	14·9
∞	0·08	0·24	0·53	0·98	1·5	2·1	2·8	3·4	4·2	5·0	5·7	6·3	7·0	7·6	8·1	8·6	9·1	9·5	9·9	10·3	10·9	11·5	11·9	12·3	12·7	13·3	13·7	14·2	15·0
0	6°	11°	17°	22°	27°	31°	35°	39°	42°	45°	48°	50°	52°	54°	56°	58°	60°	61°	62°	63°	66°	67°	69°	70°	72°	74°	76°	79°	90°

ANGLE OF OBSTRUCTION

ANALYSIS

To determine the sky component for a "standard" window (as shown in figure 16-6), calculate the *W/D* and the *H/D*, and look up the sky component from figure 16-5 or 16-7.

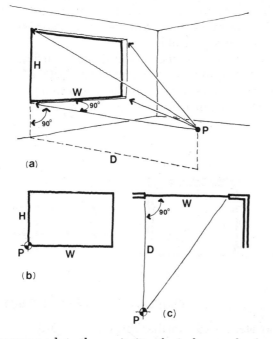

(a)

(b)

(c)

16-6. *Perspective and elevation of "standard" window showing H, D, and W, in relationship to reference point P.*

In order to accommodate the majority of window and reference location combinations that do not match the "standard" relationship, the sky component (SC) for the real window is determined by adding and/or subtracting the SC of two or more hypothetical "standard" windows, as shown in figure 16-8. Notice that only areas of the window where the sky is visible from *P* are included in the SC (i.e., window areas through which external obstructions are seen are excluded).

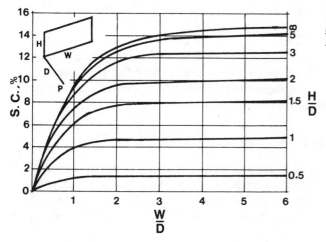

16-7. *Graph of sky components (%) for vertical glazed windows for C.I.E. standard overcast sky. (After Hopkinson, 1966)*

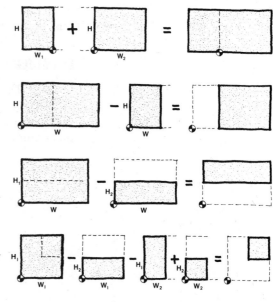

16-8. *Method of determining the sky component of a "real" window by adding and/or subtracting the sky components of two or more hypothetical "standard" windows.*

EXTERNAL REFLECTED COMPONENT (OVERCAST SKY)

To determine the ERC, determine the SC for the window area through which external obstructions are visible from *P*, and multiply this value times 0.1 (this assumes an approximately vertical surface with an average reflectance of 20 percent, illuminated by half of the skydome). Window areas extending below the height of *P* (horizontal reference plane) are ignored because that area is not visible from the reference plane.

If the window area used for the ERC is smaller than that used for the SC, it can be ignored as insignificant. Note, however, that the SC is still based on the area of sky visible above the obstruction (ignoring the contribution of an obstruction must not result in an increase in the SC).

16-9. Determining the "standard" window to be used for the ERC.

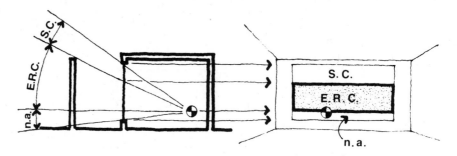

INTERNAL REFLECTED COMPONENT (OVERCAST SKY)

The IRC (%) is determined from the table in figure 15-10.

DAYLIGHT FACTOR (OVERCAST SKY)

The uncorrected daylight factor (DF) = SC + ERC + IRC. This is corrected by multiplying by one or more of the following correction factors:

■ Dirt factor (0.5 for industrial atmosphere to 0.9 for regular maintenance)

■ Glazing transmittance if other than clear single (see manufacturer's data)

■ Area of mullions (0.75 to 0.9)

INTERIOR ILLUMINANCE (OVERCAST SKY)

To determine the interior illuminance under an overcast sky for a particular time and date, use the illuminance overlay (for horizontal slope, overcast sky, Appendix C) over the appropriate sun angle chart (Appendix B), and multiply this illuminance (horizontal exterior) times the DF.

DAYLIGHT FACTOR METHOD (CLEAR SKY)

Bryan (1983) has developed a series of sixty-five nomographs for determining the sky component for clear sky conditions. An example can be found in figure 16-10. *W/D* and *H/D* are determined as above for overcast sky conditions. The procedures for determining the ERC and IRC are described in chapter 15.

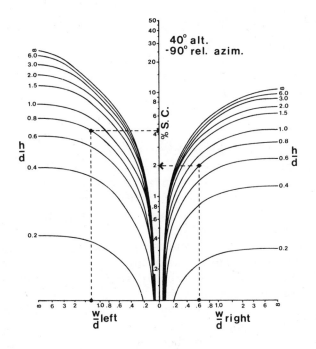

16-10. Nomograph for determining sky component for clear sky conditions: solar altitude = 40°; relative solar azimuth = −90°. (After Kroner, Bryan, and Leslie, 1981)

REFERENCES

Bryan, H. "Development of an Integrated Design Methodology." In *Progress in Passive Solar Energy Systems*, Vol. 8, pt. 1, edited by Hayes, J., and Anrejko, D. A. Boulder CO: American Solar Energy Society, 1983.

Daylighting Committee of the I.E.S. "Recommended Practice of Daylighting." In *Lighting Design and Applications*, Vol. 9, p. 25., 1979.

Kaufman, J. *I.E.S. Lighting Handbook, 1981 Reference Volume.* New York: Illuminating Engineering Society of North America, 1981.

Chapter 17
Annual Savings

The preceding portions of this book have addressed the quantity and quality of daylight illumination at one specific instant in time. They have attempted to define the illumination performance of a building design under a set of prescribed sky conditions (overcast or clear). This results in if . . . then conclusions: "*if* a 1000 footlambert equivalent overcast sky condition exists, *then* daylight illuminance at a point will be 27 footcandles, and 13 footcandles additional electric illumination will be required to reach the design illuminance." While these if . . . then conclusions are useful for comparing design alternatives, they tell us nothing about the annual savings that can be expected due to local climatic conditions.

To predict annual lighting energy savings, it is necessary to know the relative frequency of various sky conditions during the hours of operation of the building. The traditional method has been to base projections on the relative frequency of clear and overcast conditions as recorded by weather bureau observers. This method may be further refined if this information is available for various workday time periods; estimates of this data have been developed recently and considerably improve the potential accuracy of such annual estimates. Researchers have also begun to question the applicability of weather station observation data for daylighting calculations.

ANNUAL DAYLIGHTING PERCENTAGE

Robbins and Hunter (1982) have developed a method for estimating the annual energy savings attributed to daylight based on predicting the percentage of the year that the electric lighting system is not in use. This percentage is a function of the electric lighting control strategy used (dimming or various types of switching), standard working hours, local weather data, and the amount of daylight (expressed as a daylight factor) reaching a given reference point in the building. The weather data used are based on recent daylight and sunlight availability research for selected cities in the U.S. (Robbins and Hunter, 1982b and 1982c). The method is as follows:

A *standard work year* is defined as 365 days for any of 12 workday periods. These include combinations of three beginning times (0700, 0800, and 0900) and four closing times (1600, 1700, 1800, and 1900).

The daylight factor (as used in this method) is defined as the ratio of horizontal interior illuminance to glazing plane exterior illuminance (expressed as a percentage), or:

$$DF\,(\%) \;=\; \frac{E_{int}}{E_{ext}} \;\times\; 100\%. \qquad (17.1)$$

The design illuminance E_{des} represents the illuminance value used by the designer to design the lighting systems for a room or space, including both electric and daylight. Figure 17-1 represents this graphically for a 0800–1800 workday. Different values of E_{des} can exist for different rooms or spaces in a building.

Equation 17-1 can be rewritten to determine the interior illuminance if the DF and the exterior illuminance are known:

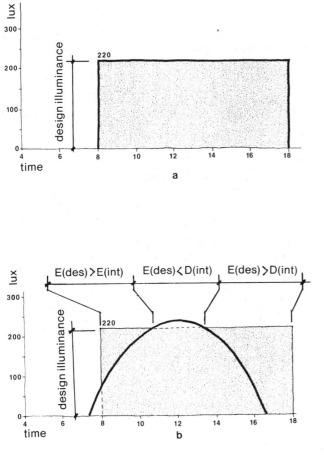

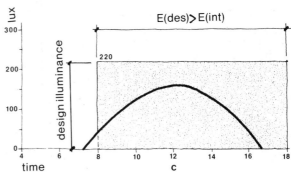

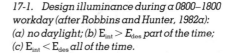

17-1. *Design illuminance during a 0800–1800 workday (after Robbins and Hunter, 1982a): (a) no daylight; (b) $E_{int} > E_{des}$ part of the time; (c) $E_{int} < E_{des}$ all of the time.*

$$E_{int} = E_{ext} \times \frac{DF}{100} \qquad (17.2)$$

Supplementary electric lighting can be controlled by continuous dimming or by switching. The switching can be two-step (off/on), three-step (off, half on, and all on), four-step (off, one-third on, two-thirds on, and all on), and five-step (off, one-fourth on, one-half on, three-fourths on, and all on). Figure 17-2 shows how these various control strategies respond to various daylighting levels.

Begin by calculating the exterior threshold illuminance (ET) required to yield the interior design illuminance E_{des}:

$$ET = \frac{E_{des}}{DF} \times 100 \qquad (17.3)$$

Next, look up the maximum exterior illuminance (E_{max} = largest single illuminance value occurring during a standard work year, expressed in lux) from Robbins and Hunter (1982a) for diffuse, illuminance, horizontal, clear conditions. A sample portion of this data for Denver (0800–1800) is shown in figure 17-3. For Denver for this workday period, E_{max} = 16,594 lux. (1 footcandle = 10.76 lux; 1 lux = 0.093 footcandles.) Two possible scenarios allow daylight illumination to displace electric lighting energy: (1) where the threshold illuminance (ET) is greater than the maximum exterior illuminance (E_{max}) during some or all of the work year, and (2) where ET is always less than E_{max} during the entire work year.

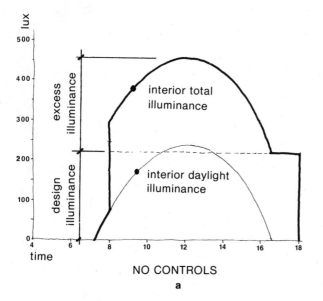

NO CONTROLS

a

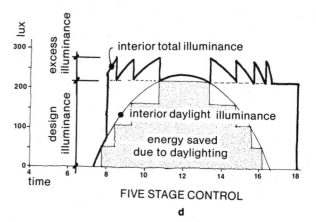

17-2. *Response of various control strategies to a selected interior design illuminance for various daylight conditions (after Robbins and Hunter, 1982a): (a) no controls; (b) two-stage (on/off) control; (c) three-stage control; (d) five-stage control; (e) continuous dimming.*

FIVE STAGE CONTROL

d

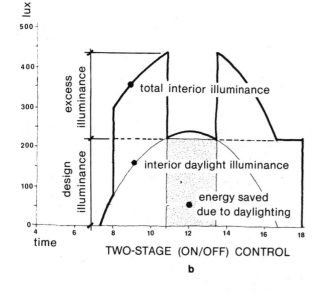

TWO-STAGE (ON/OFF) CONTROL

b

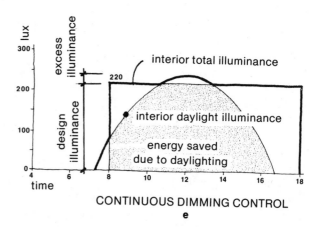

CONTINUOUS DIMMING CONTROL

e

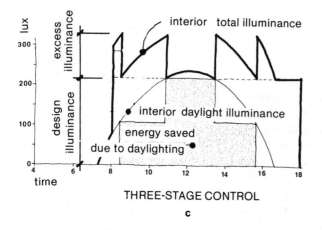

THREE-STAGE CONTROL

c

CASE 1: WHERE ET < E_{max} SOME OR ALL OF THE WORK YEAR

Calculate the fraction of lighting energy saved when $E_{int} > E_{des}$ using data from Robbins and Hunter (1982a):

$$F = C_0 + (C_1 \times ET) + (C_2 \times ET^2) + (C_3 \times ET^3) \quad (17.4)$$

where:

$$F = \text{fraction of the work year that } E_{des} \text{ is exceeded,}$$
$$C_0, C_1, \text{ and } C_2 = \text{dimensionless equation coefficients (from Robbins and Hunter, 1982a), and}$$
$$ET = \text{threshold illuminance.}$$

For example, assume diffuse, clear sky, Denver data, a DF of 2.75 at a given point in a room due to horizontal skylights (determined by previous methods from chapters 13, 14, or 15), and a design illuminance at that point of 220 lux (20 footcandles). The estimate of the lighting energy saved when the sky is clear can be determined by Equations 17-3 and 17-4 as follows:

$$ET = \frac{220}{2.75} \times 100 = 8000 \text{fc.}$$

$$
\begin{aligned}
F_{clr} = {} & 92.69 + (1.793 \times 10^{-3}) \times (8000) \\
& + (-1.052 \times 10^{-6}) \times (8000)^2 \\
& + (3.803 \times 10^{-4}) \times (8000)^3 \\
= {} & 59.17\%.
\end{aligned}
$$

(Note: the equation coefficients in the Robbins-Hunter tables are presented in scientific notation: 9.23E + 02 = 923.0.)

Thus, for 59.17% of the standard work year under clear sky conditions, daylighting alone would meet the design illuminance of 220 lux (20 footcandles). Using the coefficients from figure 17-3 for horizontal overcast, F_{oc} is computed in the same way as F_{clr}:

$$
\begin{aligned}
F_{oc} = {} & 87.72 + (-8.364 \times 10^{-4}) \times (8000) \\
& + (-1494 \times 10^{-7}) \times (8000)^2 \\
& + (2.693 \times 10^{-12}) \times (8000)^3 \\
= {} & 72.84\%.
\end{aligned}
$$

The total fraction of lighting energy saved (F) is the average of F_{clr} and F_{oc} weighted by the fractions of the year that are clear (P_{clr}) and overcast (P_{oc}), calculated as follows:

$$F = F_{clr} \times P_{clr} + F_{oc} \times P_{oc}. \quad (17.5)$$

The value for P_{clr} for Denver, 0800–1800 is found in Robbins and Hunter (1982b) to equal 0.750, and

$$P_{oc} = 1 - P_{clr} = 0.250.$$

Thus:

$$
\begin{aligned}
F = {} & 59.17\% \times .750 + 72.84\% \times .250 \\
= {} & 62.59\%.
\end{aligned}
$$

DENVER ,CO	ILLUMINANCE	SKY CONDITION	ORIENTATION	C0	C1	C2	C3	MEAN	G/D	MAXIMUM
(0800-1800)	DIRECT	CLEAR	NORMAL	9.861E+01	-9.771E-04	3.173E-08	-3.377E-13	70580		96311
	GLOBAL	CLEAR	NORTH	9.240E+01	4.458E-04	-6.111E-07	1.784E-11	10002	2.249	20181
	GLOBAL	CLEAR	NE/NW	1.134E+02	-7.829E-03	1.911E-07	-1.574E-12	13343	3.000	53439
	GLOBAL	CLEAR	EAST/WEST	1.019E+02	-4.479E-03	8.830E-08	-6.363E-13	23636	5.313	73415
	GLOBAL	CLEAR	SE/SW	9.686E+01	-2.757E-03	5.339E-08	-4.545E-13	33448	7.519	75814
	GLOBAL	CLEAR	SOUTH	9.340E+01	-5.919E-04	-1.711E-08	1.210E-13	38119	8.569	78843
	DIFFUSE	CLEAR	VERTICAL	9.269E+01	3.587E-03	-4.207E-06	3.042E-10	4448		8297
	GLOBAL	OVERCAST	VERTICAL	8.772E+01	-1.394E-03	-4.151E-07	1.247E-11	8594		18218
	GLOBAL	CLEAR	HORIZONTAL	9.253E+01	-2.898E-04	-1.393E-08	7.844E-14	50249	5.648	100372
	DIFFUSE	CLEAR	HORIZONTAL	9.269E+01	1.793E-03	-1.052E-06	3.803E-11	8897		16594
	GLOBAL	OVERCAST	HORIZONTAL	8.772E+01	-8.364E-04	-1.494E-07	2.693E-12	14323		30363

17-4. *Sunlight availability by standard work year for Denver.* $P_{clr} = SA - S$. *(From Robbins and Hunter, 1982b)*

SUNLIGHT AVALABILITY
BY
STANDARD WORK YEAR
FOR
DENVER , CO

STANDARD WORK YEAR	JAN	FEB	MAR	APR	MAY	JUN	JUL	AUG	SEP	OCT	NOV	DEC	ANNUAL (SA_S)
07:00-16:00	.705	.644	.792	.732	.758	.795	.843	.788	.842	.799	.683	.732	.760
07:00-17:00	.708	.652	.783	.722	.746	.786	.827	.782	.834	.804	.690	.740	.756
07:00-18:00	.649	.610	.774	.716	.735	.780	.821	.777	.829	.760	.632	.678	.730
07:00-19:00	.599	.564	.715	.678	.726	.774	.819	.743	.765	.702	.584	.626	.691
08:00-16:00	.784	.700	.792	.730	.753	.796	.837	.784	.842	.856	.759	.814	.787
08:00-17:00	.779	.703	.782	.719	.740	.786	.820	.778	.832	.856	.759	.814	.781
08:00-18:00	.708	.653	.773	.712	.729	.779	.814	.773	.827	.803	.690	.740	.750
08:00-19:00	.649	.598	.708	.672	.720	.772	.813	.736	.758	.736	.632	.678	.706
09:00-16:00	.804	.709	.790	.726	.748	.794	.828	.779	.844	.857	.763	.821	.789
09:00-17:00	.796	.711	.779	.715	.735	.783	.810	.773	.833	.856	.762	.821	.781
09:00-18:00	.717	.655	.769	.707	.723	.776	.804	.768	.827	.798	.686	.739	.747
09:00-19:00	.652	.596	.699	.663	.714	.769	.804	.728	.752	.726	.624	.672	.700

If two-step (off/on) switching is used, 62.59% represents the fraction of lighting energy saved due to daylighting. Thus:

$$F_2 = F = 62.59\%.$$

However, if continuous dimming or switching with three or more steps is used, additional lighting energy can be saved during those parts of the work day where $E_{int} < E_{des}$ as shown in figure 17-2.

$$F_3 = 1.1 \times F = 66.85\% \quad \text{(three-step switching).} \tag{17.6}$$

$$F_4 = 1.2 \times F = 75.11\% \quad \text{(four-step switching).} \tag{17.7}$$

$$F_5 = 1.3 \times F = 81.37\% \quad \text{(five-step switching).} \tag{17.8}$$

$$F_{dim} = 1.45 \times F = 90.76\% \quad \text{(continuous dimming).} \tag{17.9}$$

CASE 2: WHERE ET $>$ E_{max} THE ENTIRE WORK YEAR

This condition may occur where the DF is low and/or the availability of daylight is low. Under these conditions, energy savings are possible only with a continuous dimming control system or with switching, where the threshold for the first step is less than E_{max}. Under these conditions, the annual fractions can be approximated as follows:

$$F_{dim} = \frac{E_{max}}{2 \times ET} \tag{17.10}$$

$$F_5 = \frac{E_{max}}{3 \times ET} \qquad \text{where } ET > E_{max} > 0.8\,ET \tag{17.11}$$

$$F_4 = \frac{E_{max}}{4 \times ET} \qquad \text{where } ET > E_{max} > 0.6\,ET \tag{17.12}$$

$$F_3 = \frac{E_{max}}{4 \times ET} \qquad \text{where } ET > E_{max} > 0.8\,ET \tag{17.13}$$

MODIFICATION FOR CLEAR SKY/CLEAR GLAZING

The above method is directly applicable only for conditions where the DF remains constant regardless of time of day. This only occurs under continuously overcast sky conditions or where the fenestration is completely diffusing (i.e., translucent glazing). The DF for a specific interior location will vary considerably with clear glazing and clear sky conditions. For these conditions, use the average of the clear sky daylight factors for 9 A.M., noon, and 3 P.M. on March 21. (If these DF values are determined from model studies, ensure that direct sunlight does not strike the interior sensor.)

MODIFICATION FOR MULTIPLE ORIENTATIONS

If fenestration contributing to the total DF faces more than one orientation, calculate the total fraction (F) for each orientation based on the total DF. F is then computed as the *average* of the F percentages for each orientation, weighted by the DF contributed by each orientation.

For example, assume that a building is sidelighted by a south-facing window contributing a DF_{south} of 2 percent and an east-facing window contributing a DF_{east} of 6 percent. The total DF (DF_{total}) is thus 8 percent. Assume that F_{south} is then computed to be 50 percent (based on a DF of 8 percent, using south-facing clear and overcast coefficients). Also assume F_{east} to be 35 percent (based on a DF of 8 percent and east coefficients). Then:

$$F = F_{(south)}\left(\frac{DF_{(south)}}{DF_{(total)}}\right) + F_{(east)}\left(\frac{DF_{(east)}}{DF_{(total)}}\right)$$

$$= 50\left(\frac{2}{8}\right) + 35\left(\frac{6}{8}\right) = 38.75\%.$$

MODIFICATION FOR TILTED FENESTRATION

Compute separate Fs for vertical and for horizontal. Interpolate in linear proportion to slope. For example, if $F_{hor} = 50\%$ and $F_{vert} = 20\%$, then the F_s for a 60° slope = 30%.

ANNUAL ENERGY SAVINGS

Robbins and Hunter (1982a) describe the following method for determining annual energy savings due to daylighting. The *lighting power budget* (P_R) of an individual room or space is determined as follows:

$$PR = A \times UPD \times RF \times SUF \tag{17.14}$$

where:

PR = lighting power budget for a room or space,
A = floor area,
UPD = unit power density,
RF = room factor, and
SUF = space utilization factor.

The *room factor* (*RF*) is a multiplying factor (between 1.0 and 2.0) that adjusts the base UPD for spaces of various dimensions to account for the effect of room configuration on lighting efficiency.

The *space utilization factor* (*SUF*) is a multiplying factor (between 0.4 and 1.0) that adjusts the allowable room power budget downward when the total area of all visual tasks within the room is less than 50 percent of the room area. Since the majority of properly planned spaces utilize more than 50 percent of the room area for work locations, this step may frequently be omitted (*SUF* = 1.0 is used).

Equation 17-14 can be rewritten for a room or space that is daylit for some fraction F_t (i.e., F_{dim}, F_2, F_3, F_4, or F_5 as previously calculated):

$$P_R = (A \times UPD \times SUF \times RF \times (1 - F_t)) + (A \times UPD_{day} \times F_t) \qquad (17.15)$$

where:

$$UPD_{day} = \text{unit power density of daylight}$$
$$= \frac{E_{des}}{125} \text{ (based on an average efficacy of daylight}$$
$$= 125 \text{ watts/lumen).}$$

Assume that the previous Denver example used a continuous dimming control strategy ($F_t = F_{dim} = 90.76\%$) and had the following characteristics:

$$A = 150 \text{ square feet,}$$
$$UPD = 1.5 \text{ W/sf,}$$
$$RF = 1.6,$$
$$SUF = 0.65, \text{ and}$$
$$UPD_{day} = 0.16 \text{ W/sf.}$$

The power budget would then be:

$$P_R = (150 \times 1.5 \times 1.6 \times 0.65 \times (1 - 0.908))$$
$$+ (150 \times 0.16 \times 0.908) = 43.3 \text{ watts.}$$

If the space were nondaylit, the P_R would have been:

$$P_R = 150 \times 1.5 \times 1.6 \times 0.65 = 234 \text{ watts.}$$

Base UPD Values for Lighting Power Limit Calculations. *

Task or Area	Base UPD — Watts per Square Meter	Watts per Square Foot	Note
Office			
Accounting	34.44	3.2	f
Drafting	50.59	4.7	f
Filing (Active)	21.53	2.0	
Filing (Inactive)	8.61	0.8	
Graphic Arts	32.29	3.0	f
Office Machine Operation			
Computer Machinery	18.30	1.7	
Duplicating Machines	7.53	0.7	
EDP I/O Terminal (Internally Illuminated)	7.53	0.7	
EDP I/O Terminal (Room Illuminated)	18.30	1.7	
Typing and Reading	23.68	2.2	f
Residential			
Bath	46.28	4.3	d
Bedroom	15.07	1.4	a, d
Finished Living Spaces	23.68	2.2	d
Garage	5.38	0.5	d
Kitchen	43.06	4.0	d
Laundry	10.76	1.0	d
Unfinished Living Spaces	5.38	0.5	d

Task or Area	Base UPD — Watts per Square Meter	Watts per Square Foot	Note
Commercial and Institutional			
Armories			
Drill	6.46	0.6	
Exhibitions	8.61	0.8	
Seating Area	4.31	0.4	
Art Galleries	17.22	1.6	a
Banks			
Lobby, General	24.76	2.3	
Posting and Keypunch	50.59	4.7	
Tellers' Stations	50.59	4.7	
Bar (Lounge)	11.84	1.1	b
Barber Shops and Beauty Parlors	40.90	3.8	
Church and Synagogues, Main Worship Area	24.76	2.3	a
Club and Lodge Rooms	11.84	1.1	
Courtrooms	9.69	0.9	

See page 4–6 for footnotes.

17-5. Sample UPD values for various task areas; see Reference for complete tables. (Reprinted, by permission, from I.E.S., 1981)

17-6. Sample room factor values for various sized rooms; see Reference for complete tables. (Reprinted, by permission, from I.E.S., 1981)

Dimensions* (feet) W	L	8	8.5	9	10	11	12	14	16	18	20+	Dimensions (meters) W	L
24	24	1.15	1.15	1.20	1.25	1.30	1.35	1.50	1.65	1.80	1.95	7.3	7.3
24	36	1.10	1.10	1.15	1.20	1.25	1.25	1.35	1.45	1.60	1.70	7.3	11.0
24	48	1.10	1.10	1.10	1.15	1.20	1.25	1.30	1.40	1.50	1.60	7.3	14.6
24	60	1.05	1.10	1.10	1.15	1.15	1.20	1.30	1.35	1.45	1.55	7.3	18.3
24	72	1.05	1.05	1.10	1.10	1.15	1.20	1.25	1.35	1.40	1.50	7.3	21.9
24	96	1.05	1.05	1.10	1.10	1.15	1.15	1.25	1.30	1.40	1.45	7.3	29.3
24	120	1.05	1.05	1.05	1.10	1.15	1.15	1.20	1.30	1.35	1.45	7.3	36.6
24	144	1.05	1.05	1.05	1.10	1.10	1.15	1.20	1.25	1.35	1.40	7.3	43.9
24	240	1.05	1.05	1.05	1.10	1.10	1.15	1.20	1.25	1.30	1.35	7.3	73.2
24	240+		1.05	1.05	1.05	1.10	1.10	1.15	1.20	1.25	1.30	7.3	73.2+
30	30	1.10	1.10	1.15	1.15	1.20	1.25	1.35	1.45	1.55	1.65	9.1	9.1
30	45	1.05	1.05	1.10	1.10	1.15	1.20	1.25	1.35	1.40	1.50	9.1	13.7
30	60	1.05	1.05	1.05	1.10	1.15	1.15	1.20	1.30	1.35	1.45	9.1	18.3
30	75	1.05	1.05	1.05	1.10	1.10	1.15	1.20	1.25	1.30	1.40	9.1	22.9
30	90		1.05	1.05	1.05	1.10	1.10	1.20	1.25	1.30	1.35	9.1	27.4
30	120		1.05	1.05	1.05	1.10	1.10	1.15	1.20	1.25	1.30	9.1	36.6
30	150			1.05	1.05	1.10	1.10	1.15	1.20	1.25	1.30	9.1	45.7
30	180			1.05	1.05	1.05	1.10	1.15	1.20	1.25	1.30	9.1	54.9
30	300				1.05	1.05	1.10	1.10	1.15	1.20	1.25	9.1	91.4
30	300+				1.05	1.05	1.10	1.10	1.15	1.20	1.20	9.1	91.4+
40	40	1.05	1.05	1.05	1.10	1.15	1.15	1.20	1.30	1.35	1.45	12.2	12.2
40	60		1.05	1.05	1.05	1.10	1.10	1.15	1.20	1.25	1.30	12.2	18.3
40	80				1.05	1.05	1.10	1.15	1.20	1.20	1.25	12.2	24.4
40	100				1.05	1.05	1.10	1.10	1.15	1.20	1.25	12.2	30.5
40	120				1.05	1.05	1.05	1.10	1.15	1.20	1.20	12.2	36.6
40	160					1.05	1.05	1.10	1.10	1.15	1.20	12.2	48.8
40	200						1.05	1.05	1.10	1.15	1.20	12.2	61.0
40	240					1.05	1.05	1.05	1.10	1.15	1.20	12.2	73.2
40	400						1.05	1.05	1.10	1.15	1.15	12.2	122.0
40	400+							1.05	1.10	1.10	1.15	12.2	122+
60	60						1.05	1.05	1.10	1.15	1.15	18.3	18.3
60	90						1.05	1.05	1.10	1.10	1.15	18.3	27.4
60	120							1.05	1.10	1.10	1.15	18.3	36.6
60	150							1.05	1.05	1.10	1.10	18.3	45.7
60	180							1.05	1.05	1.10	1.10	18.3	54.9
60	240								1.05	1.05	1.10	18.3	73.2
60	300								1.05	1.05	1.10	18.3	91.4
60	360								1.05	1.05	1.10	18.3	110.0
60	600								1.05	1.05	1.05	18.3	183.0
60+	600+									1.05	1.05	18.3	183+
Ceiling Height (meters)		2.4	2.6	2.7	3.0	3.4	3.7	4.3	4.9	5.5	6.1+	W	L

* W = width, L = length.

Energy equals power × time. The time in this example can be calculated as follows:

$$T = 10 \text{ hr/day} \times 5 \text{ days/week} \times 52 \text{ weeks/year}$$
$$= 2600 \text{ hours/year}.$$

Thus, the annual energy usage (E) of the daylighted system is:

$$E = 43.3 \times 2600 = 112,320 \text{ WH} = 112.3 \text{ KWH}.$$

For the nondaylit alternative, the annual energy usage is:

$$E = 234 \times 2600 = 608,400 \text{ WH} = 608.4 \text{ KWH}.$$

Average unit power density is used for the design of the heating and cooling systems for buildings. Continuing with the above example, the average unit power density of the daylit space would be:

$$\text{UPD}_{av} = \frac{PR}{A} = \frac{43.2}{150} = 0.288 \text{ W/sf,} \qquad (17.16)$$

while the nondaylit alternative would have an average unit power density of:

$$\text{UPD}_{av} = \frac{234}{150} = 1.56 \text{ W/sf.}$$

ANNUAL ENERGY COSTS

In residential buildings, energy savings translate directly to energy cost savings because utility charges are based only on energy consumed. For commercial buildings, however, utility costs include a charge for the maximum *rate* of consumption during the rate period (demand charge) in addition to actual energy consumed. This charge is significant in commercial buildings, typically averaging 60 percent of the total utility charges for office buildings. The demand charge is justified from the standpoint of the utility company because peak demand is the factor that determines the generating capacity required (capacity that is idle during nonpeak periods). It does, however, require that designers consider not only how much energy the building will consume, but also that they seek strategies to "level out the peaks" during the rate period.

In a nondaylit commercial office building, peak demand typically occurs on a warm day, in the early afternoon, when demands for lighting, cooling, and equipment are at a simultaneous maximum. Daylighting reduces the lighting demand (less electric lighting required) and the cooling demand (because daylight efficacy is higher than that of electric lighting, less heat is introduced in the building for a comparable amount of light). During winter months, south-oriented daylighting can also provide passive solar heating, reducing peak heating demand.

Ternoey, et al. (1983) have presented an analysis that illustrates the potential of daylighting for reducing demand charges by comparing the energy costs of a base-case typical office building with a design alternative for Pittsburgh (fig. 17-7). The project assumptions included:

■ Client is a developer of speculative office building

■ Project objectives include profit on sale of building after three years with the highest positive cash flow during the three-year construction and lease-up period

- Loan structure: three-year construction loan on 80 percent of the project costs at 20 percent per annum; interest only due annually

- Average lease term: three years

- Occupancy rate: 80 percent in first six months; 95 percent thereafter

- Leaseable space: 51,000 sf, or 85 percent of 60,000 sf building

- Fuel escalation rate: 30 percent/year

- Desired Internal Rate of Return: 20 percent of full cost of energy-related improvements

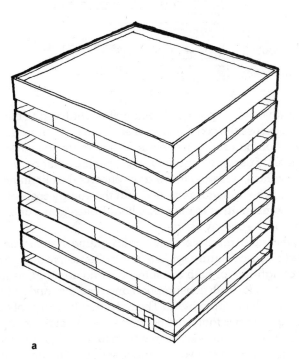

17-7. (a) Base case building, isometric; (b) base case typical floor plan; and (c) alternative typical floor plan. (After Ternoey, et al., 1983)

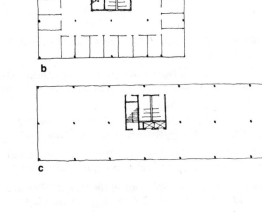

17-8. Pittsburgh design alternative, elimination parametric study: (a) base case building; (b) design alternative. (After Ternoey, et al., 1983)

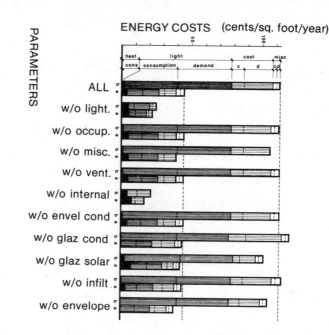

The alternative, energy-saving design was analyzed using elimination parametrics to assess the contribution of each energy feature separately (fig. 17-8). (Elimination parametrics are a series of analyses whereby a single major parameter is assumed equal to zero, and the other parameters are set at reasonable values, allowing the relative effect of the eliminated parameter to be assessed.) The analysis revealed that the energy costs of the building were relatively insensitive to envelope heat losses/gains and that internal loads dominated the energy usage.

Following the initial analysis, the electric lighting system was redesigned. The improved electric lighting system in the alternative design reduced the annual cost of lighting for both consumption and demand, reduced the annual cost of cooling for both consumption and demand, and reduced the size and initial cost of the cooling plant. The only disadvantage of the improved electric lighting system is that it did not break the coincidence of peak cooling needs and peak lighting needs that resulted in the building's monthly peak demand charge. Daylighting was found to reduce the annual lighting consumption and demand charges as well as the annual cost for cooling in both the consumption and demand categories. Unlike improved electric lighting, daylighting was found to separate the peak cooling and electric lighting periods, resulting in a reduction of the total building demand. The major disadvantage of daylighting was the increased construction cost associated with a very narrow building form.

REFERENCES

Kaufman, J. *IES Lighting Handbook, 1981 Reference Volume.* New York: Illuminating Engineering Society of North America, 1981.

Robbins, C. L., and Hunter, K. C. "A Method for Predicting Energy Savings Attributed to Daylighting." SERI report TR-254-1687. Golden, CO: Solar Energy Research Institute, 1982a.

Robbins, C. L., and Hunter, K. C. "Hourly Availability of Sunlight in the United States." SERI report TR-254-1687. Golden, CO: Solar Energy Research Institute, 1982b.

Robbins, C. L., and Hunter, K. C. "A Model for Illuminance on Horizontal and Vertical Surfaces." SERI report TR-254-1687. Golden, CO: Solar Energy Research Institute, 1982c.

Ternoey, S., Bickle, L., Robbins, C., Busch, R., and McCord, P. *The Design of Energy-Responsive Commercial Buildings.* Golden, CO: Solar Energy Research Institute, 1983.

Chapter 18
Computer Programs

Several programs for daylighting analysis have recently been developed for programmable calculators, microcomputers, and mainframe computers.

PROGRAMMABLE CALCULATOR PROGRAMS

QUICKLITE I

Bryan, et al. (1981a and 1981b) have described *Quicklite I,* a program for the TI-59 hand-held programmable calculator. The program utilizes the C.I.E. sky luminance functions for overcast and clear skies. The light reaching the interior point being considered is separated into two components. Light arriving directly from the sky (sky component) is calculated using a source area formula. Light reflected from external and internal surfaces (reflected component) is calculated using the split flux approach. The total of these two components is given as either the daylight factor or as illuminance (in footcandles) for the point(s) being considered. Up to nine points may be calculated per run.

The program is simple to use and relatively fast running. Its results compare well with other daylight calculation procedures and with physical model measurements. The program does not compute the effect of direct sunlight in the room or the contribution of skylights. A complete listing and documentation of the program are available (Bryan, et al., 1981a). Bryan and Clear (1981b) have described the algorithms used in the program.

MICROCOMPUTER PROGRAMS

MICROLITE I

Bryan and Kringel (1982) have developed an enhanced version of *Quicklite I* for use on Apple II+ and I.B.M. PC microcomputers. *Microlite I* is a design-oriented program developed around a set of input "menus," in which design parameters can be created, stored, changed, or replaced to determine the effects of design alternatives. Like *Quicklite I,* it has provisions for both clear and overcast sky conditions and is limited to window openings (i.e., the contribution of skylights cannot be analyzed). The output from the program offers several graphic formats in the familiar architectural representafjtion of plan, section, and axonometric projection. The program on disk with documentation is available at nominal cost through the Designers' Software Exchange (see reference).

An earlier version of the program (without the graphic output) is available as a listing for TRS-80 microcomputers with 16K RAM (Selkowitz, 1981).

ENERGY

D. DiLaura of Lighting Technologies, Inc. (see reference) has developed a daylighting analysis program for IBM PC microcomputers called *Energy.* It predicts the daylight illumination under overcast or clear sky conditions, based on algorithms developed by Bryan and Clear (1981b). It also calculates annual energy savings due to daylighting based on local daylight availability, using various control strategies. The energy savings component can also receive user input from model studies or more sophisticated mainframe programs.

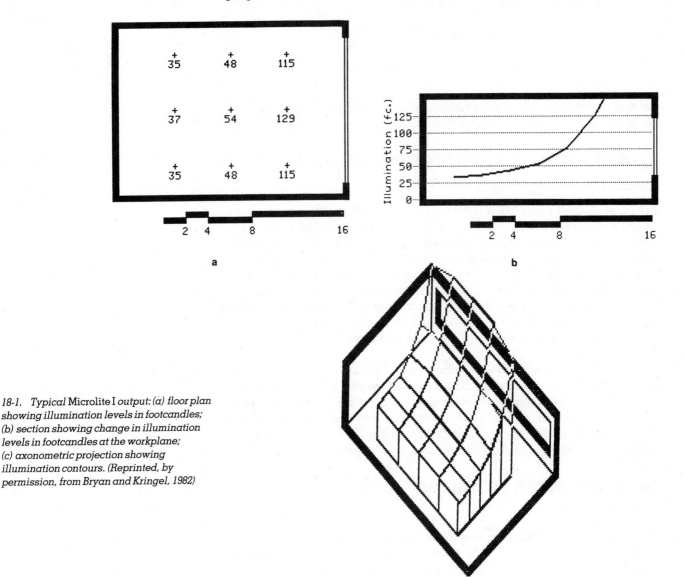

18-1. Typical Microlite I output: (a) floor plan showing illumination levels in footcandles; (b) section showing change in illumination levels in footcandles at the workplane; (c) axonometric projection showing illumination contours. (Reprinted, by permission, from Bryan and Kringel, 1982)

DAYLITE

C. L. Robbins and W. Ashton (SolarSoft, see reference) have developed a system of programs for daylighting analysis. *Daylite* calculates daylight factors for a room using the flux transfer method, with a point-specific IRC algorithm, for overcast and clear sky conditions (including direct sunlight contribution). It can accommodate light shelves, overhangs, vertical exterior fins, saw-toothed roofs, monitors, and tilted glazing. Glare and contrast can be analyzed for specific locations. An electric lighting subroutine allows the specification of overhead task/ambient or task/background electric lighting, performing energy analysis on the system to complement daylighting performance. The room configurations can be stored on disk.

Graphic outputs illustrate daylight penetration, design illuminance, and percent of space illuminated to design level using either a two- or three-dimensional format. Annual energy performance is calculated for any of 244 cities, using the Robbins-Hunter method described in the previous chapter.

MAINFRAME COMPUTER PROGRAMS

SUPERLITE

Selkowitz, et al. (1982) have described *Superlite,* a large computer model that predicts the spatial distribution of the illuminance in a building based on exterior sun and sky conditions, site obstructions, fenestration and shading device details, and interior room properties. It is compatible with DOE-2. 1B (see below), which estimates annual energy use and peak load impact. The mathematical bases for the *Superlite* algorithms have been described by Modest (1981) and are based on a uniform sky, C.I.E. standard overcast sky, and C.I.E. standard clear sky, with and without direct sun.

Based on the luminance distribution of a given sky, the luminances of the ground, adjacent buildings, and other external obstructions are calculated. Then the luminances of each interior surface are determined. From this the workplane illuminance is determined by integrating the surface luminances over the appropriate solid angles.

Compared with other daylighting computational models, the major advantage of *Superlite* is its ability to model nonrectangular surfaces and other complex geometries. Arbitrary room shapes (e.g., L-shaped), internal partitions, windows of various shapes and tilts, and overhangs and fins with various opaque and translucent properties can be modeled. Improvements in progress include provisions for complex shading devices (such as eggcrates and louvers) and the capability of modeling electric systems.

Luminance and illuminance values from the program can be output in tabular form or as contour plots of illuminance levels. Daylight factors can be generated by an auxiliary graphics program. The program has been extensively validated against physical model studies under a twenty-four-foot-diameter artificial skydome and against other computer programs. The program is in the public domain and is expected to be available with documentation in late 1985 through Lawrence Berkeley Laboratory (see references).

DOE-2.1B

Selkowitz, et al. (1982) have also described *DOE-2.1B,* a revision of *DOE-2* (a mainframe program that has been used extensively by larger architectural and engineering firms). *DOE-2.1B* contains a daylighting analysis model for the estimation of annual energy use and peak load impact of daylighting strategies based on hour-by-hour analysis of daylight availability, site conditions, window management in response to sun control and glare, and various lighting control strategies. The thermal interaction of daylighting strategies is automatically accounted for within the program. The program is publicly available with documentation through Lawrence Berkeley Laboratory (see references).

The calculation has three main stages. In the first stage, a preprocessor calculates daylight factors for later use in the hourly loads calculation. The user specifies the coordinates of one or two reference points within the space. *DOE-2.1B* then integrates over the area of each window to obtain the contribution of direct light from the window to the illuminance at the reference points and the contribution of reflected light from the walls, floor, and ceiling to the reference points. Such factors as the luminance distribution of the sky, window size and orientation, glass transmittance, inside surface reflectances, sun control devices such as blinds and overhangs, and external obstructions are also taken into account. The calculation is carried out for standard C.I.E. clear and overcast sky conditions for a series of twenty different solar altitude and azimuth values covering the annual range of U.S. sun positions. Analogous daylight factors for discomfort glare are also calculated and stored.

In stage two, an hourly daylighting calculation is performed for every hour of the year that the sun is up. The illuminance from each window is found by interpolating the stored daylight factors using the current-hour sun position and cloud cover, then multiplying by the current-hour exterior horizontal illuminance. If the glare-control option has been specified, the program will automatically close window blinds or drapes in order to decrease glare below a predefined comfort level. A similar option is available to use window shading devices to control solar gain automatically.

In stage three, the program simulates the lighting control system (which may be stepped or dimmed continuously) to determine the electrical lighting energy needed to make up any difference between the daylighting and the design illuminance. Each thermal zone can be divided into two independently controlled lighting zones. Both uniform lighting and task ambient systems can be modeled. Finally, the zone lighting electrical requirements are passed to the *DOE-2* thermal calculation which determines hourly heating and cooling loads and monthly and annual energy use.

LUMEN III

Lumen III is a sophisticated daylight illumination calculation program using the flux transfer algorithms described by DiLaura and Hauser (1978). It is an enhanced version of *Lumen II,* retaining the electric lighting analysis capability of that predecessor. Room illuminance can be calculated for overcast or clear sky conditions. It can accommodate clear and diffuse glazing, overhangs, and certain controls (such as venetian blinds). The program is significant for its detailed accommodation of external obstructions (including adjacent sunlit surfaces) and other sunlit and skylit surfaces in and out of the room.

Lumen III is available only as a time-sharing service (Computer Sharing Services, see reference), making it suitable for small and medium-sized professional offices.

UWLIGHT

Bedrick, et al. (1978) have described *Uwlight,* a mainframe program for the study of the control and use of natural and electric illumination in buildings. Given the geometry of a room, the reflectances of its interior surfaces, and the configuration of windows and/or electric lighting fixtures, the program determines the pattern of illuminance levels on the interior surfaces and at specified workplane heights. The program's measurement of daylight illumination is based on the C.I.E. concept and definition of daylight factor for both overcast and clear sky conditions. The contribution of electric lighting is calculated from manufacturer's photometric data (input by user or from a computer tape of previously recorded tables). The program is publicly available (see reference).

Uwlight operates in two stages. The first, or initial distribution stage, subdivides the room surfaces into rectangular areas called *nodes.* The amount of light that reaches the center point of each node directly from the sources is then computed. The second stage is an iterative process used to simulate the light being reflected from the room. During each iteration, each node is studied and the amount of light it receives from every other node is calculated and added to its running total. The number of iterations is specified by the user. Each successive iteration assumes that some light is absorbed by the surface and so adds less light to the node than did the previous iteration. Thus a final distribution is approached asymptotically.

REFERENCES

Bryan, H., Clear, R., Rosen, J., and Selkowitz, S. "*Quicklite I:* New Procedure for Daylighting Design." *Solar Age* 6: (1982) 37–47. (Also available as LBL-12248 preprint, Lawrence Berkeley Laboratory, University of California, Berkeley, CA.)

Bryan, H., and Clear, R. "Calculating Interior Daylight Illumination with a Programmable Hand Calculator." *Journal of the Illuminating Engineering Society,* 10: (1981) 219–227. (Also available as LBL-11687 EEB-W-80-16 report, Lawrence Berkeley Laboratory, University of California, Berkeley, CA.)

Bryan, H., and Kringel, D. "*Microlite I:* A Microcomputer Program for Daylighting Design." In *Proceedings, Seventh National Passive Solar Conference, Vol. I,* edited by Hayes, J., and Winn, C. B., pp. 405–410. New York: American Solar Energy Society, 1982.

Bedrick, J. R., Millet, M. S., Spencer, G. S., Heerwagen, D. R., and Varey, G. B. "The Development and Use of the Computer Program *Uwlight* for the Simulation of Natural and Artificial Illumination in Buildings." In *Proceedings, Second National Passive Solar Conference,* edited by Prowler, D., pp. 365–370. New York: American Solar Energy Society. (For information on the availability of *Uwlight,* contact D. R. Heerwagen, Department of Architecture, University of Washington, Seattle, WA 98105.)

Computer Sharing Services, Inc., 7535 East Hampden Avenue, Suite 200, Denver, CO 80231, Attn: Thomas Rollins.

Designer's Software Exchange, c/o H. Bryan, Department of Architecture, M.I.T., Cambridge, MA 02139.

DiLaura, D., and Hauser, G. "On Calculating the Effects of Daylighting in Interior Spaces." *Journal of the Illuminating Engineering Society* 7:219–27.

Lighting Technologies, Inc., 3060 Walnut Street, Suite 203, Boulder, CO 80301, Attn: David DiLaura.

Modest, W. F. "Daylighting Calculations for Non-Rectangular Interior Spaces with Shading Devices." LBL Report 12599, Windows and Daylighting Program, Lawrence Berkeley Laboratory, 1981.

Selkowitz, S. "Memo to *Quicklite* Users: Availability of *Quicklite I* Basic Listings." Window and Daylighting Program, Lawrence Berkeley Laboratory, 1981.

Selkowitz, S. "The *DOE-2* and *Superlite* Daylighting Programs." In *Proceedings, Seventh National Passive Solar Conference, Vol. I,* edited by Hayes, J., and Winn, C. B., pp. 417–422. New York: American Solar Energy Society, 1982.

SolarSoft, Inc., Box 124, Snowmass, CO, 81654, Attn: William Ashton.

Appendix A:
Sundials

(See chapter 6 for discussion)

A-1. *Sundial for 28° north latitude.*

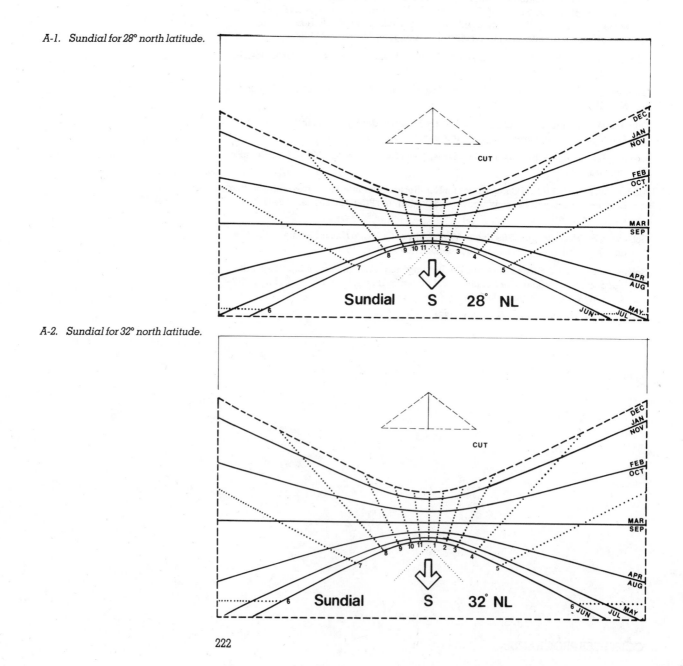

A-2. *Sundial for 32° north latitude.*

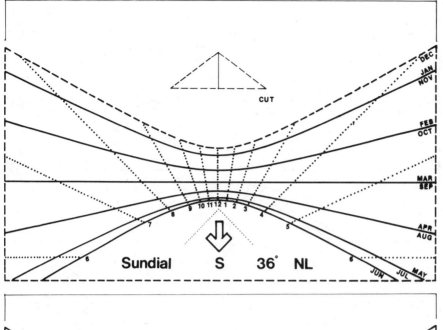

A-3. Sundial for 36° north latitude.

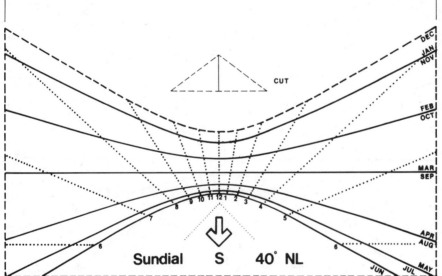

A-4. Sundial for 40° north latitude.

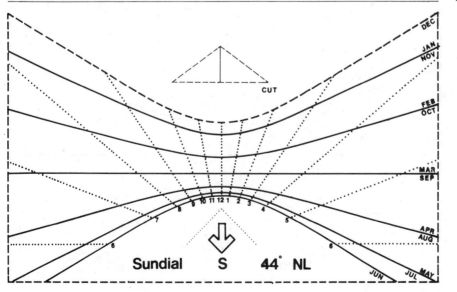

A-5. Sundial for 44° north latitude.

A-6. Sundial for 48° north latitude.

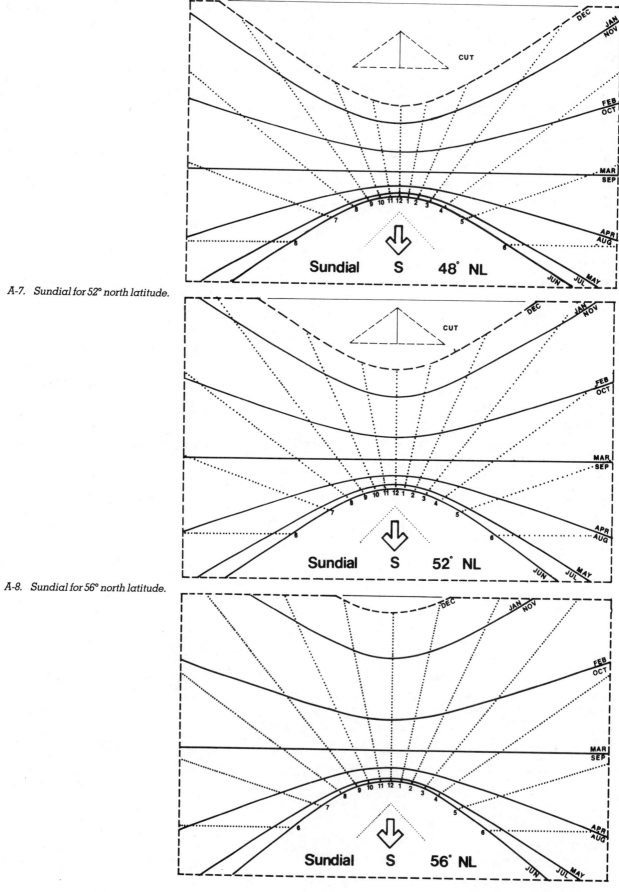

A-7. Sundial for 52° north latitude.

A-8. Sundial for 56° north latitude.

Appendix B:
Sun Path Charts, Mask Protractor, and Daylight Factor Dot Charts

(For convenience, these may be converted to overlay format by copying onto a transparent material.)

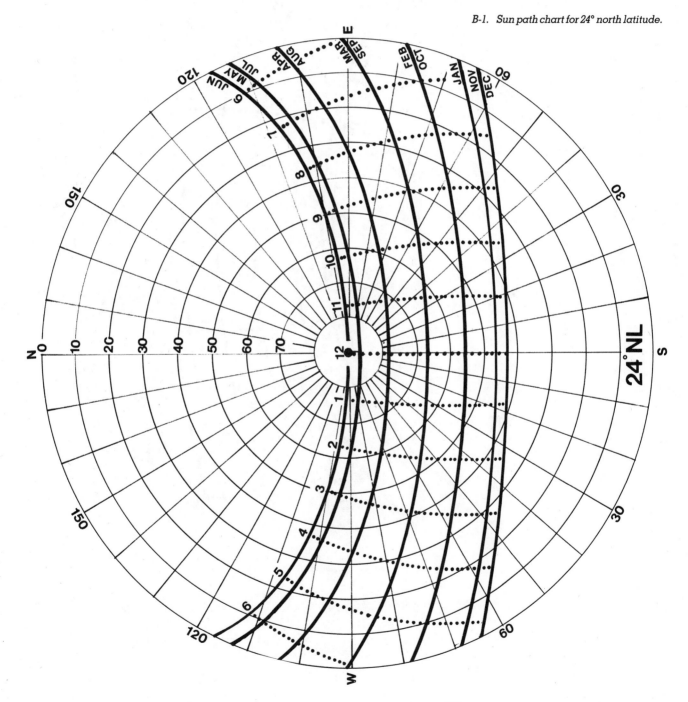

B-1. Sun path chart for 24° north latitude.

B-2. Sun path chart for 28° north latitude.

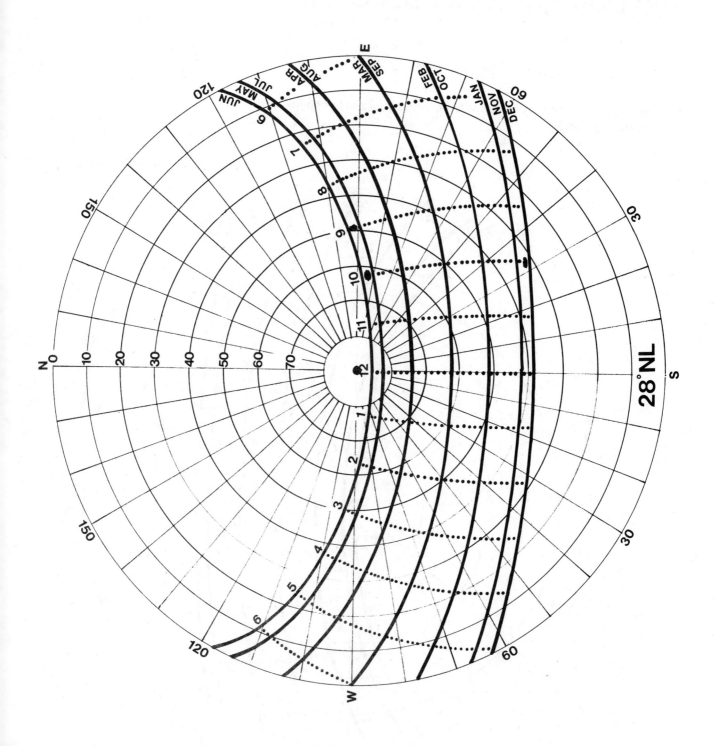

B-3.   Sun path chart for 32° north latitude.

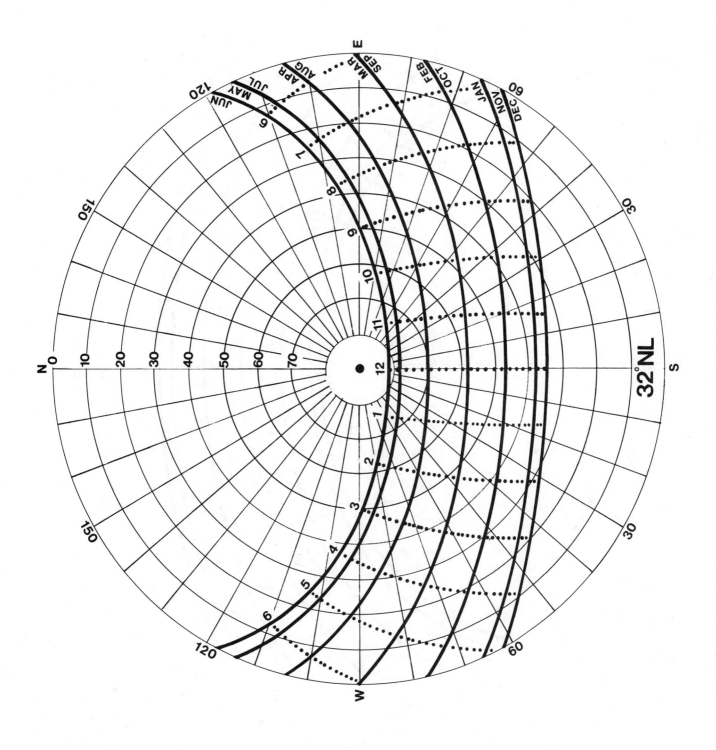

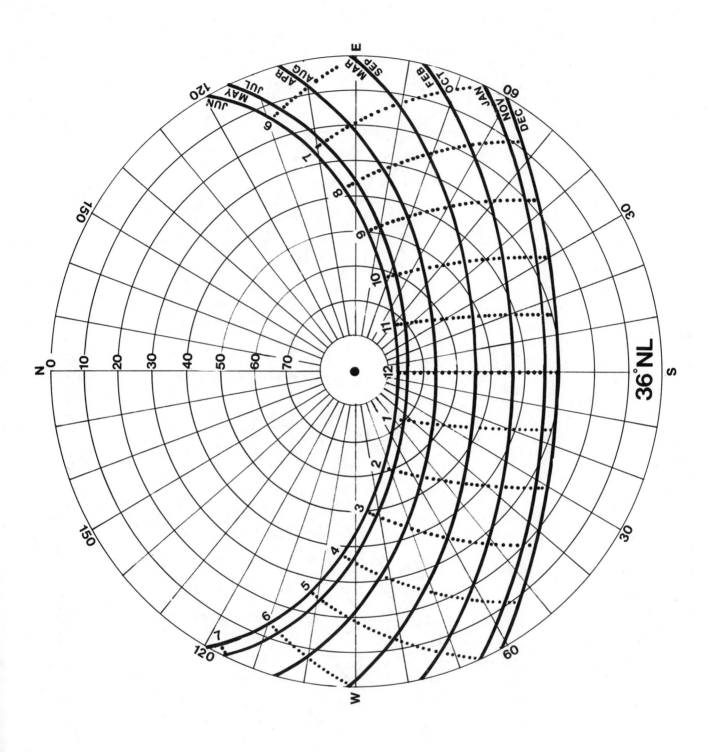

B-5. Sun path chart for 40° north latitude.

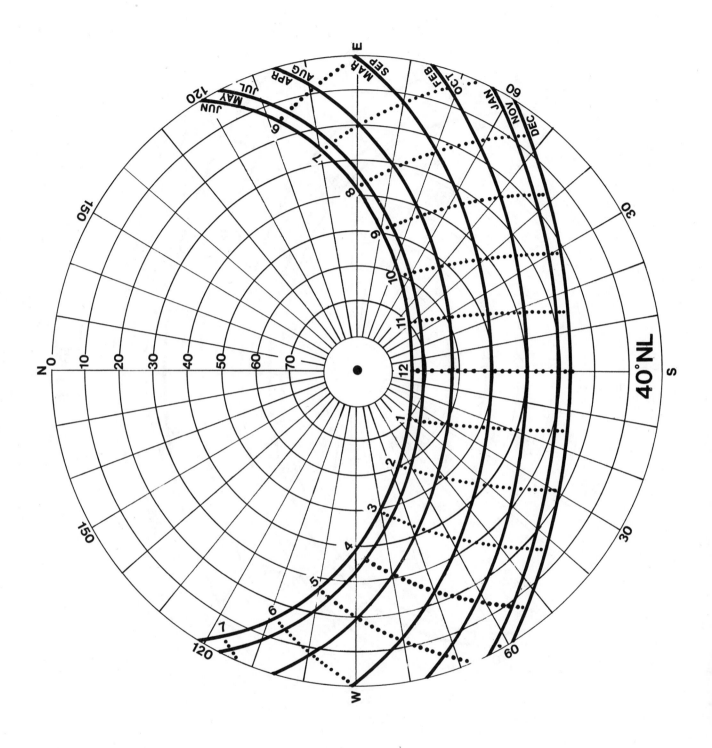

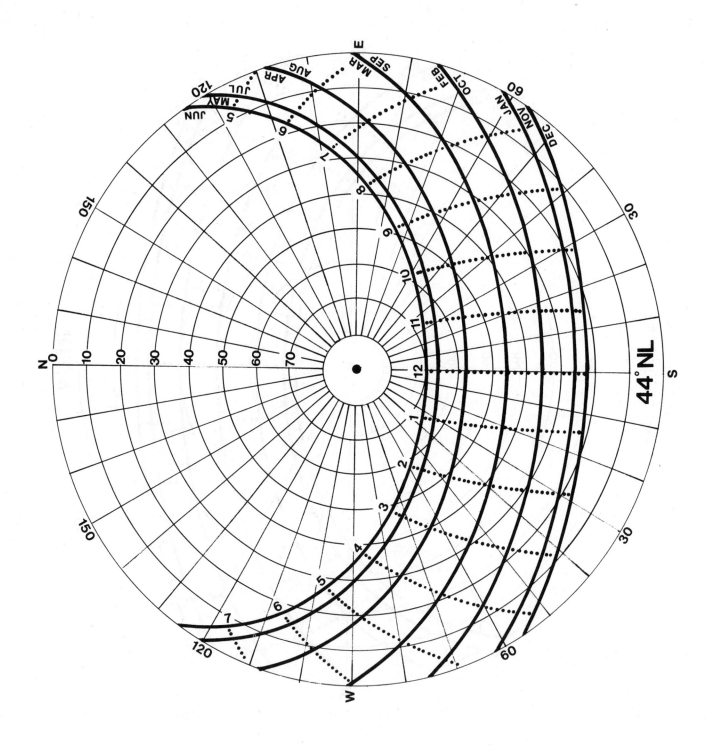

B-7. *Sun path chart for 48° north latitude.*

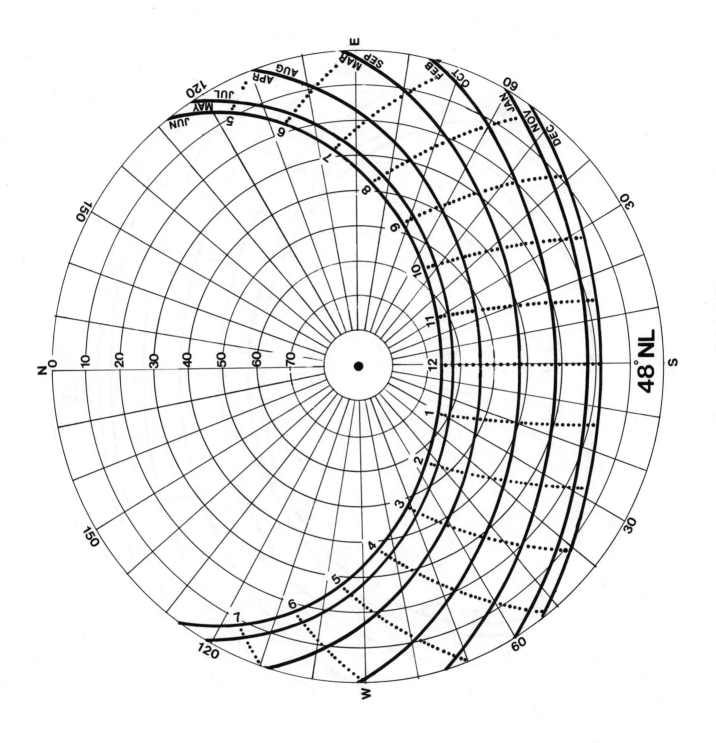

B-8. Sun path chart for 52° north latitude.

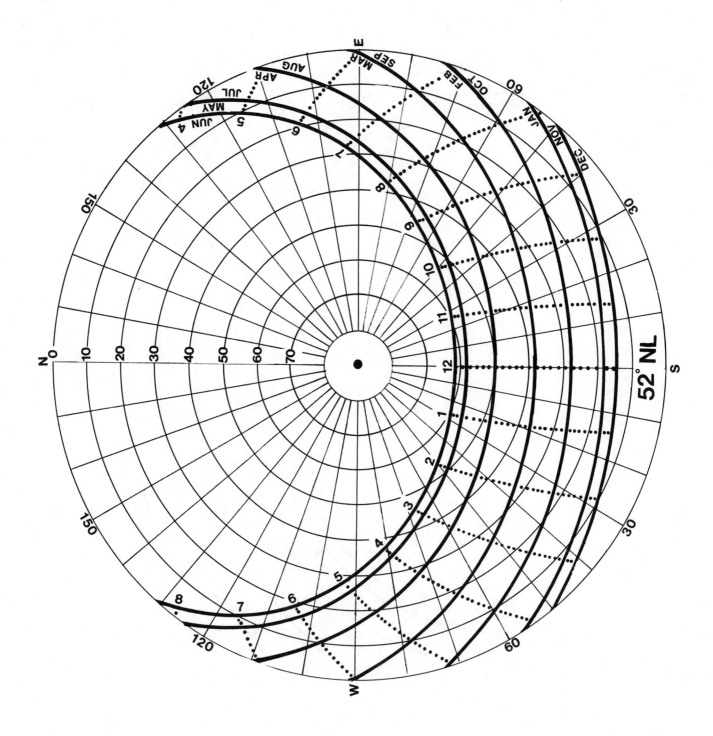

B-9. *Obstruction mask protractor.*

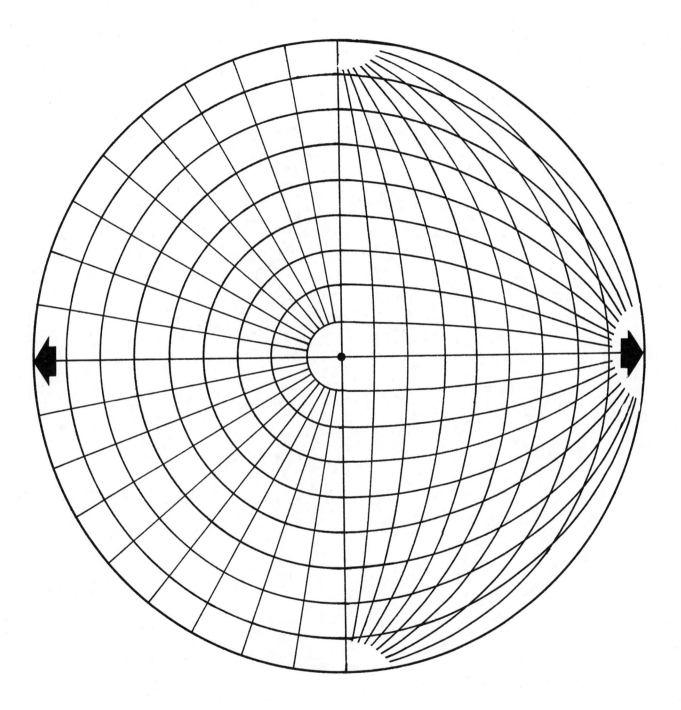

APPENDIX B

B-11. *External reflected component dot chart (overcast sky, unglazed aperture). For use with obstruction mask. North orientation. Each dot = 0.1 percent daylight factor.*

B-12. *Sky component dot chart, 15° solar altitude (clear sky, unglazed aperture). For use with obstruction mask. Arrow points toward solar azimuth. Each dot = 0.1 percent daylight factor.*

B-13. Sky component dot chart, 30° solar altitude (clear sky, unglazed aperture). For use with obstruction mask. Arrow points toward solar azimuth. Each dot = 0.1 percent daylight factor.

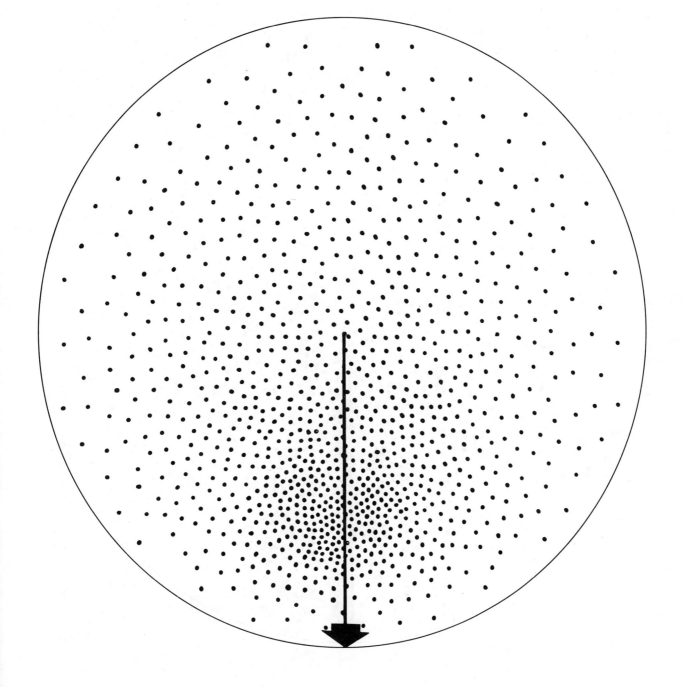

B-14. *Sky component dot chart, 45° solar altitude (clear sky, unglazed aperture). For use with obstruction mask. Arrow points toward solar azimuth. Each dot = 0.1 percent daylight factor.*

B-15. Sky component dot chart, 60° solar altitude (clear sky, unglazed aperture). For use with obstruction mask. Arrow points toward solar azimuth. Each dot = 0.1 percent daylight factor.

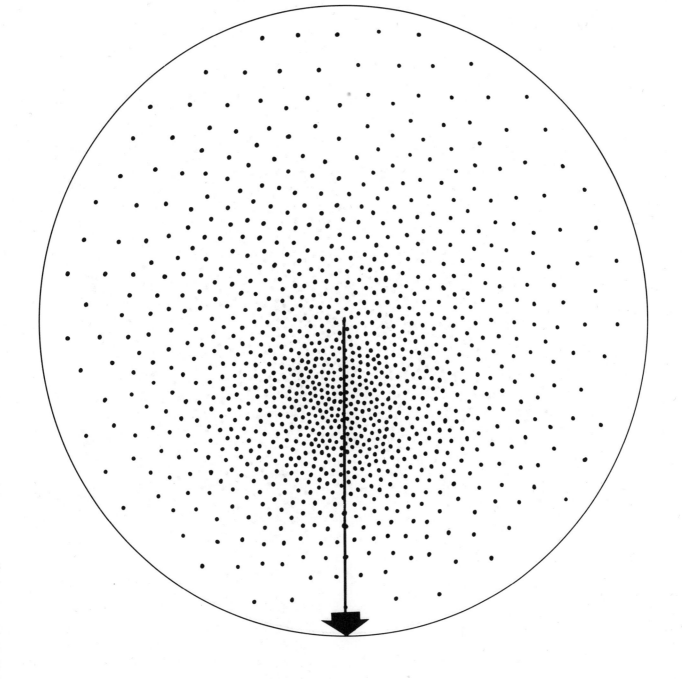

B-16. Sky component dot chart, 75° solar altitude (clear sky, unglazed aperture). For use with obstruction mask. Arrow points toward solar azimuth. Each dot = 0.1 percent daylight factor.

240

B-17. *Sky component dot chart, 90° solar altitude (clear sky, unglazed aperture). For use with obstruction mask. North orientation. Each dot = 0.1 percent daylight factor.*

B-18.   *External reflected component dot chart
(clear sky, unglazed aperture). For use with
obstruction mask. Requires obstruction
surface illuminance multipliers.*

Appendix C:
Exterior Illuminance Overlays

(For convenience, these may be copied onto a transparent sheet.)

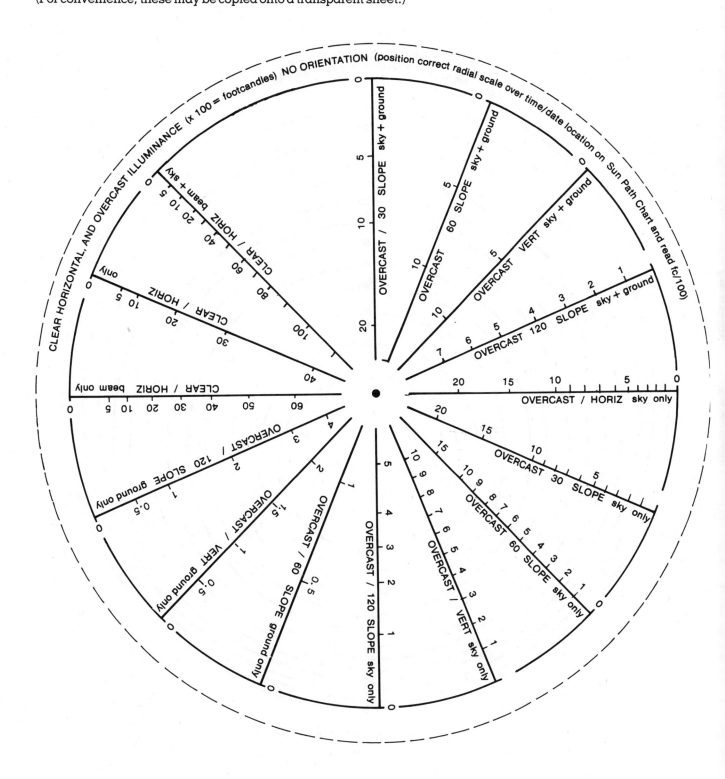

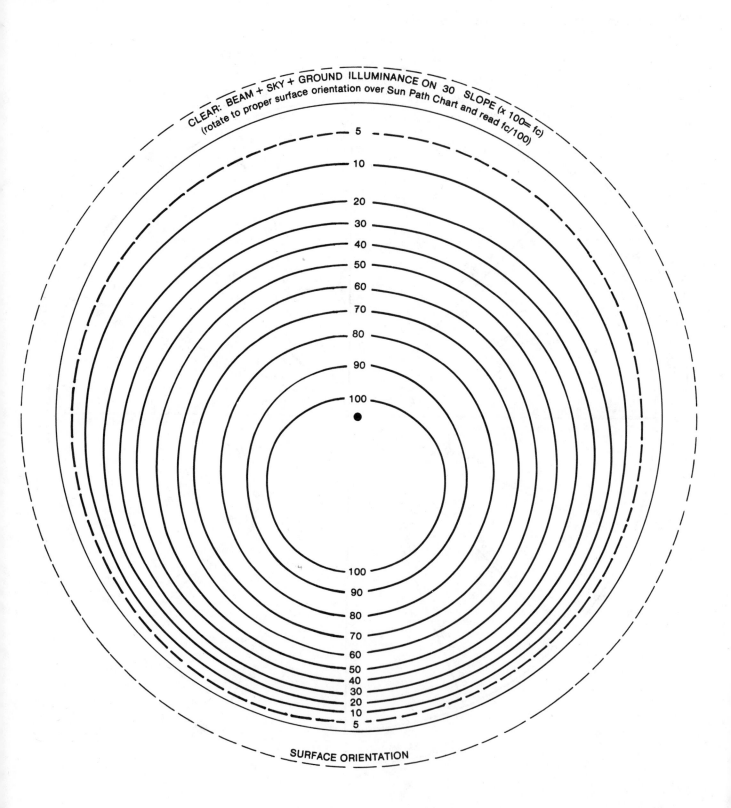

CLEAR: BEAM + SKY + GROUND ILLUMINANCE ON 30° SLOPE (x 100= fc)
(rotate to proper surface orientation over Sun Path Chart and read fc/100)

5
10
20
30
40
50
60
70
80
90
100

100
90
80
70
60
50
40
30
20
10
5

SURFACE ORIENTATION

APPENDIX C

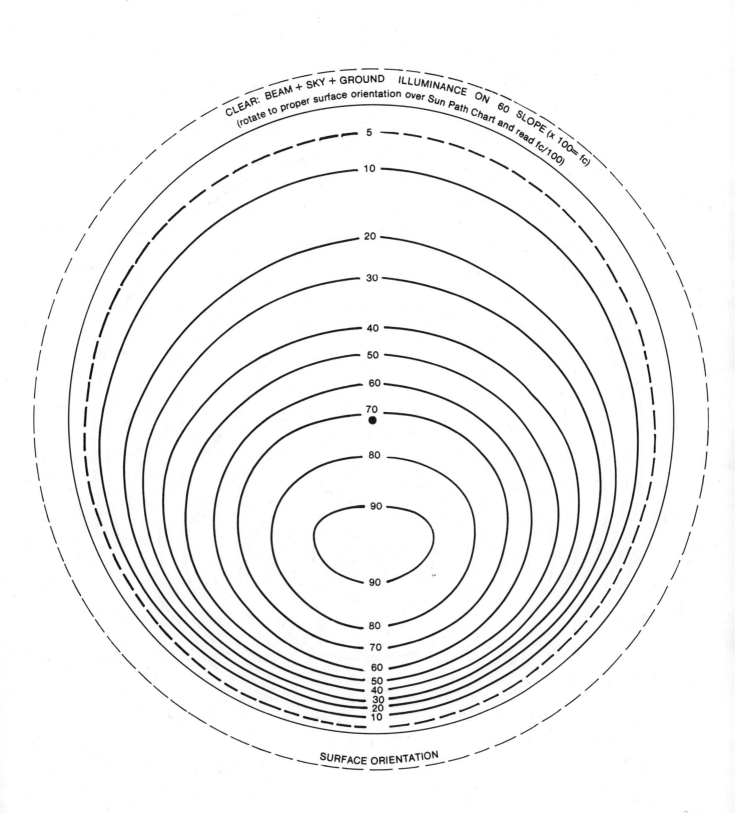

CLEAR: BEAM + SKY + GROUND ILLUMINANCE ON 60 SLOPE (x 100= fc)
(rotate to proper surface orientation over Sun Path Chart and read fc/100)

SURFACE ORIENTATION

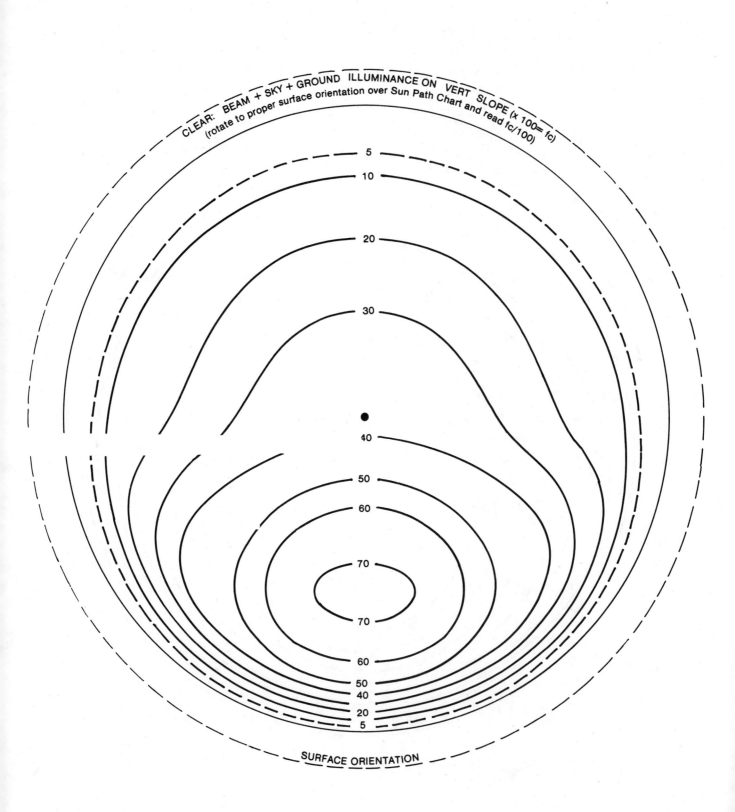

CLEAR: BEAM + SKY + GROUND ILLUMINANCE ON VERT SLOPE (x 100= fc)
(rotate to proper surface orientation over Sun Path Chart and read fc/100)

5
10
20
30
40
50
60
70
70
60
50
40
20
5

SURFACE ORIENTATION

APPENDIX C

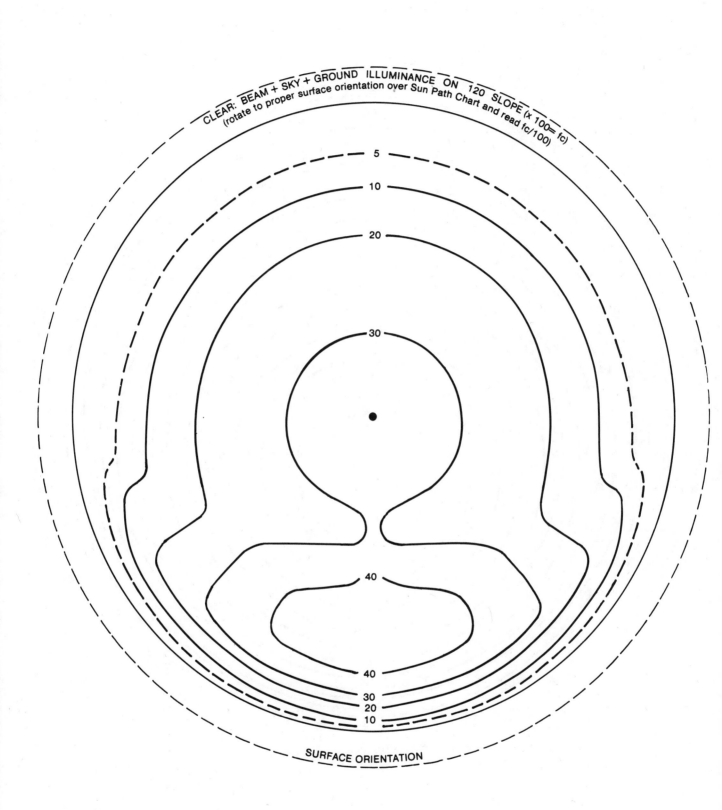

CLEAR: BEAM + SKY + GROUND ILLUMINANCE ON 120 SLOPE (x 100= fc)
(rotate to proper surface orientation over Sun Path Chart and read fc/100)

5

10

20

30

40

40

30
20
10

SURFACE ORIENTATION

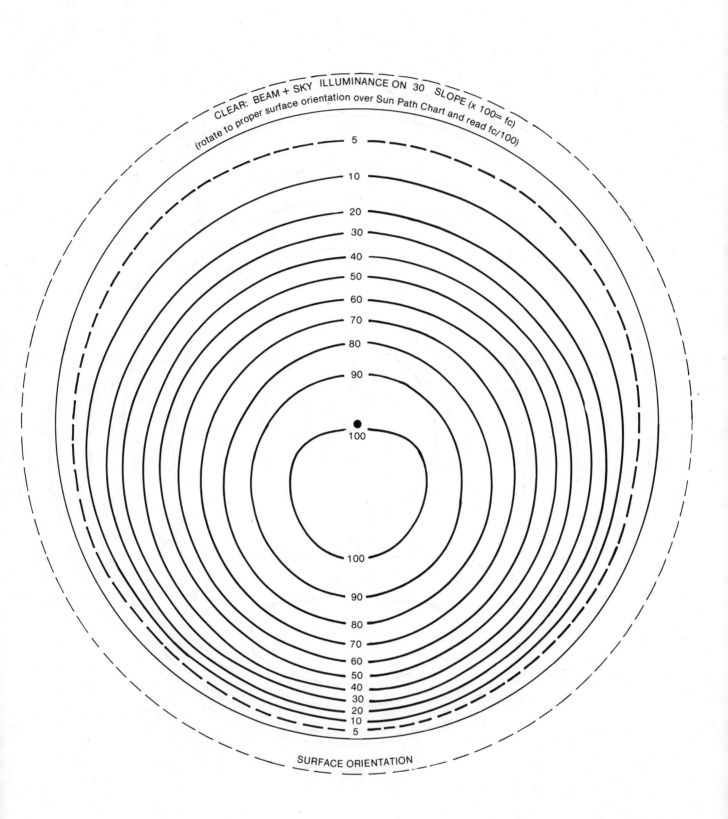

CLEAR: BEAM + SKY ILLUMINANCE ON 30 SLOPE (x 100= fc)
(rotate to proper surface orientation over Sun Path Chart and read fc/100)

SURFACE ORIENTATION

APPENDIX C

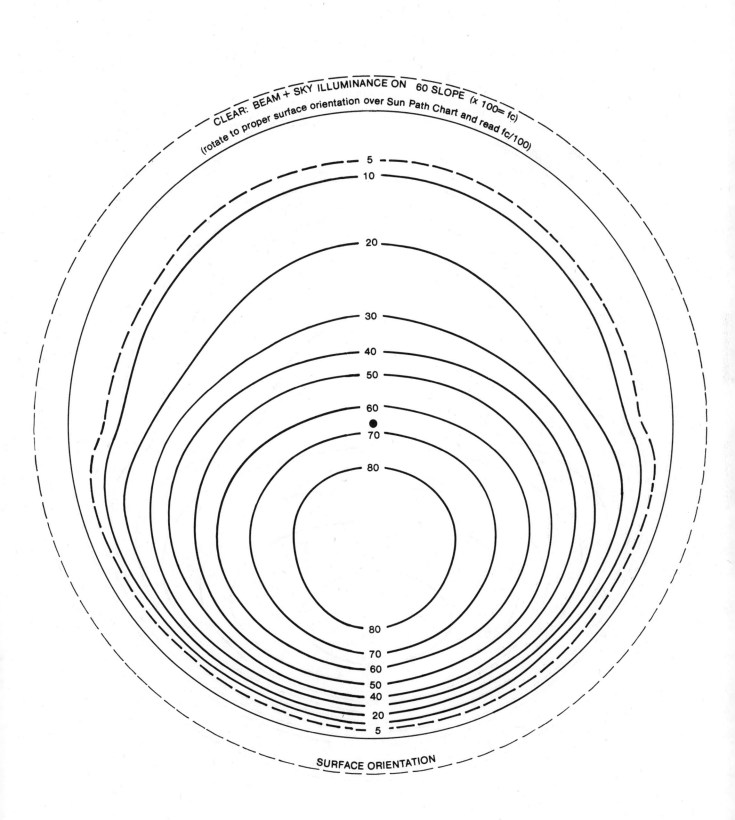

CLEAR: BEAM + SKY ILLUMINANCE ON 60 SLOPE (x 100= fc)
(rotate to proper surface orientation over Sun Path Chart and read fc/100)

5

10

20

30

40

50

60

70

80

80

70

60

50

40

20

5

SURFACE ORIENTATION

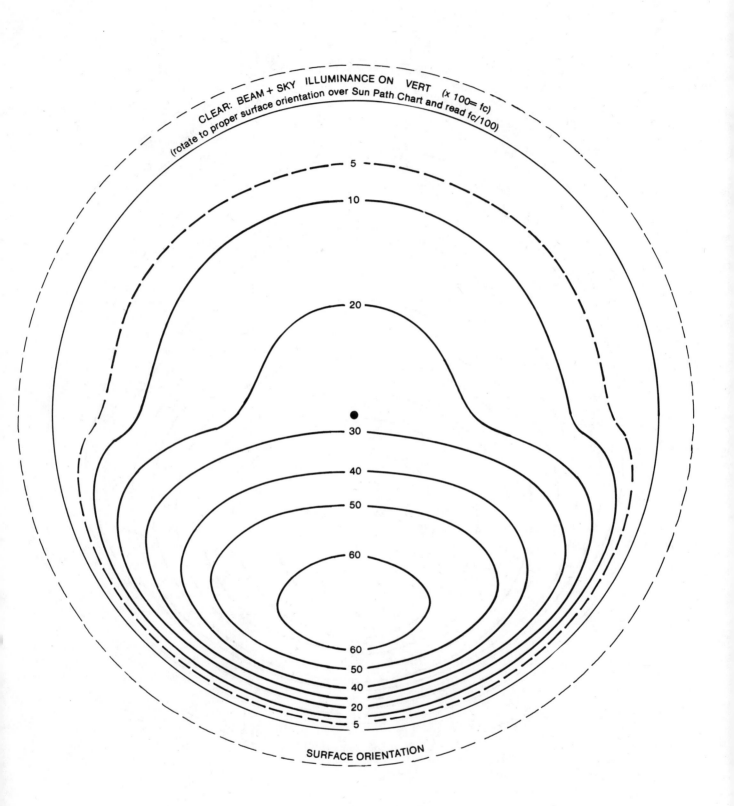

CLEAR: BEAM + SKY ILLUMINANCE ON VERT (x 100= fc)
(rotate to proper surface orientation over Sun Path Chart and read fc/100)

5

10

20

30

40

50

60

60

50

40

20

5

SURFACE ORIENTATION

APPENDIX C

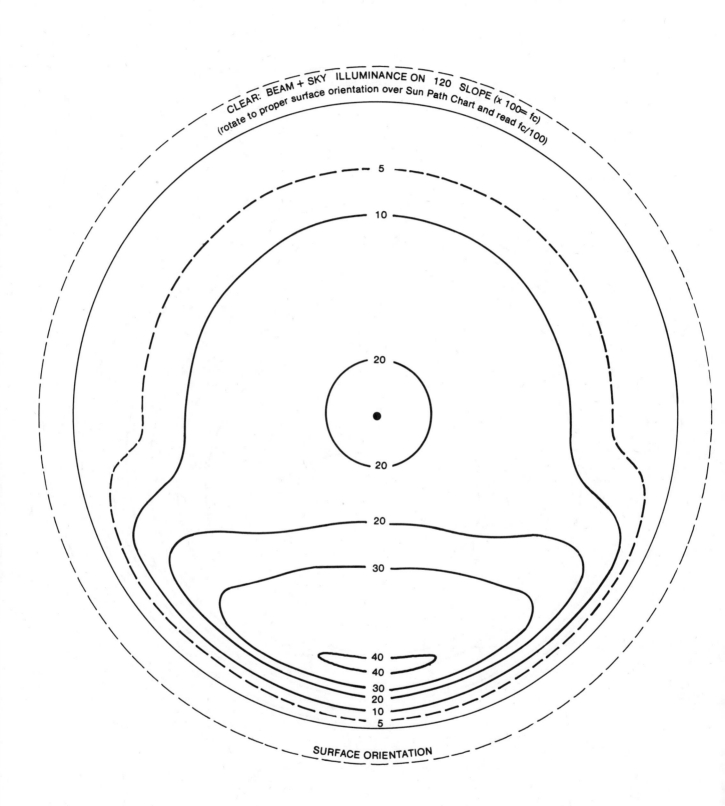

CLEAR: BEAM + SKY ILLUMINANCE ON 120 SLOPE (x 100= fc)
(rotate to proper surface orientation over Sun Path Chart and read fc/100)

5

10

20

20

20

30

40
40
30
20
10
5

SURFACE ORIENTATION

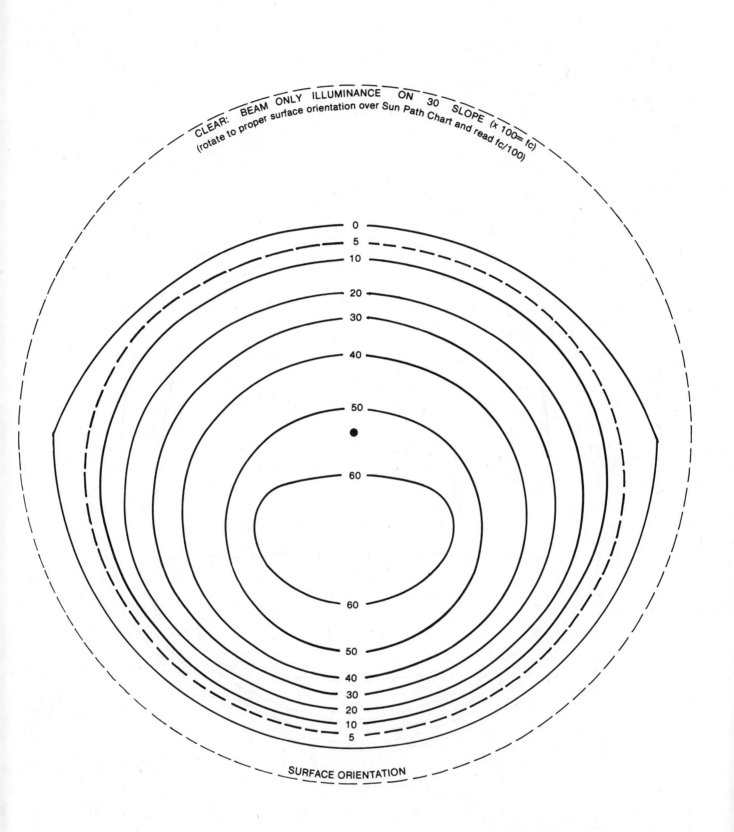

CLEAR: BEAM ONLY ILLUMINANCE ON 30 SLOPE (x 100= fc)
(rotate to proper surface orientation over Sun Path Chart and read fc/100)

0
5
10
20
30
40
50
60
60
50
40
30
20
10
5

SURFACE ORIENTATION

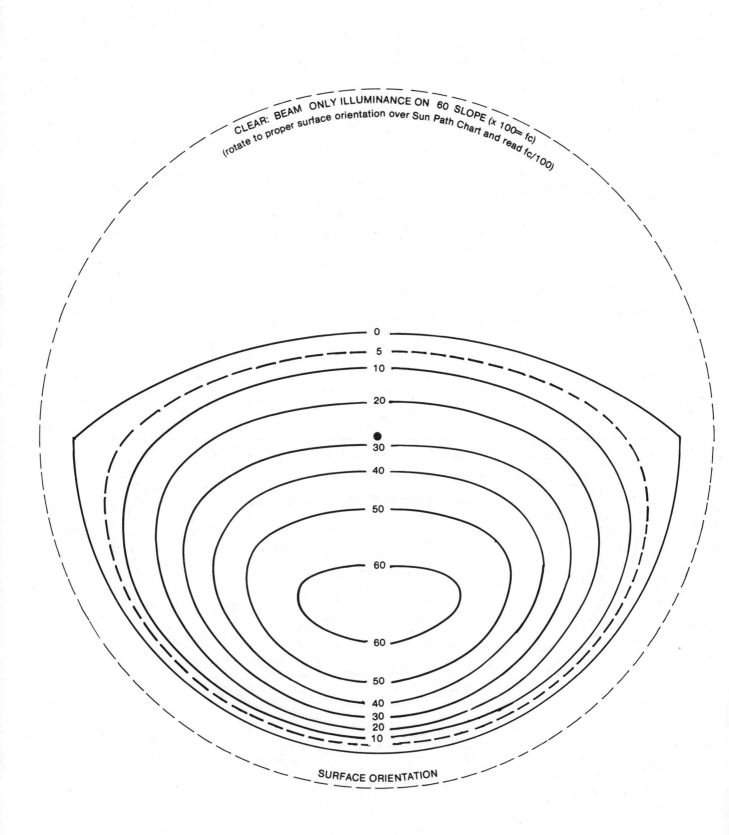

CLEAR: BEAM ONLY ILLUMINANCE ON 60 SLOPE (x 100= fc)
(rotate to proper surface orientation over Sun Path Chart and read fc/100)

0
5
10
20
30
40
50
60
60
50
40
30
20
10

SURFACE ORIENTATION

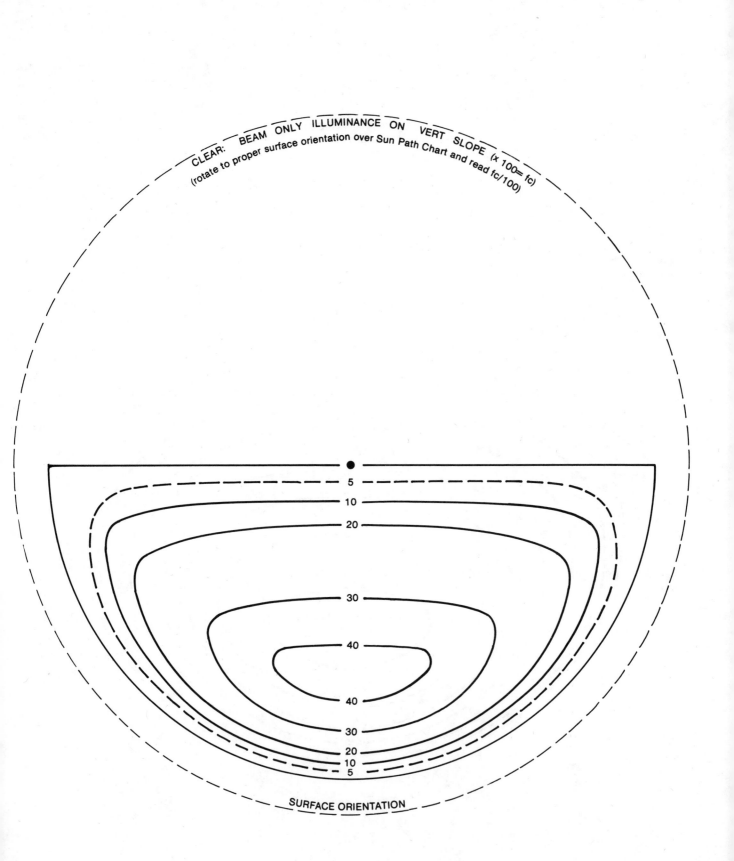

CLEAR: BEAM ONLY ILLUMINANCE ON VERT SLOPE (x 100= fc)
(rotate to proper surface orientation over Sun Path Chart and read fc/100)

5
10
20

30

40

40

30
20
10
5

SURFACE ORIENTATION

APPENDIX C

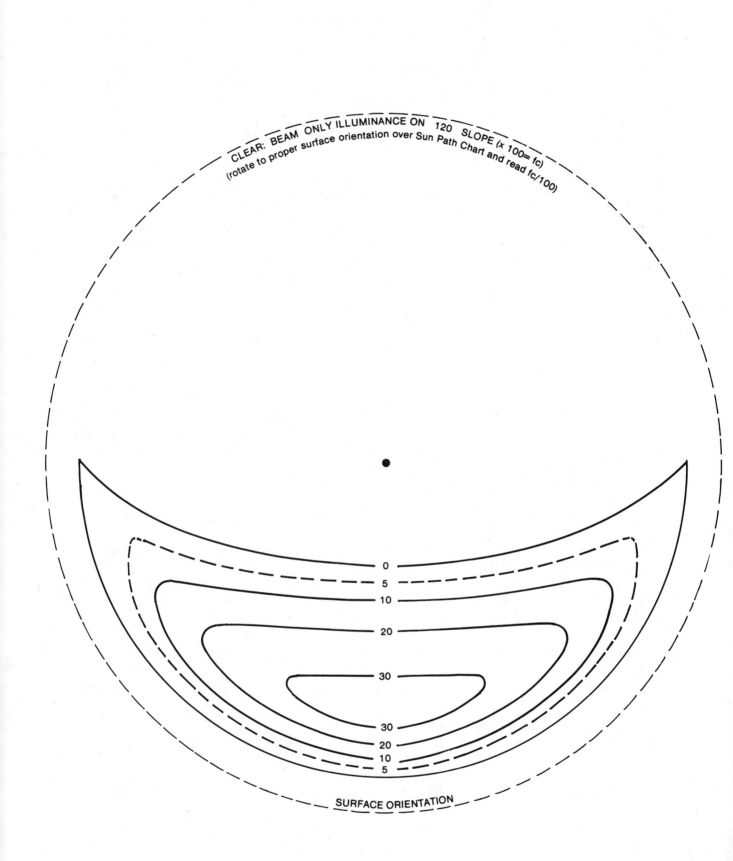

CLEAR: BEAM ONLY ILLUMINANCE ON 120 SLOPE (x 100= fc)
(rotate to proper surface orientation over Sun Path Chart and read fc/100)

0
5
10

20

30

30
20
10
5

SURFACE ORIENTATION

A computer program was written to determine the illuminance on an exterior surface when the sun was at every location in the skydome relative to the orientation of the surface. These data were plotted onto polar coordinates using equidistant skydome projection (i.e., L.O.F. sun angle calculator format). These plots form a chart that can be used as an overlay over the sun angle chart for the appropriate latitude (see Appendix B). The surface illuminance for a given time can be read from the overlay at the sun angle chart sun location for that time (figs. 15-24 and 15-25).

The values for nonhorizontal clear sky conditions are orientation dependent and can be indicated by isolux contours (see fig. 15-24). The values for horizontal clear sky and all overcast sky conditions are independent of surface orientation; the isolux contours for these conditions are concentric about the center of the chart and are plotted as several "spokes" on a single chart to save space (fig. 15-25).

The following charts for various combinations of clear (beam, sky, and ground) and overcast (sky and ground) conditions for five surface slopes (0-, 30-, 60-, 90-, and 120-degree slopes, where 0 degrees = horizontal and 90 degrees = vertical). The 120-degree "post-vertical" slope can be used to approximate the average illuminance on a window with an overhang having a 60-degree profile angle. Shorter overhangs can be approximated by interpolation between values for 120- and 90-degree slopes.

Note that these charts yield surface illuminances and do not include glazing transmission losses, which should be subtracted for interior calculations.

The Robbins-Hunter (1983) low turbidity algorithm was used for the clear day contours. The date-dependent parameters were interpolated based on solar altitude. The I.E.S. (1979) charts for horizontal and vertical overcast illuminance were interpolated to generate the overlays for overcast conditions. Ground reflectance was assumed to be 0.2.

REFERENCES

Daylighting Committee of the IES. "Recommended Practice of Daylighting." *Lighting Design and Applications,* 9 (1979): 25.

Robbins, C. L., and Hunter, K. C. "A Model for Illuminance on Horizontal and Vertical Surfaces." SERI report TR-254-1703. Golden, CO: Solar Energy Research Institute, 1983.

Appendix D:
Construction of a "Mirror-Box"
Artificial Overcast Sky

Airy (1983) has described the design, construction, calibration, and use of a "mirror-box" artificial overcast sky at the University of Washington. A summary of her findings follows.

DESIGN AND CONSTRUCTION

While in principle the design of a rectilinear sky is quite simple, there are few guidelines available for proportioning the various elements. Published descriptions and illustrations suggest vastly different designs, from tall enclosures to very flat boxes with plan dimensions nearly three times their height.

For the artificial sky at the University of Washington, a shape between these extremes was chosen: a box of near-cubic proportions, measuring four feet by five feet in plan, and five feet high, with the upper twelve inches reserved for the lamp housing. The basic construction is ⅜-inch plywood, framed at the edges for stiffness. Mirrored squares line all four walls, one of which is movable to provide access. The light source consists of twenty-four four-foot, forty-watt Vita-Lite fluorescent lamps, chosen specifically for their close approximation of the natural daylight spectrum; they are arranged in parallel on twelve ballasted fixtures and spaced to provide an even output distribution. Eight inches below the lamps is an acrylic diffuser of ⅛-inch Plexiglass, supported along the edges; the middle is supported at the one-third and two-thirds span points with suspended transparent buttons. The sides of the lamp housing are also lined with mirrors. Although fluorescent lamps are comparatively cool in operation, this arrangement generates 960 watts and thus overheating (with reduced efficiency) is a potential problem. To prevent this, several small holes are drilled in the plywood roof panel near the heat-generating ballasts, and two five-inch, propeller-type fans are mounted on the back panel of the lamp enclosure. The floor is painted a neutral concrete gray to approximate ground reflectance.

CALIBRATION OF THE U. W. SKY

Fully overcast skies give up to 2000 footcandles of illumination. In the University of Washington sky, initial tests of horizontal illumination with a Vactec illumination photometer showed values of about 1500 footcandles. Thus, even as lamp output diminished, a high level of illumination would be maintained.

Since the natural sky is a fluctuating light source, the formula for the C.I.E. standard overcast sky (Hopkinson, 1966, p. 44) was adopted as a stable reference:

$$B_o = B_z \frac{1 + 2 \sin Al}{3}$$

where: B_o is the luminance at altitude angle Al, and

B_z is the zenith luminance.

D-1. Luminance distribution of University of Washington artificial sky compared with C.I.E. standard overcast sky. (After Airy, 1983)

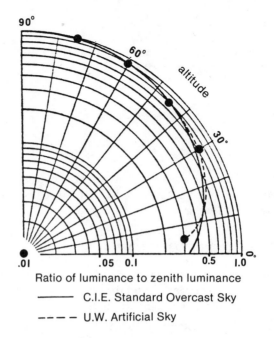

D-1. Luminance distribution of University of Washington artificial sky compared with C.I.E. standard overcast sky. (After Airy, 1983)

The luminance calibration measurements were obtained using a hand-held Minolta one-degree Spotmeter (a luminance meter), with an "angle-finder" level mounted on top for reading elevation angles. The luminance tests showed generally good results, with some variation according to test height and azimuth direction.

MODEL TESTING UNDER THE U. W. SKY

In constructing models for indoor testing it is necessary to keep in mind that the luminance distribution under the artificial sky varies when viewed from different positions. Thus, in a model that is too large, widely separated points within tend to "see" different skies. For an artificial sky of this size, model dimensions kept to eighteen inches or less produce good results.

To reduce the effect of a model's mirror image on the horizon, model exteriors should be white.

UTILIZATION OF THE U. W. SKY

The U. W. artificial sky has proven suitable for design studies and some daylighting research. Model studies under the artificial sky have been compared with results obtained with computer simulations of analogous rooms employing the *Uwlight* program (Bedrick, et al., 1978). While neither procedure has been fully checked against "real" conditions, the resulting correlation tends to verify both. The U. W. artificial sky was built in September, 1978 and has been in continuous operation since that time.

CONSTRUCTION DETAILS

The base (floor) of the sky is extended beyond the confines of the chamber to form a five-inch ledge. A small element of this edge slides out to provide a recessed channel for instrument leads.

The entire sky box is raised and mounted on a three-foot platform with a trapdoor (opening downward) so that the experimenter can get inside the sky chamber to move photocells or alter the model without opening the large front door panel and removing the model.

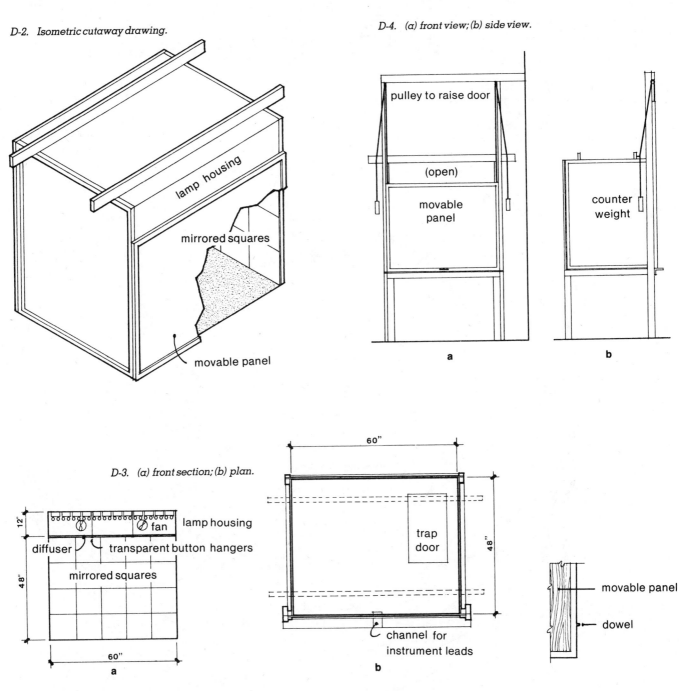

D-2. *Isometric cutaway drawing.*

lamp housing

mirrored squares

movable panel

D-4. *(a) front view; (b) side view.*

pulley to raise door

(open)

movable panel

counter weight

a

b

D-3. *(a) front section; (b) plan.*

12"

lamp housing

fan

diffuser   transparent button hangers

4'8"

mirrored squares

60"

a

60"

trap door

4'8"

channel for instrument leads

b

movable panel

dowel

a

mirror

track

dowel seat

b

The front door panel is mounted on wooden tracks and hung from pulleys with counterweights equivalent to the door weight, so that the door can easily be pushed out of the way for placing or removing test models. The vertical edges of the door panel each have two small pins (wooden dowels) to guide the door in the vertical tracks. The tracks are designed so that the door is held ⅜-inch out from the sky chamber (to protect the mirrors) until it is in the fully closed position; then the dowel pins fall forward into "seats," and the door is secured with simple casement window latches in its light-tight position.

REFERENCES

Airy, A. "An Artificial Sky for Daylighting Studies." In *Workbook: Daylighting Design Tools Workshop,* pp. 35–45. Washington, DC: American Institute of Architects Service Corporation, 1983.

D-5. *Movable door and tracks: (a) front view; (b) side view.*

Appendix E:
B.R.S. Protractors (Overcast Sky)

2
(SECOND SERIES)

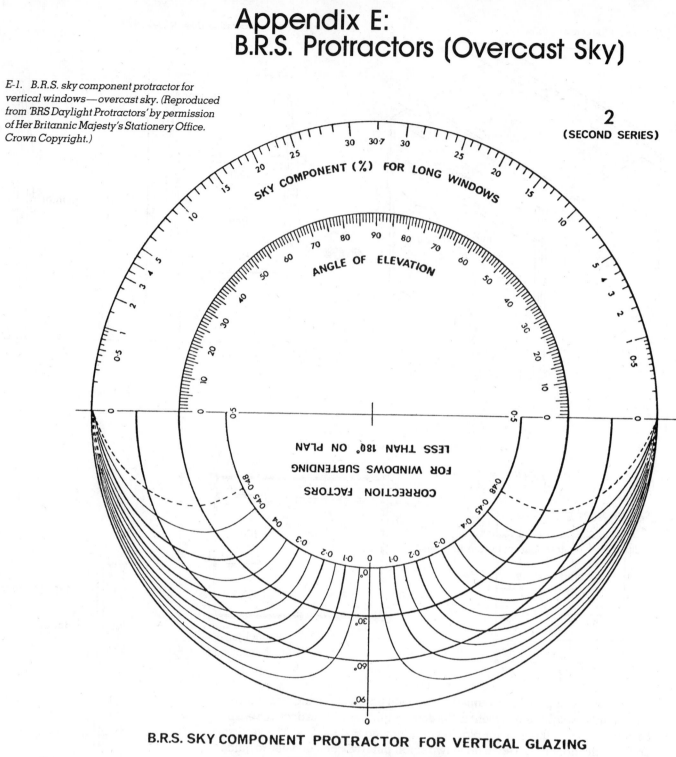

B.R.S. SKY COMPONENT PROTRACTOR FOR VERTICAL GLAZING

(C.I.E. OVERCAST SKY)

260

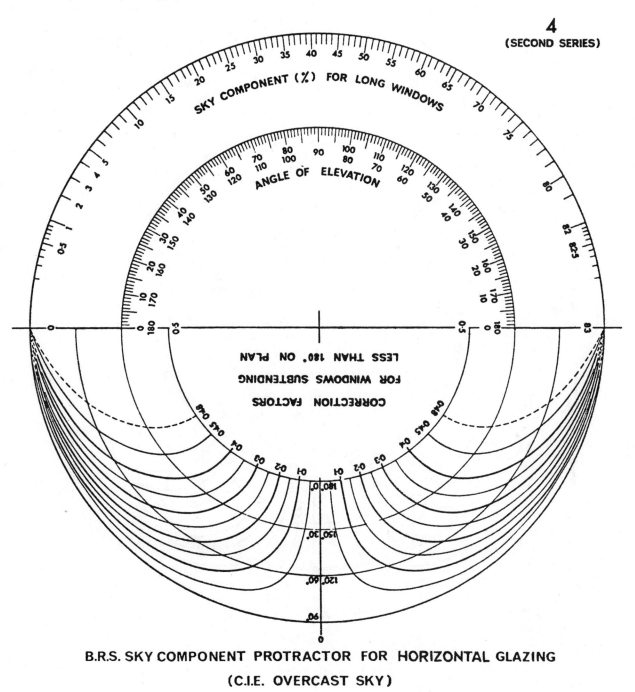

B.R.S. SKY COMPONENT PROTRACTOR FOR HORIZONTAL GLAZING

(C.I.E. OVERCAST SKY)

*E-3. B.R.S. sky component protractor for 30°
sloped windows—overcast sky. (Reproduced
from 'BRS Daylight Protractors' by permission
of Her Britannic Majesty's Stationery Office.
Crown Copyright.)*

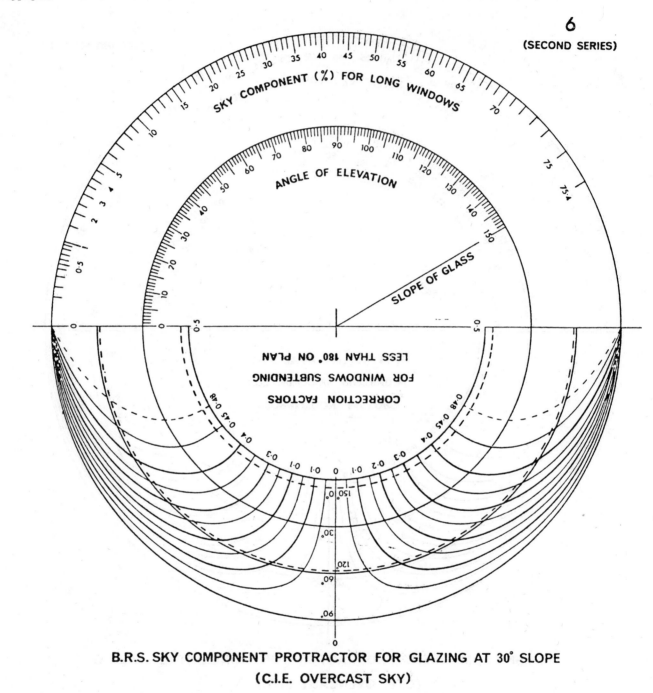

B.R.S. SKY COMPONENT PROTRACTOR FOR GLAZING AT 30° SLOPE
(C.I.E. OVERCAST SKY)

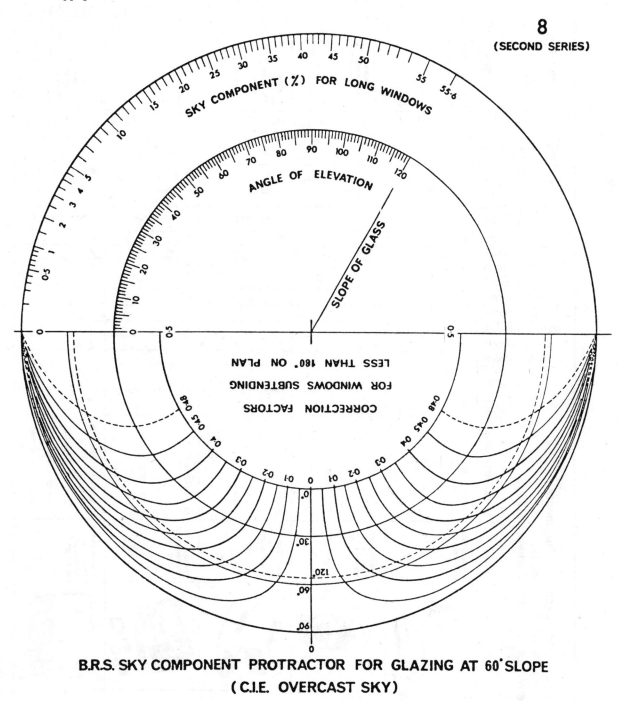

8
(SECOND SERIES)

B.R.S. SKY COMPONENT PROTRACTOR FOR GLAZING AT 60° SLOPE
(C.I.E. OVERCAST SKY)

Appendix F:
Survey of Lighting Instrumentation

F-1. Survey of lighting instrumentation. (Reproduced courtesy of Lawrence Berkeley Laboratory, University of California)

Survey of Light Measuring Instruments
Lawrence Berkeley Laboratory
University of California, Berkeley 94720

May 1983 Update LBL-12897

Attribute	Pritchard 1980A Photometer	Litemate/Spotmate System 500	1605 Spectra-spot Photometer/Radiometer; 1610	Spectra Photometer Model FC-200	Spectra Digital Photometer/Radiometer Model 301
MANUFACTURER	PHOTO RESEARCH DIV. OF KOLLMORGEN CORPORATION 3000 N. Hollywood Way Burbank, CA 91505 (213) 843-6100				
SENSITIVITY RANGE	$2 \times 10^{-5} - 2 \times 10^{7}$ fc	$10^{-1} - 1.999 \times 10^{4}$ fc / $10^{-2} - 1.999 \times 10^{4}$ fl*	$10^{-1} - 2 \times 10^{5}$ fl / $10^{-2} - 2 \times 10^{6}$ fl	$10^{-1} - 3 \times 10^{4}$ fc / $10^{-1} - 3 \times 10^{4}$ fl	$1.999 \times 10^{-2} - 1.999 \times 10^{4}$ fc / $1.999 \times 10^{0} - 1.999 \times 10^{6}$ fl** / **Luminance with 10° field
COSINE CORRECTION	●	●		●	●
CIE PHOTOPIC % DEVIATION					±1%*
SENSOR SIZE					
SILICON SENSOR		●	● ●		●
SELENIUM SENSOR				●	
DIGITAL DISPLAY	●	●		●	●
ANALOG DISPLAY			●	●	
LUMINANCE	●			●	●
ILLUMINANCE	●			●	●
METRIC			● ●		●
ENGLISH	●		● ●	●	●
SIZE	19¾" × 6¼" × 9"		12¼" × 6½" × 5½"	11¼" × 8½" × 4"	13¾" × 10¼" × 4¼"
WEIGHT	20½ lbs.	1½-2 lbs.	8½ lbs.	6 lbs.	8 lbs.
PORTABLE		●	● ●	●	●
LENGTH OF CORD SENSOR TO READOUT	5'		5"	6'	6'
COST / DATE	$13000 / 5/83	$950 / 5/83	$6400 / 5/83	$1355 / 5/83	$2900 / 5/83
COMMENTS	Photometer requires accessories for full range luminance and illuminance readings.	Handheld photometer and a luminance spotmeter with a 1° acceptance angle. *With Spotmate attached.	Photometer/radiometer ½° measuring field. *With optional illuminance accessories. 1° measuring.	Low-cost, portable, solid-state, multi-ranging photometer.	Model 301 provides direct measurement readings of illuminance, luminance, irradiance, radiance, radiant power, & integrated energy. Additional features: auto-null ambient light control, zero reset button, meter reading button & zero adjust for temperature & drift control. % dev. depends on individual sensor/filter combination.

(reproduced by permission)

Survey of Light Measuring Instruments
Lawrence Berkeley Laboratory
University of California, Berkeley 94720

Manufacturer	Model	Sensitivity Range	Cosine Correction	CIE Photopic % Deviation	Sensor Size	Silicon Sensor	Selenium Sensor	Digital Display	Analog Display	Luminance	Illuminance	Metric	English	Size	Weight	Portable	Length of Cord Sensor to Readout	Cost	Date	Comments
EG&G ELECTRO-OPTICS, 35 Congress St., Salem, MA 01970, (617) 745-3200	550-1 Radiometer/Photometer	$1.999\times10^{-3}-1.999\times10^{5}$ fc; $19.99\times10^{-3}-19.99\times10^{3}$ fl	●	±1%	1 cm²	●		●		●	●	●	●	9"×11"×3"	7 lbs.		5'	$1900	5/83	Optional 550-2 Type B Silica Multiprobe $750; System price: $2650.
GOSSEN, Berkey Marketing Companies, 25-20 Brooklyn-Queens Expressway West, Woodside, NY 11377, (212) 932-4040	Gossen Panlux Electronic Foot-candle & Foot-lambert Meter	$5\times10^{-2}-1.2\times10^{4}$ fc; $1.5\times10^{0}-3.6\times10^{5}$ fl	●		2¼" diam.		●		●	●	●		●	4¼"×3"×1¾"	13 oz.	●	1 m	$300	5/83	
INTERNATIONAL LIGHT, INC., Dexter Industrial Green, Newburyport, MA 01950, (617) 465-5923	IL410 Photometer	$3\times10^{-1}-10^{3}$ fc	●	±2%		●			●		●				2¼ lbs.		7'	$458	5/83	Compact low profile probe available. Comes with probe below.
	SC 110	$3\times10^{0}-10^{4}$ fc									●									High illumination probe.
	IL510A Research Photometer	$10^{-2}-10^{4}$ fc		±2%	1⅝"×1¾"	●			●		●			5.2"×11.2"×8.0"	7½ lbs.		7'	$1551	5/83	Programming switch reads currents in amps.
	IL710A Research Photometer	$2\times10^{-3}-5\times10^{4}$ fc		±2%		●		●			●			11"×5"×9"	15 lbs.	●	7'	$1938	5/83	Research photometer range as low as 4×10^{-8} with photomultiplier

(reproduced by permission)

Survey of Light Measuring Instruments
Lawrence Berkeley Laboratory
University of California, Berkeley 94720

MANUFACTURER	MODEL	SENSITIVITY RANGE	COSINE CORRECTION	CIE PHOTOPIC % DEVIATION	SENSOR SIZE	SILICON SENSOR	SELENIUM SENSOR	DIGITAL DISPLAY	ANALOG DISPLAY	LUMINANCE	ILLUMINANCE	METRIC	ENGLISH	SIZE	WEIGHT	PORTABLE	LENGTH OF CORD SENSOR TO READOUT	COST	DATE	COMMENTS
KRATOS ANALYTICAL INSTRUMENTS 24 Booker St. Westwood, NJ 07675 (201) 664-7263	M 460 Photomultiplier Photometer	100 microamps–100 picoamps*		±2%		●	●		●					5½"×8½"×10"	10 lbs.	●		$1980	5/83	*Not calibrated in fc or ft; no direct conversion.
LI-COR, INC. 4421 Superior Street P.O. Box 4425 Lincoln, NE 68504 (402) 467-3576	LI-210SB Photometric Sensor		●		1" diam. × 1" height	●											5	$265	5/83	2003S mounting fixture optional.
	LI-185B Quantum/Radiometer/Photometer	3×10¹–3×10⁶ lux							●		●	●		5"×7"×2.5"	2.44 lbs.	●		$495	5/83	Uses either batteries or AC adapter.
	LI-188B Integrating Quantum/Radiometer/Photometer	0–1.999×10⁶ lux						●			●	●		5.7"×10"×5.9"	4.25 lbs.	●		$990	5/83	Uses either batteries or AC adapter.
LICTMESSTECHNIK LMT GmbH Berlin u. Co., KG Helmholtzstr. 9 D-1000 Berlin 10 West Germany 030-393 40 28	Pocket-Lux Portable Illuminance Meter	10⁻¹–1.999×10⁶ lux	●	±1%	10mm diameter			●	with adapter		●	●		40mm × 80mm × 135mm	350 g	●		DM 1,490	3/81	Automatic ranging system. Storage of measured display. Special option—DM 1,790 with ext. photovoltaic cell and 3m connection cable. Uses either batteries or AC adapter.

(reproduced by permission)

Survey of Light Measuring Instruments
Lawrence Berkeley Laboratory
University of California, Berkeley 94720

MANUFACTURER	PHOTO	MODEL	SENSITIVITY RANGE	COSINE CORRECTION	CIE PHOTOPIC % DEVIATION	SENSOR SIZE	SILICON SENSOR	SELENIUM SENSOR	DIGITAL DISPLAY	ANALOG DISPLAY	LUMINANCE	ILLUMINANCE	METRIC	ENGLISH	SIZE	WEIGHT	PORTABLE	LENGTH OF CORD SENSOR TO READOUT	COST	DATE	COMMENTS
MEGATRON LTD. 165 Marlborough Road Hornsey Road London N19 4NE England		Architectural Model Luxmeter	0–10⁴ lux	●	2.96%	1.6 cm		●		●		●	●		13"×13"×4½"	7 lbs.	●	2 m	£650	3/81	12 individually operated photocells allow 12 simultaneous measurements ideal for model work.
		BRS Daylight Photometer	0–10⁶ lux	●	2.96%	2.5 cm		●		●		●	●		13"×8½"×5"	7½ lbs.	●	5 m	£450	3/81	Reads daylight factor directly 0–5%, 1–10%, 0–20%.
		B.R.E. Cylindrical Illuminance Meter	0–10⁴ lux	●	2.96%	2 cm × 4 cm		●		●		●	●		13"×5"×3"	3 lbs.	●	2 m	£265	3/81	Toggle switch to allow for cylindrical or planar measurement. Also potentiometer for zero drift correction.
		DA 5 Luxmeter	2.5×10⁻¹–2.5×10¹ lux	●	2.96%	6.7		●		●		●	●		10½"×5"×2½"	2 lbs.	●	2 m	£160	3/81	Low level illuminance meter. Portable, lightweight.
		Spatial Illumination Meter Mark 2	0–2.5×10⁴ lux	●	2.96%	2.5 cm									6"×13½"×8"	13½ lbs.	●	10 m	£490	3/81	

(reproduced by permission)

Survey of Light Measuring Instruments
Lawrence Berkeley Laboratory
University of California, Berkeley 94720

May 1983 Update
LBL-12897

MANUFACTURER	PHOTO	MODEL	SENSITIVITY RANGE	COSINE CORRECTION	CIE PHOTOPIC % DEVIATION	SENSOR SIZE	SILICON SENSOR	SELENIUM SENSOR	DIGITAL DISPLAY	ANALOG DISPLAY	LUMINANCE	ILLUMINANCE	METRIC	ENGLISH	SIZE	WEIGHT	PORTABLE	LENGTH OF CORD SENSOR TO READOUT	COST	DATE	COMMENTS
OPTRONIC LABORATORIES, INC. 730 Central Florida Parkway Orlando, FL 32809 (305) 857-9000		730A Radiometer/Photometer	10^{-6}–10^6 fc		±5%	1 cm²	●		●			●		●	15"×5"×9"	8 lbs.		4-6'	$2750	5/83	Direct reading in 14 units. Autoranging radiometer/photometer. Detector spectral response cal. 250-1100 nm. Radiometric & photopic filters, BCD output, and pulse integrator.
		85 Cosine Receptor		●															$265	5/83	Optional receptor for 730A.
		80 Relay Lens	10^0–10^6 fc									●		●					$825	5/83	Optical lens enables luminance and radiance measurements.
PHOTODYNE INC. 5356 Sterling Center Dr. Westlake Village, CA 91361 (213) 889-8770		88XLA Radiometer/Photometer			±6%		●		●			●		●		.6 kg	●	3"	$825	5/83	Range achieved with sensor model 650/750. *With 3001 Extension Head & cable ($95).
		650 Photometric Sensor Head	10^{-4}–10^3 fc		±6%	•	●					●	●	●	1" diam., 1¼" length				$295	5/83	Sensor heads may be set to match CIE curve at specific wavelength.

(reproduced by permission)

Survey of Light Measuring Instruments
Lawrence Berkeley Laboratory
University of California, Berkeley 94720

May 1983 Update — LBL-12897

MANUFACTURER	PHOTO	MODEL	SENSITIVITY RANGE	COSINE CORRECTION	CIE PHOTOPIC % DEVIATION	SENSOR SIZE	SILICON SENSOR	SELENIUM SENSOR	DIGITAL DISPLAY	ANALOG DISPLAY	LUMINANCE	ILLUMINANCE	METRIC	ENGLISH	SIZE	WEIGHT	PORTABLE	LENGTH OF CORD SENSOR TO READOUT	COST / DATE	COMMENTS
TEKTRONIX, INC. P.O. BOX 500 BEAVERTON, OR 97077 (503) 644-0161		J16 Photometer/Radiometer			NA				●		●	●	optional	●	2.4" × 4.6" × 8"	3.3 lbs.	●		$1180 5/83	Digital photometer/radiometer. Battery powered.
		J6511 Illuminance Probe	10^{-3}–1.999×10^3 fc	●	±2%		●					●	optional	●	*	11 oz.	●	25'	$540 5/83	*Probe consists of 2 pieces, 1½" × 6¾" × 1⅞" and 2½" × 1½" × 2½".
		J6503 8° Luminance Probe	10^{-1}–1.999×10^5 fl		±2%		●		●		●		optional	●	1⅞" × 6¾" × 1½"	4 oz.	●		$545 5/83	
		J6523 1° Luminance Probe	10^{-1}–1.999×10^6 fl		±2%		●		●		●		optional	●	5" × 9¼" × 2¼"	2¼ lbs.	●		$575 5/83	

(reproduced by permission)

Survey of Light Measuring Instruments
Lawrence Berkeley Laboratory
University of California, Berkeley 94720

May 1983 Update — LBL-12897

MANUFACTURER	MODEL	SENSITIVITY RANGE	COSINE CORRECTION	CIE PHOTOPIC % DEVIATION	SENSOR SIZE	SILICON SENSOR	SELENIUM SENSOR	DIGITAL DISPLAY	ANALOG DISPLAY	LUMINANCE	ILLUMINANCE	METRIC	ENGLISH	SIZE	WEIGHT	PORTABLE	LENGTH OF CORD SENSOR TO READOUT	COST	DATE	COMMENTS
UNITED DETECTOR TECHNOLOGY 3939 Landmark Street Culver City, CA 90230 (213) 204-2250	40X Opto-Meter	10^{-3}–10^4 fc / 10^{-2}–10^5 fl	●	±2%	1 cm²	●			●	●	●	●	●		3 lbs.	●	2 m	$495	5/83	Model 1153 Accessory Lens for luminance. Standard 248 sensing head optional $395
	181 PIC Radiometer/Photometer	10^{-4}–10^3 fc / 10^{-4}–10^6 fl	●	±2%	1 cm²	●		●		●	●	●	●		6 lbs.	●	2 m	$1545	5/83	Offers plug in calibration modules, with programmable decimal points. Standard 248 sensing head optional $395
	111A Radiometer/Photometer	10^{-2}–10^3 fc	●	±2%	1 cm²	●		●		●	●	●	●		6 lbs.		2 m	$1495	5/83	Laboratory standard. Model 1153 lens for luminance. Standard 248 sensing head optional $395
	3300 Digaphot Photometer	0–9.99×10² fc	●	±2%		●		●			●		●		9 oz.	●	2 m	$445	5/83	Rechargeable battery available. #1606 carrying case optional $25

(reproduced by permission)

Appendix G:
Daylighting Formulae

CONVERSIONS

1 meter = 3.2808 feet (1 foot = 0.30480 meters).

1 square meter = 10.7639 square feet (1 square foot = 0.092903 square meters).

1 degree = .01745329 radians (1 radian = 57.2957795 degrees).

1 solid degree = 0.0003046 steradians (1 steradian = 3282.8062 solid degrees).

natural log base e = 2.7182812.

1 lumen = 0.0014614 watts (1 watt = 683 lumens).

1 lumen = 0.004999 Btu/h (1 Btu/h = 200.04 lumens).

1 watt = 3.41443 Btu/h (1 Btu/h = 0.2931 watts).

1 candela = 1 lumen per steradian.

1 candela = 0.0014641 watts/steradian (1 watt = 683 candelas/steradian).

1 footcandle = 1 lumen per square foot.

1 lux = 1 lumen per square meter.

1 lux = 0.0001 phot = 0.1 milliphot.

1 footcandle = 10.763910 lux (1 lux = 0.9290304 footcandles).

1 footcandle = 0.0013959 langley/hour (1 langley = 716.3836 footcandles/hour).

1 footlambert = 3.426258 candelas/square meter (1 candela/square meter = 0.2918636 footlamberts).

1 candela/square meter = 1 nit = 10,000 stilbs.

1 candela/square meter = 3.14159 Apostilbs (asb) = 3.14159 blondels.

1 footcandle = illuminance on horizontal plane under sky of 1 footlambert uniform illuminance.

C.I.E. STANDARD OVERCAST SKY LUMINANCE DISTRIBUTION

(MOON AND SPENCER, 1942, ADOPTED BY C.I.E. IN 1955)

$$L_p = L_z \frac{1 + 2 \cos P_{al}}{3}$$

where:

L_p = sky luminance at any point P,

L_z = sky luminance at the zenith (overhead), and

P_{al} = altitude angle of point P (above the horizon).

C.I.E. STANDARD CLEAR SKY LUMINANCE DISTRIBUTION (KITTLER, 1965, ADOPTED BY C.I.E. IN 1973)

$$L_p = L_z \frac{\left(1 - e^{-0.32 \sec (P_z)}\right)\left(0.91 + 10\, e^{-3\, P_s}\right)\left(0.45^{\cos^2 (P_s)}\right)}{0.27385\,(0.91 + 10\, e^{-3S_z} + 0.45 \cos^2(S_z))}$$

where:

L_p = sky luminance at any point P,

L_z = sky luminance at zenith,

P_z = angle of point P from zenith,

P_s = angle of point P from sun (radians), and

S_z = angle of sun from zenith (radians).

ANGLE BETWEEN SUN AND ANY POINT IN THE SKY

$$P_z = \arccos\,(\cos(S_{az} - P_{az})\cos(S_{al})\cos(P_{al}) + \sin(S_{al})\sin(P_{al}))$$

where:

S_{az} = solar azimuth angle,

S_{al} = solar altitude angle,

P_{az} = point azimuth angle, and

P_{al} = point altitude angle.

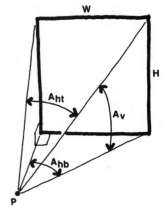

G-1. Illumination at a point P on a horizontal plane from a vertical rectangular window WH.

SKY COMPONENT—OVERCAST SKY (HOPKINSON, ET AL., 1966)

$$SC = ((.0682\,(A_{hb} - A_{ht})\cos\,(A_v))$$

$$+ (0.9095 \arcsin\,(\sin\,(A_{hb})\sin\,(A_v))$$

$$- (0.04547 \sin\,(2 \times A_v)\sin\,(A_{ht}))) \times 100\%$$

where: angles are in radians, and other terms are as shown in fig. G-1.

SOLAR DECLINATION

$$D_s\,(\text{in degrees}) = 23.45 \times \sin\,(0.9863013\,(284 + N))$$

where:

D_s = solar declination, and

N = Julian day of the year.

SOLAR HOUR ANGLE

$$A_{hs} \text{ (in degrees)} = 15 \times (12 - H)$$

where:

$$A_{hs} = \text{Solar hour angle, and}$$

$$H = 24 \text{ hour time.}$$

SOLAR ALTITUDE ANGLE

$$S_{al} = \arcsin (\sin (Lat) \sin (D_s) + \cos (Lat) \cos (D_s) \cos (A_{hs}))$$

where:

$$S_{al} = \text{solar altitude angle,}$$

$$Lat = \text{latitude,}$$

$$D_s = \text{solar declination, and}$$

$$A_{hs} = \text{solar hour angle.}$$

SOLAR AZIMUTH ANGLE

$$S_{az} = \arcsin \frac{\cos (D_s) \sin (A_{hs})}{\cos (S_{al})}$$

where:

$$S_{az} = \text{solar azimuth angle,}$$

$$D_s = \text{solar declination,}$$

$$A_{hs} = \text{solar hour angle, and}$$

$$S_{al} = \text{solar altitude angle.}$$

VERTICAL PROFILE ANGLE

$$A_p = \arctan \frac{\tan (S_{al})}{\cos (S_{az} - W_{az})},$$

where: A_p = vertical profile angle, and other terms are as shown in figure G-2.

G-2. *Vertical profile angle.*

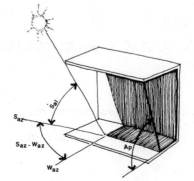

RATIO OF BEAM ILLUMINANCE ON A TILTED SURFACE TO THAT ON A HORIZONTAL SURFACE

$$R_b = \frac{\cos(Lat - SL)\cos(D_s)\cos(A_{hs}) + \sin(Lat - SL)\sin(D_s)}{\cos(Lat)\cos(D_s)\cos(A_{hs}) + \sin(Lat)\sin(D_s)}$$

where:

R_b = ratio of beam tilted to beam horizontal,

Lat = latitude,

D_s = solar declination,

A_{hs} = solar hour angle, and

SL = surface slope angle (90° = vertical).

REFERENCES

Hopkinson, R. G., Petherbridge, P., and Longmore, J. *Daylighting.* London: William Heinemann Ltd., 1966.

Kittler, R. "Standardization of Outdoor Conditions for the Calculation of the Daylight Factor with Clear Skies." In *Proceedings of the C.I.E. Intersessional Meeting on Sunlight.* Newcastle-upon-Tyne, 1965.

GLOSSARY OF DAYLIGHTING TERMS

absorptance The ratio of radiant flux absorbed by a medium to the incident radiant flux. See *absorption*.

absorption A process by which incident radiant flux is converted to another form of energy, usually (and ultimately) heat.

accent lighting Directional lighting designed to emphasize a particular object or to draw attention to a part of the field of view.

accommodation The process by which the eye changes focus from one distance to another.

adaptation The process by which the visual system becomes accustomed to more or less light, resulting from a change in the sensitivity of the eye to light.

altitude The vertical angular distance of a point in the sky above the horizon. Altitude is measured positively from the horizon to the zenith, from 0 to 90 degrees.

ambient lighting Lighting throughout an area that produces general illumination. See *task lighting*.

angle of collimation The angular size of a light source from a point on an irradiated surface.

angular size The solid angle subtended by a surface where the vertex is at a selected reference point.

apostilb (asb) A unit of luminance equal to 0.3183101 candela per square meter. One lumen per square meter leaves a surface whose luminance is 1 apostilb in all directions within a hemisphere. The use of this unit is deprecated.

apparent size The angular size of a surface as "seen" from a selected point location.

artificial sky An enclosure that simulates the luminance distribution of a real sky for the purpose of testing physical daylighting models. See *hemispherical dome artificial sky* and *mirror-box artificial sky*.

atmospheric transmissivity The ratio of the directly transmitted flux incident on a surface after passing through unit thickness of the atmosphere to the flux that would be incident on the same surface if the flux had passed through a vacuum.

average luminance (of a surface) The total luminous flux (lumens) leaving the surface per unit solid angle and unit area.

azimuth The horizontal angular distance between the vertical plane containing a point in the sky and true south.

baffle A single opaque or translucent element used to shield a source from direct view at certain angles or to absorb unwanted light.

beam component That component of flux received directly (or by specular reflection or transmission) from a point source (such as the sun or small lamp). It is a direct component.

blinding glare Glare that is so intense that, for an appreciable length of time after it has been removed, no object can be seen.

brightness The subjective perception of luminance. See *subjective brightness, luminance, veiling luminance.*

candela (cd) The SI unit of luminous intensity (formerly called the *candle*). One candela equals one lumen per steradian—the luminous intensity, in a given direction, of a source that emits monochromatic radiation at a frequency of 540E12 hertz and of which the radiant intensity in that direction is $\frac{1}{683}$ watts per steradian.

candlepower Luminous intensity expressed in candelas.

candlepower (intensity) distribution curve A curve, generally polar, representing the variation of luminous intensity of a lamp, luminaire, or fenestration in a plane through the light center.

cavity ratio (CR) A number indicating cavity proportions calculated from length, width, and height:

$$CR = \frac{5H(L + W)}{LW}$$

where:

$$H = \text{height of cavity,}$$

$$L = \text{room length, and}$$

$$W = \text{room width}$$

ceiling area lighting A general lighting system in

which the entire ceiling is, in effect, one large light source.

ceiling cavity The cavity formed by the ceiling, the plane of the luminaires, and the wall surfaces between these two planes.

central (foveal) vision The seeing of objects in the central or foveal part of the visual field approximately two degrees in diameter. Foveal vision allows one to see much finer detail than does peripheral vision.

chromaticity (of a color) Refers to the dominant or complementary wavelength and purity aspects of the color taken together, or of the aspects specified by the chromaticity coordinates of the color taken together.

C.I.E. method (for calculating daylighting illuminance) See *daylight factor method.*

clear sky (U.S. Weather Bureau) A sky that has less than thirty percent cloud cover. See *clear sky, C.I.E. standard.*

clear sky (C.I.E. Standard) A reference cloudless sky condition, having the greatest luminance near the sun and least luminance 90 degrees from the sun, as specified by a formula proposed by Kittler (1965) and adopted by the Commission Internationale de l'Eclairge (C.I.E.) in 1973.

clerestory That part of a building rising clear of the roofs or other parts, whose walls contain windows for lighting the interior.

cloudy sky (U.S. Weather Bureau) A sky having more than 70 percent cloud cover.

coefficient of attenuation The decrement in flux per unit distance in a given direction within a medium.

coefficient of beam utilization (CBU) The ratio of luminous flux (lumens) reaching a specified area directly from a source to the total beam luminous flux (lumens).

coefficient of utilization (CU) The ratio of luminous flux (lumens) from a source calculated as received on the workplane to the luminous flux emitted by the source alone.

color temperature (of a source) The absolute temperature of a blackbody radiator having a chromaticity equal to that of the light source.

Commission Internationale de l'Eclairge (C.I.E.) International lighting commission whose commission whose standards, procedures, and definitions are in general use in Europe, but less widely accepted in North America.

complete diffusion Diffusion in which the diffusing medium redirects the incident flux by scattering so that none of it is in an image-forming state.

cone A retinal receptor that dominates the retinal response when the luminance level is high and provides the basis for the perception of color.

contrast Luminance differences.

contrast sensitivity The ability to detect the presence of luminance differences.

cosine law The law that the illuminance on any surface varies as the cosine of the angle of incidence. (The angle of incidence is the angle between the normal to the surface and the direction of the incident light.)

cut-off angle The critical viewing angle beyond which a source can no longer be seen because of an obstruction (such as a baffle or overhang).

dark adaptation The process by which the retina becomes adapted to a luminance of less than 0.01 footlamberts.

daylight factor (DF) The ratio of daylight illumination at a given point on a given plane due to the light received directly or indirectly from a sky of assumed or known luminance distribution, to the illumination on a horizontal plane due to an unobstructed hemisphere of this sky, expressed as a percentage. Direct sunlight is excluded for both values of illumination. The daylight factor is the sum of the sky component, the external reflected component, and the internal reflected component. The interior plane is usually horizontal. If the sky condition is the C.I.E. standard overcast condition, then the DF will remain constant, regardless of absolute exterior illuminance. If used in conjunction with other than standard overcast conditions, the sky conditions should be specified. The term is also informally applied to the ratio of horizontal interior to exterior illuminance in the fenestration plane; under clear sky conditions, the DF remains constant only if the fenestration is completely diffusing (such as an ideal opalescent glass).

daylight factor method A method for calculating the daylighting illuminance in buildings. Based on theoretical principles (as compared with the lumen method, which is based on empirical studies), the daylight factor is computed by adding the sky component, the external reflected component, and the internal reflected component. Also known as the C.I.E. or the B.R.S. methods.

densitometer A photometer for measuring the optical density (common logarithm of the reciprocal of the transmittance) of materials.

diffuse lighting Lighting provided on the workplane or on an object that is not predominantly incident from any particular direction.

diffuse reflectance The ratio of the flux leaving a surface or medium by diffuse reflection to the incident flux.

diffuse reflection The process by which incident flux is redirected over a range of angles.

diffuse transmission The process by which the incident flux passing through a surface or medium is scattered.

diffuse transmittance The ratio of the diffusely transmitted flux leaving a surface or medium to the incident flux.

diffusing surfaces and glazings Those surfaces and glazings that redistribute some of the incident flux by scattering in all directions.

direct component That portion of flux, from sources such as the sky or sun, that arrives at a specified location without further diffusion.

direct glare Glare resulting from high luminances or insufficiently shielded light sources in the field of view. Direct glare is usually associated with bright areas, such as the sky, that are outside the visual task or region being viewed.

direct sky light That portion of daylight that arrives at a specified location directly from the skydome without further diffusion.

direct sunlight (beam sunlight) That portion of daylight that arrives at a specified location directly from the sun without diffusion.

disability glare Glare resulting in reduced visual performance and visibility. Often accompanied by discomfort glare.

disability glare factor (DGF) A measure of the visibility of a task in a given lighting installation in comparison with its visibility under reference lighting conditions, expressed in terms of the ratio of luminance contrasts having an equivalent effect upon task visibility. The value of DGF takes into account the equivalent veiling luminance produced in the eye by the pattern of luminances in the task surround.

discomfort glare Glare producing discomfort. Does not necessarily interfere with visual performance or visibility.

discomfort glare factor The numerical assessment of the capability of a single source of brightness in a given environment for producing discomfort. (This term is obsolete and usually applied to electric lighting.)

discomfort glare rating (DGR) A numerical assessment of the capacity of a number of sources of luminance in a given visual environment for producing discomfort. The DGR is the net effect of the individual values of the index of sensation for all of the luminous areas in the field of view. Primarily applicable to electric lighting; the *glare index* is preferred for daylighting applications. See also *discomfort glare factor*.

effective ceiling cavity reflectance A number giving the combined reflectance effect of the walls and ceiling of the ceiling cavity. See *ceiling cavity ratio*.

effective floor cavity reflectance A number giving the combined reflectance effect of the walls and floor of the floor cavity. See *floor cavity ratio*.

efficacy A measure of the luminous efficiency of a radiant flux, expressed in lumens per watt as the quotient of the total luminous flux by the total radiant flux. For daylighting, this is the quotient of visible flux incident on a surface to radiant flux on that surface. For electric sources, this is the quotient of the total luminous flux emitted by the total lamp power input.

efficiency See *efficacy*.

electromagnetic spectrum A continuum of electric and magnetic radiation encompassing all wavelengths.

elevation The altitude of the angular center of a distributed daylight source (such as the sky visible through a window from a reference point).

emissivity The ratio of radiance (for directional emissivity) or radiant exitance (for hemispherical emissivity) of an element of surface on a temperature radiator to that of a blackbody at the same temperature. By Kirchoff's Law, for a given wavelength of the electromagnetic spectrum, emissivity of a surface equals its absorptivity (and is the reciprocal of its reflectivity).

emittance The ratio of the radiance in a given direction (for directional emittance) or radiant exitance (for hemispherical emittance of a sample of a thermal radiator) to that of a blackbody radiator at the same temperature.

equivalent sphere illumination (ESI) The level of sphere illumination that would produce task visibility equivalent to that produced by a specific lighting environment. The presence of veiling reflections on a task surface reduces the ESI.

exitance (luminous) The density of luminous flux leaving a surface at a point. Formerly *luminous emittance*.

external reflected component (of the daylight factor) The ratio of that part of the daylight illumination at a point on a given plane that is received directly from external reflecting surfaces illuminated directly or indirectly by a sky of assumed or known luminance distribution, to the illumination on a horizontal plane due to an unobstructed hemisphere of this sky, expressed as a percent. In the case of clear sky conditions, the contribution of external surface luminance due to direct sunlight, if present, is included; however, the contribution of direct sunlight to the illumination of the exterior and interior reference planes is excluded. Note that the inclusion of the sunlit contribution to exterior surface illuminance is contrary to practice in Europe, but is proposed as more applicable to North American climates.

fenestration Any opening or arrangment of openings (normally filled with glazing media) for the admission of daylight, including any devices in the immediate proximity of the opening that affect distribution (such as baffles, louvers, draperies, overhangs, light-shelves, jambs, sills, and other light-diffusing materials).

fixture Informal substitute term for *luminaire.*

floor cavity The cavity formed by the workplane, the floor, and the wall surfaces between these two planes.

floor cavity ratio A number indicating floor cavity proportions calculated from length, width, and height:

$$FCR = \frac{5H\,(L\,+\,W)}{LW}$$

where:

H = floor cavity height,

L = room length, and

W = room width.

flux The time rate of flow. For example, volume per hour is the flux of a fluid.

flux trar.sfer theory A method of calculating the illuminance in a room by taking into account the interreflection of the light flux from the room surfaces based on the average flux transfer between surfaces.

footcandle (fc) The unit of illuminance when the foot is taken as the unit of length. One footcandle equals one lumen per square foot (or the illuminance produced on a surface all points of which are at a given distance from a directionally uniform point source of one candela). One footcandle of illuminance is received by a horizontal surface under an unobstructed sky having a uniform luminance of one footlambert.

footcandle meter See *illuminance meter.*

footlambert (fL) A unit of luminance equal to 0.3183010 candela per square foot, or to the uniform luminance of a perfectly diffusing surface emitting or reflecting light at a rate of one lumen per square foot, or to the average luminance of a surface emitting or reflecting light at that rate. An unobstructed sky of one footlambert uniform luminance contributes one footcandle of illuminance on a horizontal plane.

fovea A small region at the center of the retina, subtending about two degrees and forming the site of the most distinct vision and greatest color discrimination.

general lighting Lighting designed to provide a uniform level of illumination throughout an area, exclusive of any provision for local lighting requirements.

glare The sensation produced by luminance within the visual field that is sufficiently greater than the luminance to which the eye is adapted to cause annoyance, discomfort, or loss in visual performance and visibility. The magnitude of this sensation depends on such factors as the size, position, and luminance of a source, the number of sources, and the luminance to which the eyes are adapted. See *blinding glare, direct glare, disability glare,* and *discomfort glare.*

glare index A method of predicting the presence of discomfort glare due to daylighting. Factors affecting the *glare index* include the size and relative position of fenestration, sky luminance, and interior luminances. Most widely used in Europe, the *glare index* is similar to the *index of sensation* and the *discomfort glare rating,* which are used in North America for electric lighting applications.

goniophotometer A photometer for measuring the directional light distribution characteristics of sources, luminaires, media, and surfaces.

ground light Visible radiation from the sun and sky reflected by exterior surfaces below the plane of the horizon. See *external reflected component.*

hemispherical dome artificial sky A dome-shaped enclosure that is illuminated to simulate the luminance distribution of a sky for the purposes of testing physical models.

hemispherical reflectance The ratio of all of the flux leaving a surface or medium by reflection to incident flux. (Note: if reflectance is not preceded by an adjective descriptive of other angles of view, hemispherical reflectance is implied.)

hemispherical transmittance The ratio of all of the flux leaving a surface or medium by transmission to incident flux. (Note: if transmittance is not preceded by an adjective descriptive of other angles of view, hemispherical transmittance is implied.)

hue (of a perceived color) The attribute of a color that allows it to be classified as red, yellow, blue, and so on.

illuminance The density of the luminous flux incident on a surface, expressed in units of footcandles (or lux).

illuminance meter A photometer for measuring illuminance from visible flux on a plane. It must be color-corrected (that is, sensitivity must match that of the human eye) and cosine-corrected (have a flat receiving surface, usually with a special edge configuration to compensate for increased diffusion disk reflection at high angles of incidence).

Illuminating Engineering Society (of North America) A professional society devoted to the dissemination of knowledge relating to the art and science of illumination.

illumination The act of illuminating or state of being illuminated. This term has been used for density of luminous flux on a surface (illuminance) but such use is deprecated.

incandescence The self-emission of visible flux due to the thermal excitation of molecules.

index of sensation (M) (of a source) A number that expresses the effects of source luminance, apparent (angular) size, position in the field of view, and field luminance on the discomfort glare rating.

indirect component The portion of luminous flux arriving at the workplane after being diffused by terrestrial materials (such as interior and exterior diffuse reflective surfaces and translucent glazing materials).

indirect sources Surfaces which, after being illuminated by other sources (direct sources such as the sun, sky, or electric light, or other indirect sources), have measurable luminance and, in turn, become sources themselves.

infrared radiation Radiation with wavelengths too long to be perceived by the human eye (that is, longer than 0.77 microns) and less than 1,000 microns. *Room IR* is infrared radiation in the 7.7–8.0 micron region and typical of that radiated from surfaces near room temperature.

integrating photometer A photometer that enables total luminous flux from all directions to be determined by a single measurement.

intensity A shortening of the terms *luminous intensity* and *radiant intensity*. Often misused for level of illuminance.

interflection (interreflection) The multiple reflection of light by various surfaces prior to reaching a designated point.

internal reflected component The ratio of that part of the daylight illumination at a point on a given plane that is received from internal reflecting surfaces (the sky being of assumed or known luminance distribution) to the illumination on a horizontal plane due to an unobstructed hemisphere of this sky, expressed as a percent. The contribution of direct sunlight to the luminances of internal reflecting surfaces and to the illumination of the comparison plane is excluded.

inverse-square law The law stating that the illuminance at a point on a surface varies directly with the intensity of a point source, and inversely as the square of the distance between that source and that surface.

irradiance (E) The density of radiant flux incident on a surface.

isocandela line A line plotted on any appropriate set of coordinates to show directions in space, about a source of light, in which the intensity is the same. A series of such curves, usually in equal increments of intensity, is called an *isocandela diagram*.

isodaylight factor line A line plotted on any appropriate set of coordinates to show all the points on a surface where the daylight illuminance is the same and measured as daylight factor. A series of such lines for various illuminance values plotted on a building floor plan is called an *isodaylight factor* (or more informally *isolux*) *plan*.

isolux (isofootcandle) line A line plotted on any appropriate set of cordinates to show all the points on a surface where the illuminance is the same. A series of such lines for various illuminance values is called an *isolux (isofootcandle) diagram*.

lambert (L) A unit of luminance equal to 0.3183101 candela per square centimeter. One lumen per square centimeter leaves a surface whose luminance is one lambert in all directions within a hemisphere. The use of this unit is deprecated.

light Radiant energy that is capable of exciting the retina and producing a visual sensation. The visible portion of the electromagnetic spectrum (light) extends from about 0.38 to 0.77 microns.

light adaptation The process by which the retina becomes adapted to a luminance greater than about 1.0 footlambert.

light loss factor (LLF) A factor used in calculating the illuminance after a given period of time and under given conditions. It takes into account temperature and voltage variations, lamp depreciation (of electric luminaires), dirt accumulation on luminaire and room surfaces, maintenance procedures and atmosphere conditions. Formerly called *maintenance factor*.

light shelf A horizontal shelf positioned (usually above eye level) to reflect daylight onto the ceiling and to shield direct glare from the sky.

local lighting Lighting designed to provide illuminance over a relatively small area without providing any significant general surrounding lighting.

localized general lighting Lighting that utilizes sources above the visual task and also contributes to the illumination of the surround.

louver A series of baffles used to shield a light source from view at certain angles or to absorb unwanted light. The baffles are usually arranged in a geometric pattern.

louver shielding angle The angle between the horizontal plane of the baffles or louver grid and the plane at which the louver conceals all objects above.

lumen (lm) The luminous flux emitted within a unit solid angle (one steradian) by a point source having a uniform luminous intensity of one candela.

lumen-hour (lmh) The quantity of light delivered in one hour by a flux of one lumen.

lumen method (daylighting) A method of estimating the interior illuminance due to window daylighting at three locations within a room. Based on empirical studies, the use of this method is primarily limited to North America.

luminaire A complete electric lighting unit including housing, lamp, and focusing and/or diffusing elements; informally referred to as *fixture*.

luminance Luminous intensity of a surface in a given direction. More precisely, the quotient of the luminous intensity in the given direction of an infinitesimal element of the surface containing the point under consideration, by the orthogonally projected area of the element on a plane perpendicular to the given direction. Formerly *photometric brightness.*

luminous flux The time rate of flow of light.

luminous intensity The luminous flux per unit solid angle in the direction in question. Units are candelas or lumens per steradian.

lux (lx) The SI unit of illuminance equal to one lumen per square meter.

matte surface Surface from which the reflection is predominantly diffuse, with or without a negligible specular component. See *diffuse reflection.*

micron 0.000001 meter (one million microns = one meter).

mired A unit of reciprocal color temperature; 1/Tk × 1,000,000, where *Tk* is color temperature in degrees Kelvin.

mirror-box artificial sky A rectangular enclosure having a luminous ceiling and mirror walls for the purpose of simulating the luminance distribution of the sky by specular interreflection, for the purpose of physical model daylighting study.

monitor A raised section of roof that includes a vertically (or near-vertically) glazed aperture for the purpose of daylight illumination.

near infrared (solar infrared) The region of the electromagnetic spectrum between 0.77 to 1.4 microns. Most of the infrared solar radiation falls into this region. This near infrared (or *solar IR*) region is transmitted, absorbed, and reflected in a similar manner to visible light by most glazing and nonmetallic building materials.

nit (nt) Unit of luminance equal to one candela per square meter.

no-sky line A line that separates all points in the workplane at which the sky is directly visible from those at which no section of the sky is directly visible.

orientation The relation of a building with respect to compass directions. Exterior wall orientation is the compass direction that the exterior surface of a wall faces.

overcast sky (C.I.E. Standard Condition) A sky luminance distribution three times brighter near the zenith than at the horizon, as defined by a formula proposed by Moon and Spencer in 1942 and adopted by the Commission Internationale de l'Eclairge in 1955 (see Appendix G).

overcast sky (U.S. Weather Bureau) Sky that has 100 percent cloud cover (sun is not visible).

overhang A horizontal building projection, usually above a window, for the purpose of shading.

partly cloudy sky Sky that has 30 to 70 percent cloud cover.

peripheral vision The seeing of objects displaced from the primary line of site and outside of the central visual field.

phot (ph) The unit of illuminance equal to one lumen per square centimeter.

photometer An instrument for measuring photometric quantities such as luminance, luminous intensity, luminous flux, and illuminance.

photometric brightness A term formerly used for *luminance.*

photometry The science of the measurement of quantities associated with light.

point method A method of estimating the illuminance

at various locations in a building using photometric data.

polar angle Angular measurement in a polar coordinate system.

polar coordinates Numbers that locate a point in a plane by its distance from a fixed point on a line and the angle this line makes with a fixed line.

pupil The opening in the iris of the eye that admits light.

pyranometer An instrument for measuring irradiance in a plane. Usually calibrated for measurement of beam and diffuse solar radiation and mounted in the horizontal plane.

pyrheliometer An instrument for measuring radiant flux from a point source (such as the sun). For solar applications, the instrument is typically mounted in a motorized tracking device.

radiant energy (radiation) Energy traveling in the form of electromagnetic waves. Measured in units of energy such as joules, ergs, or kilowatt-hours.

radiation See *radiant energy.*

reflectance The ratio of reflected flux to incident flux.

reflectance factor (R) The ratio of the radiant (or luminous) flux reflected in delimited directions to that reflected in the same directions by a perfectly reflecting diffuser identically irradiated (or illuminated).

reflected glare Glare resulting from specular reflection of high luminances in polished or glossy surfaces in the field of view. See *veiling reflection.*

reflection The process by which incident flux leaves a surface or medium from the incident side, without change in frequency.

refraction The process by which the direction of light changes as it passes obliquely from one medium to another in which its speed is different.

regular reflection See *specular reflection.*

regular transmission See *specular transmission.*

retina A light-sensitive membrane lining the posterior part of the inside of the eye.

rods Retinal receptors that respond to low levels of luminance but cannot distinguish hues. Not present in the center of the foveal region.

room cavity The cavity formed by the plane of the luminaires, the workplane, and the wall surfaces between these two planes.

room cavity ratio (RCR) A number indicating room

cavity proportions:

$$RCR = \frac{5H\,(L\,+\,W)}{LW}$$

where:

H = height of luminaire/workplane,

L = room length, and

W = room width.

room ratio (RR) A number indicating room proportions, equal to 5.0/room cavity ratio.

room utilization factor (RUF) The ratio of lumens received on the workplane in a room to that emitted by the luminaire or fenestration.

shade A screen made of opaque or translucent material to prevent a light source from being directly visible at normal angles of view.

shielding angle See *cut-off angle.*

sky component The ratio of that part of the daylight illumination at a point on a given plane that is received directly from a sky of assumed or known luminance distribution, to the illuminance on a horizontal plane due to an unobstructed hemisphere of this sky, expressed as a percent.

skydome An imaginary hemispherical dome representing the sky overhead.

sky factor The sky component of the daylight factor if the sky has uniform luminance distribution.

sky light Daylight from the skydome only.

skylight A relatively horizontal glazed roof aperture for the admission of daylight.

skyvault See *skydome.*

solid angle A measure of that portion of space about a point bounded by a conic surface whose vertex is at that point. It can be measured as the intercepted surface area of a sphere centered at that point to the square of the sphere's radius. Expressed in steradians.

spectrophotometer An instrument for measuring the transmittance and reflectance of surfaces and media as a function of wavelength.

spectroradiometer An instrument for measuring radiant flux as a function of wavelength.

specular angle The angle of mirror reflection (angle of incidence equals angle of reflectance).

specular reflection The process by which incident light is redirected at the specular (mirror) angle.

specular transmission The process by which incident flux passes through a surface or medium without scattering.

sphere illumination The illumination of a task from a source providing equal luminance in all directions about that task, such as an illuminated sphere with the task located at the center.

steradian (sr) (unit solid angle) One steradian equals the solid angle subtended at the center by $\frac{1}{4}\pi$ of the surface area of a sphere of unit radius.

stilb A unit of luminance equal to one candela per square centimeter. The use of this term is deprecated.

subjective brightness The subjective perception of luminance.

sun bearing angle The solar azimuth angle relative to the horizontal direction a building surface is facing. Often referred to as the *relative solar azimuth.*

sunlight Light directly from the sun excluding light from other portions of the sky.

talbot (T) A unit of light equal to one lumen-second.

task-lighting Light used to illuminate visually demanding activities, such as reading.

transmission The process by which incident flux leaves a surface or medium on a side other than the incident side, without change in frequency.

transmissometer A photometer for measuring transmittance.

transmittance The ratio of transmitted flux to incident flux.

ultraviolet radiation (uv) Any radiant energy within the wavelength range of 0.001 to 0.38 microns.

veiling luminance Luminance superimposed on the retinal image that reduces its contrast.

veiling reflection Specular reflection superimposed upon diffuse reflection from an object that partially or totally obscures the details to be seen by reducing the contrast. Controlled by distributing the source over a larger area, relocating the source out of the reflected field of view, changing the task surface specular reflectance or tilt, or relocating the observer.

visibility The quality or state of being perceivable to the eye.

visibility (meteorological) The greatest distance that selected objects (visibility markers) or lights of moderate intensity (twenty-five candelas) can be seen and identified under specified conditions of observation.

visual acuity A measure of the ability to distinguish fine details.

visual angle The angle subtended by an object or detail at the point of observation.

visual comfort probability (VCP) The rating of a lighting system expressed as a percentage of the people who, when viewing from a specified location and in a specified direction, will be expected to find it comfortable in terms of discomfort glare.

visual field The locus of objects or points in space that can be perceived when the head and eyes are kept fixed.

visual perception The quantitative assessment of impressions transmitted from the retina to the brain in terms of information about a physical world displayed before the eye.

visual performance The quantitative assessment of the performance of a visual task, taking into consideration speed and accuracy.

visual surround All portions of the visual field except the task.

visual task Those details and objects that must be seen for the performance of a given activity, including the immediate background of the details or objects.

wavelength The distance between periodic radiation waves.

workplane The plane at which work is usually done and on which the illuminance is specified and measured. Unless otherwise indicated, this is assumed to be a horizontal plane thirty inches (0.76 meters) above the floor.

zenith The point on the skydome directly overhead; 90-degree solar altitude angle.

INDEX